T0150807

PRAI

Raver Girl

"Can you get high from reading a book? A few pages into Samantha Durbin's *Raver Girl*, and you'll swear this coming-of-age memoir is laced with at least one of the arsenal of drugs Durbin inhaled, snorted, or swallowed as a 16-year-old immersed in the San Francisco Bay Area's '90s rave scene. The details and dialogue of this mind-altering memoir feel vivid and authentic, thanks in part to Durbin's dictaphone recordings from attending over 100 raves in the late '90s. *Raver Girl* is a wild ride through first-time sexual encounters, hallucinogenic experiences, and the thrills and pitfalls of high school. Give it a read if you loved *Euphoria* but thought it could use more JNCO jeans and a happier ending."

—POPSUGAR

"Dust off your JNCOs and glowsticks! If you weren't a Bay Area raver during the '90s, reading this book is the closest you'll get. And if you were at these parties, you probably forgot all the incredible details that Durbin packed into this thrilling book. Crank up the bass, and get ready to relive some magic."

—Liam O'Donoghue, host/producer of the
East Bay Yesterday podcast

"Psychedelic, twisting, and never less than real, *Raver Girl* is a remarkable work of auto-documentary in which Durbin fearlessly reconstructs the highs and lows of her singular adolescence at the epicenter of '90s Bay Area rave culture. I read this book in one ravenous sitting, wholly under the influence of its addictive voice. Just when I thought I couldn't be more engrossed, shocked, or transported, I turned the page and found myself in yet another new world. With vulnerability, compassion, and a wicked sense of possibility, Durbin has crafted a true-life bildungsroman that is a trip like none other."

—Lisa Locascio, author of *Open Me*

"Finally, a story from a young woman's point of view on learning the ins and outs of drug, rave, and psychedelic culture—without falling into the traps of stigma or stereotypes. *Raver Girl* is of its time and universal, the often untold story of teenage experimentation, learning how and how not to use drugs for fun, connection, and self-exploration."

—Michelle Janikian, author of *Your Psilocybin Mushroom Companion*

"Samantha Durbin is an exciting new voice. She shares an engaging, rave-fueled tribute to growing up in the '90s, and the teenage angst which accompanies it."

—Kat Odell, author of *Unicorn Food* and *Day Drinking*

"Durbin balances her portrait of the gritty scene of teen sex, drugs, and house music—before helicopter parents, iPhones, and YouTube cordoned following generations into danger-free zones—with the sweetness of a traditional coming-of-age story. A wild ride."

—Barbara Herman, author of *Scent and Subversion: Decoding a Century of Provocative Perfume*

"*Raver Girl* takes you on a hedonistic roller coaster ride of teen angst and discovery, whilst navigating you through the bastion of the last major international youth culture explosion: rave. If you were there, it's a memory-inducing maelstrom; if you weren't, you're going to wish you were . . ."

—Chelsea-Louise Berlin, artist and author of *Rave Art*

"High-energy prose shines bright in this stylish memoir. *Raver Girl* beacons you to the dance floor of infamous warehouse parties of the '90s. I loved this confessional—Durbin doesn't hold back in a world of music that you must listen to and must read."

—Michelle Zaffino, librarian and author of *Librarian Detective*

RAVER GIRL

RAVER GIRL

A MEMOIR

SAMANTHA DURBIN

SHE WRITES PRESS

Published 2021
Printed in the United States of America
Print ISBN: 978-1-64742-307-0
E-ISBN: 978-1-64742-308-7
Library of Congress Control Number: 2021909387

For information, address:
She Writes Press
1569 Solano Ave #546
Berkeley, CA 94707

She Writes Press is a division of SparkPoint Studio, LLC.

Book design by Stacey Aaronson
Cover photograph by Ms. Aquamarine

For my family, then and now—
especially my dad, who taught me how to edit words and myself.

AUTHOR'S NOTE

For privacy, names and identities have been changed, except for members of the Color Club, whose colors remain authentic.

"You've always had the power, my dear, you just had to learn it for yourself."
—THE WIZARD OF OZ

1 / PARANOID ANDROID, SIDE A

'm in a major panic. I'm being pursued by helicopters and cops, speeding down Hegenberger Boulevard in Oakland as fast as a vintage Beetle can. The deafening blare of sirens is behind me, beside me, above me—I'm surrounded.

I'm flying through my hometown streets, freaking out, turning without thinking, driving like a maniac. My heart's pounding, my stomach is twisting. Red, white, and blue lights flash in my rearview mirrors. Whiz. Whirl. Whoop. I keep glancing in my mirrors, willing the lights to leave me alone.

But they're persistent. And fuck, they're there. *The po-po are after me! Is that an ambulance? A fire truck? I just ran a red light. Shit! Don't crash. E. Acid. Coke. Mushrooms. Crystal. All on me. All illegal. Where's Mr. Blue?* Wild thoughts zip through my mind as fast as my blood's racing through my veins.

My time is up. There is no way I can outrun them. I have to pull over. Raves, drugs, lies . . . it's all over. I've pushed everything too far, and I can't take this anymore. So, as if I'm acting out a chase scene from a movie, I pull into a parking lot, screech to a stop, leap out of my car, and throw my hands up in the air.

"I surrender! I surrender!" I shout into the cold air, desperate. I stand with my eyes closed and still see the flashing lights. I cover my ears with my hands. It's overwhelming, and I can't escape it. I gasp for air and open my eyes, resigning myself to my ill fate.

But no one's there. The lights and sirens disappear the moment I open my eyes. All I see is an empty parking lot and my white car parked haphazardly across yellow lines. I left my door open. My car is humming, still running. Shopping carts sprawled across the cement are my only witnesses as I wonder how I could have ditched all those cops and helicopters. *Where did they go? How could I outrun that?*

Totally bizarre.

I am alone in a parking lot, in the middle of the night, in Oakland. A sixteen-year-old girl wearing JNCO pants and a yellow North Face fleece with fancy airbrushed nails and a dolled-up prom 'do. Still in disbelief, I chuckle, embarrassed. Then, suddenly, I become aware of my surroundings and realize I'm making myself a target for other dangerous things. I quickly get back in my car.

Driving toward safety, toward the hills, I turn up a DJ Dan mixtape. It's a chilly October night—*wait, it is October, right*? I crank my window down, and a rush of air refreshes me, keeping me alert. Stoplights blast Christmas colors. The streets are empty. I'm calm, abiding all traffic laws, especially stop signs. Stars twinkle in the sky. The moon hides.

A switch flips and fear turns on again. I begin checking my rearview mirrors obsessively. A lightning bolt strikes through my open window like a beam from a UFO. Startled, I roll up my window as fast as I can, cranking the lever while tightening my grip on the steering wheel. Red, white, and blue lights reflect in my rearview mirrors for a second time, blinding me, terrifying me. *They're back.*

I shift into third, leaving calm in my wake. Once again, I remember the drugs I'm carrying. All sitting on the seat next to me in my Polo Sport satchel. I glance at my bag, thinking I could throw them out the window, but no, the cops would see them flying out of my car. I could risk stopping for a moment to throw them into a bush, but my hands hold on to the steering wheel with the voracity of a racecar driver. I'm safe in my car. I can't stop.

Another solution comes to me: *Flush the evidence.* My intuition screams, "Yes!" As I chug up a never-ending hill that leads to the 580 freeway, I decide the only thing to do is go home and get rid of the drugs by flushing them down a toilet. *My* toilet. It has to be mine, because then I'll know they're gone—the drugs, the cops, all of it. Then I'll be safe.

A sharp left curves me onto an onramp. My vision flicks between my mirrors and the road. Yellow spots linger in my eyes like after you look at the sun. On the two-lane road ahead of me, red taillights turn into hovering demon eyes, pulsating deeper and deeper. Trees loom over the way, creeping and swaying like goblins trying to capture me through a tunnel of darkness. My body jerks around to electric beats. I turn up the volume to drown out the menacing sirens. My finger stings; I realize I've unknowingly been biting my cuticles and just ripped one open. I shove my finger into my mouth. A salty, metallic taste saturates my tongue.

The freeway sign for my exit appears. The letters are distorted, but I know it by memory. Determination drives me. My jaw pops. Almost there.

A few supercharged minutes later, I screech into our garage.

Get rid of the drugs. Get to the toilet and flush them. They're after me, and if they catch me, I'll be arrested and I'll be fucked. Mom and Dad don't know, and it would crush them. Now get up to the bathroom and flush it all away before the cops ring the doorbell. Play it cool.

But my cool has evaporated like sweat off my neck.

I enter the side door and glide up the stairs, light on my feet in my Adidas, making a beeline for my bathroom. The house is dark and quiet except for muffled sounds coming from a TV downstairs. I run up a staircase and down the hallway into my room. I close every door behind me. No one stops me.

I get to my bathroom and throw my purse on the white tile counter. Digging around, I find loose capsules of Ecstasy, vials of coke, hits of acid, crystal in mini plastic baggies, some loose shroom stems and caps. The drugs escaped the confines of my makeup bag at some point. I grab it all, dump everything in the toilet, and flush.

Whites and browns and shiny plastic swirl around, drowning together. Relief washes over me. *It had to be done. To be safe. That was hundreds of dollars' worth of drugs, but whatever, I can get more.*

There's always more.

Leaning over my bathroom counter, I stare into my purse at the remaining contents of my raver life. My dictaphone, Cesar, cigarettes, a lollipop, my glittery turquoise wallet, flyers, my hot pink highlighter pipe. I'm finally able to take a deep breath and slowly let go of the panic. My cheeks are tingling, my heart is thumping.

I step into the stillness of my bedroom. I'm in my safe space, where everything is familiar. Jewel colors, torn-out magazine pages taped to the walls, and framed pictures of people I love surround me, comforting me.

I peek through my burgundy curtains and don't see any spotlights shining my way. I don't hear any sirens. Trees wave slowly at me. *I am safe.*

A vibrating noise comes from my purse. I go to check it and see that my pager is blowing up. There are multiple 911 pages from Tommy. *Where is he? Is he okay? We were together. At a rave. Did I tell him I was leaving? No, I freaked out and ditched him. I straight-up left my best friend at the party.*

As the night's events become clearer in my consciousness, I hear a knock on my bedroom door. My parents. Strung out, spaced out, I freeze.

"Sam?" my brother Justin's deep voice asks through the door.

I open the door, and Justin's standing in the hallway, his hair hanging free from its usual ponytail. "What the hell are you doing?" he asks. "It's, like, two in the morning. Are you okay?"

I stare at him, resisting the urge to hug him, still in shock.

"Good thing Mom and Dad are out of town, or you would be busted. But seriously, is everything okay?"

His presence soothes me and it finally sinks in. What happened to me tonight is something I've heard about but hadn't experienced until now: a bad acid trip.

Justin's green eyes look into me, all-knowing. *Everything is not okay.*

"Oh, shit. You had a bad trip, huh?"

Hearing it from my brother, my guru, confirms it.

"Bummer." He hugs me.

I hold him and don't want to let go. Safe in his embrace, I ask myself, *How did I get here?*

2

THE GOOD OLD DAYS

Samantha Durbin
Ms. Kulsrud
Period B
September 6, 1995

"The good old days"

The good old days were when I could run around in a bathing suit and not worry whether I looked fat or not. The good old days were when I could walk around with food on my face and not have to worry about something being stuck between my teeth. The good old days were when I could do the splits with no problem and wear little leotards with ruffles on them. The good old days were when I could take baths with my brother and squirt soap in his eye. The good old days were when I could put on fashion shows with my friends for my mom and play in her makeup. The good old days were when I could suck my thumb while watching Scooby-Doo on Saturday mornings. The good old days were when I could wear

Tinkerbell nail polish and listen to my brother's '80s tunes. The good old days were when I didn't have to worry about harmful UV rays and could swim like a star. The good old days were when I was a little girl.

3 / FRESHWOMAN

I started raving my sophomore year of high school. During my freshman year, I led a normal high school existence. I had healthy ways of channeling my teen angst then, like dying skunk stripes of bleached blond into my brunette mane. I first tried it at home with the Jolen Creme Bleach I'd used to lighten the fine hairs above my lip. The stripes—one beginning at the center of my forehead, the other two sprouting from my temples—came out a yellow squash color. My mom took one look and said, "I'm making you an appointment at the hair salon." With three foils, my hair went from botched to brilliant.

My look freshman year was "vintage skater chick," a style inspired by grunge and *Vogue* magazine: flared corduroy jeans, grandpa sweaters, baby tees, Vans, and French manicures. I was all about friends, boys, clothes, drama club, and smoking weed. In that order. And that's what I would daydream about in classes at my private Catholic high school. Perched atop a hill in Oakland, Bishop O'Dowd was near the zoo and residential areas. You didn't have to be Catholic to attend. I was half Catholic from my mom, but my family practiced liberal politics rather than organized religion.

Known for its sports teams and diversity, every shade of skin walked through the locker-lined halls at O'Dowd in 1994. Girls wore Gap sweatshirts and burgundy lipstick, boys North Face fleeces and Oakland A's baseball caps. Baggy jeans for all.

I was boy crazy, though I hadn't had a boyfriend for longer than a couple weeks in junior high. I'd had lots of crushes and plenty of French kisses but still hadn't gone past being felt up.

I usually crushed on older skater boys rather than boys my age, whom I saw as immature and awkward. When I did find myself in an intimate situation, I was quite shy and quickly felt immature and awkward myself. I pretended I was more experienced than I was.

Girl-next-door pretty, I was lithe and tall. I wore clothes well. That was where my passion shone: fashion. Obsessed with the Beastie Boys and anything sparkly, I was half street, half sophisticate. So what if I wasn't the prettiest or smartest girl in school—I was the most stylish.

Every week served up a new crush, never on guys in my own classes. There was the junior with olive-green eyes and a fancy French name (Clément). The slim, long-limbed lacrosse star sophomore with chocolate ice cream skin and a baby face. And the ultimate Adonis: the captain of the swim team, a senior with honeycomb abs, wavy brown hair, and a radiant California tan.

Then, one day in October, a new specimen walked across the quad. It was one of those time-freeze moments; The Everly Brothers' song "All I Have to Do is Dream" played in my head as he walked toward me in slow motion. His raven-black hair was brushed back with a soft-hold product, allowing strands to fall on either side of his head, nonchalant, framing his pretty-boy mug. A button nose softened his bold look. His sideways smile revealed bright whites. (I would later learn that he was part Japanese, part Black, and part white—a striking combination.)

This guy was fine, but what intrigued me the most was the way he carried his athletic 5'11" frame; his swagger was confident, strong, sexy. He seemed more like a man than a boy. A guy who looked and walked like that was what I'd been waiting for.

"Who is *that*?" I asked Naomi, my best friend from junior high, who was sitting next to me on a bench in the middle of the quad.

"Who?" she quickly replied, her brown eyes squinting to look.

"That fine guy over there." I indicated with my chin. "Black hair, navy flannel."

"Oooh yeah," she said, raising an eyebrow. "Brandon Landor. So fine."

"Is your brother friends with him?" Naomi's brother was a senior, and she already knew tons of upperclassmen.

"Sorta. He's the quarterback. And he has a girlfriend." She rolled her eyes.

My heart sank. Of course he did.

As I quietly kept dream, dream, dreaming about Brandon, I found myself disinterested in classes where a teacher lectured for an hour, sometimes writing on a chalkboard. After five minutes, I'd tune out what sounded like the teacher in the *Peanuts* cartoon's "blah blah blahs." The hairstyles of the other kids or the drifting clouds out the window were more interesting. Taking notes usually turned into drawing doodles.

I found a haven in drama class. My parents were relieved there was something at school I was excited about other than boys. After channeling my inner Rizzo from *Grease*, singing

"Look at Me, I'm Sandra Dee" at an audition for the fall production of *Evita*, I was cast as chorus and had every intention of showing off my dance skills.

I grew up dancing competitively. When I stepped into sequins and tap shoes, I razzle-dazzled on stage. I wasn't a fabulous singer, but I was loud with high energy. I helped with the production's costumes and would often sneak out the theater's back door during rehearsals to smoke cigarettes with fellow rebels on the fire escape.

One day after school, we were taking a break from practicing a dance routine. A few of us took off our shoes to get better traction on the rug of the drama club room. Warm and sweaty, I was whispering with my newest friend, Tommy. There were about twenty of us in the rectangular room bordered by instruments, microphones, and a piano. Our pony-tailed, white-haired, turtleneck-wearing director was running through another scene while us dancers relaxed when, mid-scene, he yelled, "Woooooeee! What is that smell?!" and fanned his nose.

The actors started laughing since our director was usually Mr. Serious. The rest of us looked around the room, sniffing for clues.

"It smells like stinky cheese over here," the director continued in his snarky drawl.

While giggling with Tommy, I thought of my patent leather Converse One Stars. I'd been wearing them without socks for weeks and knew they smelled sour. I hadn't even thought about it when I took them off and left them by the director's chair. I looked at them sitting on the floor, the outside shiny, the inside stinky. Heat spread into my cheeks.

"Okay," he yelled, "just start over!"

I was mortified, knowing my shoes stank like funky cheese. I hoped no one figured out they were the offenders.

Tommy leaned into me. "What's wrong?"

We were sitting next to each other, cross-legged, about ten feet from my shoes. I looked into his green eyes, then at my shoes, and his eyes followed mine. His eyes widened and he boomed a laugh that lit up the room, forcing the director to shush us.

With a broad head full of blond curls, Tommy was a teen riot. He looked like a young Jude Law, with large features that fully animated when he spoke. Friendly and outgoing, he seemed to always be smiling. Or maybe that was just me when I was with him. Everyone in drama liked him, but I was his biggest fan.

I'd never had any openly gay friends before Tommy. I admired him for coming out to his family when he was twelve. My parents had organized a movie night to watch the TV movie *And the Band Played On* when I was thirteen—a movie I'd learned a lot about LGBTQIA+ history from—and I knew not everywhere was as accepting as the San Francisco Bay Area.

The first time I went to Tommy's house in Piedmont, a city embedded in Oakland, he showed me his bedroom. Soft lighting, dark wood furniture, a just-cleaned smell, it was vanilla, which was confusing because Tommy was vivacious. My room was livelier, with its colorful bedding and magazine tears of supermodels on the walls. I was mint chip ice cream on a sugar cone.

Then Tommy flung open his closet. Top to bottom, posters and photos of the R&B group TLC adorned the inside of the door.

"These are my girls," he said, giggling. "My mom said I should keep them in the closet."

There was his truth. Tommy was more like cookies and cream with rainbow sprinkles.

Tommy was out of the closet, but his true self was behind a closet door. He dressed like a typical '90s high school kid in baggy jeans and hoodies and addressed everyone as "dude." There was no *Will and Grace* yet, Anderson Cooper was still in the closet (not that I watched the news anyway), and mainstream media hadn't begun to normalize gay people. My image of a gay man involved feather boas and tight shirts a la Freddie Mercury. But Tommy broke down that stereotype, opening my eyes to the spectrum.

He had a certain reserve about him, a tightness I didn't notice until we got high together. When we smoked weed, he shed his armor, relaxing into the funny, intelligent, sometimes spastic guy he truly was. He let go of all the things he thought he was supposed to be—what society told him to be—and showed me his true self: the boy taped up inside his closet door.

Around the time Tommy came out to his family, I smoked weed for the first time with my brother, who was fifteen when I was thirteen. It was a Friday night, and our parents were out to dinner, when he sat down next to me on the sofa while I was watching *The Fresh Prince of Bel Air*.

"You're probably going to do this sooner or later, and I'd rather have your first time be with me," he said.

Something in his hand glimmered: a pipe with green swirls

in clear glass. It was packed with a fresh bowl of green weed with teeny brown hairs in it. We stepped outside the door of the TV room and sat down at the round glass-top table outside.

"Inhale when I light the bowl, hold it in for a couple beats, and then slowly blow out the smoke," Justin said. He lit himself a hit, then gave me the pipe.

The rest of that night, in true stoned form, is forgotten. According to Justin, I had a blast laughing at everything he and the Fresh Prince said. And because I couldn't stop laughing, he couldn't put eye drops in my reddened eyes. He tucked me into bed early, before Mom and Dad came home.

The next morning, I slept until 2:00 p.m. My mom wondered if I was coming down with something.

"Bad cramps," I said.

One weekend afternoon a couple of weeks later, my dad sat down next to me as I watched TV, in the same spot on the sofa where my brother had offered me my first bowl, and said, "Your mother and I would rather have you smoke pot than cigarettes."

He'd succeeded in stealing my attention away from *Hey Dude*.

He continued, "We both used to smoke, you know, before we had you and your brothers. In the '60s. And we both quit because we learned how horrible it is for your health. But"—he stiffened—"pot is illegal. And if you or your brothers get caught with it, you're in serious shit. Not just serious with your mother and I. The *law* serious."

Even as I dwelled on how dorky it was that he called it "pot," it was clear to me that my dad knew my brothers and I had smoked it. My oldest brother, Reed, was eight years older than me, and he smoked cigarettes. I knew this from smelling his ashtray breath and seeing bright red packs of Marlboro Reds lying around in his car. And if I knew he smoked cigarettes, my parents certainly knew (and disapproved) too. It was reassuring that I wasn't the only Durbin kid who deviated from square norms.

"Okaaay," I said to my dad, wishing for parental advice hour to be over.

"Okay," he said.

He sat with me for a few more minutes, pretending to watch the cheesy teenage drama on the screen. It seemed like he was debating saying something more. But then he stood up abruptly and exited the room.

That was my dad's first attempt to advise me about drugs. What I took away from it was that I needed to hide all evidence of smoking cigarettes—something I did socially—from my parents. And that they were kinda cool with me smoking weed, but I needed to hide that from the cops. Noted.

By my freshman year of high school, I was a seasoned weed smoker. I knew the difference between kind bud and shwag. I'd smoked out some of my friends for the first time. And I had a glass pipe of my own. Weed agreed with me. Sativa. Indica. Both. It brought out my silly side or relaxed me, it got me out of my head, and it got my creative juices flowing.

4 / PASSIN' ME BY

I spent the summer between freshman and sophomore year going to high school keggers with Naomi and another friend from school, Johanna. I had a few flirtations at those parties, mostly due to being muddled from a combination of smoking weed and drinking. I was more the type of girl who would go running and yelling through a sprinkler rather than strip down in someone's back seat. Plus, I wasn't interested in my classmates—I was interested in the "hella fine" skater boys of Berkeley's Telegraph Avenue, per my journal at the time. That's who Johanna and I would stalk during leisurely summer days. We would smoke up and hang out on the sofa at the X-Large store, hoping to catch the eye of "Mr. Fine," who worked there.

X-Large was a street brand associated with the Beastie Boys in the '90s. We were obsessed with anything Beastie. The store also carried X-Girl, the offbeat girls' line started by Kim Gordon of Sonic Youth. That summer, I lived in my red X-Girl corduroys and shrunken X-Girl tees, which made me feel like the kind of cool skater girl our crushes would like. Only I didn't actually skate, and I didn't nab a hottie.

After days pretending not to be skater groupies, Johanna and I would take the bus up the winding Berkeley hills to her house. Within minutes of us stomping into Johanna's bedroom, her mom would knock on the door and ask us in her offbeat South African accent what we wanted for dinner.

Johanna's response was always "Mac n' cheese!"

Another knock twenty minutes later, and her mom carried a tray with two bowls of cheesy goodness into Johanna's bedroom. After scarfing that down, we gorged on ice cream, and then Johanna spent the next fifteen minutes in her bathroom puking up the feast. Obsessed with food and her body. Going to the bathroom after every meal. I knew the signs. She wasn't my only friend with bulimia.

We locked ourselves in her bedroom for hours at a time, talking about what life would be like when we married the Beastie Boys (she was an Adrock girl, MCA was mine, RIP) and taking Polaroid pictures of ourselves, perfecting our angles, smiles, and bitch faces. Once, after seeing *Interview with the Vampire* in the theater, we used eyeliners to draw faux veins on our faces, inspired by Brad Pitt. I knew that after doing weird stuff like that, Johanna was meant to be my friend.

Between high school parties with Naomi, trying-to-be-cool hangs with Johanna, and smoking out with Tommy, I managed to stay out of trouble that summer. I think it helped that I didn't have a driver's license or boyfriend yet.

But then sophomore year rolled around, and it was all about friends, boys, clothes, drama, smoking weed, acid, and raving. In that order.

My favorite class sophomore year was Christian Sexuality, a class taught by a funny priest. He knew the modern realities of teenagers, and instead of preaching abstinence and shaming sex, he passed around color photos of what STDs looked like. One look at the advanced stages of syphilis, and I was disgusted. Condoms were a must. But more than that, the photos solidified that having sex with just anyone wasn't for me—and it certainly wasn't worth grotesque ulcers on my face. I was holding off for someone special, something meaningful.

I liked writing papers but loathed taking tests. What always bit my GPA in the ass was low test scores. Especially in science and math. My main issue when it came to taking tests wasn't knowing the material—I did study—it was time pressure. I would get nervous when others started standing up to turn in their tests. They'd finished before me, and shit, I wasn't even halfway done. This distraction made me lose focus, and then I had to start over. When it got bad, my pulse accelerated. Restless and sweaty, I'd forget the material because I was consumed by my inability to get the job done. Performance anxiety. A vicious cycle that none of my teachers recognized.

Tommy and I were back to our drama club thrills in the production of *Godspell*. This time around, we were more obnoxious at rehearsal, snickering away, stoned half the time. I didn't have performance anxiety when I was singing and dancing on stage. When I performed creatively, I forgot about who was watching and surrendered to the high of showmanship. I never had solo parts and didn't want them—being a part of the ensemble lifted me up, gave me the courage to be my best self.

In November, a lanky, greasy-haired guy in drama asked me to the senior winter formal. Chris was cute and clever—boyfriend material. I excitedly said yes.

When the day came, I got ready for the dance at a friend from drama's house. My red silk mini dress showed off my long legs. One of my style mantras has always been "If you've got it, flaunt it." So I did. The shoes—black patent leather Mary Jane's —were Betsey Johnson, my go-to designer for dressing up. Our parents schmoozed while my friend and I curled each other's hair in the bathroom.

Finally, our dates showed up with corsages. The dads intimidated the dates, and the moms couldn't stop smiling.

When we got to the venue, Chris was so serious, a.k.a. nervous. I did my best to act cool so he would act cool. After taking our photos, we went inside the dance, and Chris flashed a flask from inside his blazer.

"Want some?" he asked, raising his brows.

A few swigs of whiskey, and he was the funny guy I knew from drama smoke sessions on the fire escape.

The venue was an old-fashioned theater with red velvet curtains and booth seating around a half moon–shaped dance floor. A crystal chandelier hung from a dome ceiling. Chris and I switched between cutting it up on the dance floor and swigging from his flask in the butterscotch leather booths.

On my way back from the bathroom, I stood on the sidelines to watch, take it all in. Silver disco ball glimmers, bodies in motion, Mariah Carey's shrill voice—I was energetically tipsy. All the girls were wearing heavier-than-usual makeup and the guys were looking sharp in their suits. Sweet-smelling perfume infused the air.

My eyes fixed on a familiar dark-haired guy looking in my direction. Brandon Landor. White lights flickered over him, casting him clearer every second. Self-conscious that he would see me staring at him, I looked down at the floor.

I'd heard Brandon was single, and I'd carved my hallway routes at school so I'd pass him often. There was a small plaza between buildings where you-know-who liked to hang. Bad boy mystique on full bore, sometimes he'd be talking with friends. Or girls. Walking through there presented opportune times for me to make a move, any move. Eye contact. A smile. A flip of my Cindy Crawford hair. But no—every day I would hold my breath and walk on by. Heart-fluttering power walking, really. I gave myself grief after every pass. *What the hell?* In my vintage KangaROOS sneakers, I was the most stylish girl in school (or so I thought), and yet I couldn't muster the nerve to flirt with Brandon.

Even though I was inspired by Naomi, who'd caught herself a junior hottie, I was frustrated by what a clueless virgin I was.

Lauryn Hill's voice rang out—was I "Ready or Not?" I looked up, holding my head high. Liquid Courage urged me to look at him again. Just in case. I blinked back in Brandon's direction and was 95 percent sure he was looking at me. Our eyes locked. I smiled a little. But I sensed another set of eyes on me. The girl sitting next to him. I blinked at her and was 100 percent sure she was looking at me, her eyes cutting through the crowd. I shifted in my Mary Jane's. However, the girl's death stare confirmed my wish. I pretended to look for my date, smiling to myself as I strutted through the dance.

I ran into my friend Dana, who was newly dating one of Brandon's senior friends. I was giddy telling her about our flirtatious exchange.

"Let's make it happen," she said through a lazy-eyed stoner smile.

☺

Soon after the dance, I was at a house party in the Oakland hills where I knew Marku, Dana's boyfriend, would be and hoped Brandon would be too. Dana, Naomi, and I accepted any cup of alcohol and joint passed outside on the deck overlooking the darkened verdure below.

Walking through the unfamiliar house, stoned and tipsy, I peeked into the rooms, hoping to find something more exciting to do than sit on the deck, and entertained myself by looking at family photos on the walls and feeling the smooth leaves of the indoor plants. I didn't know where my girls were. It was a mellow vibe.

I turned a shadowy corner into the kitchen and stumbled into something. Someone. Him. A giggle defense mechanism kicked in, and Brandon touched my arm in a gallant attempt to keep me upright.

"Oh," I mumbled. "Hey, sorry."

"That's all right." He smiled and leaned against the refrigerator. "Sophomore, right?"

"Yeah." I smiled back.

"I'm Brandon," he said, still smiling.

"Samantha," I said, searching for a prop—a drink, a cigarette, something to do with my idle hands.

He cocked his head. A strand of hair fell out of place. It practically made me jump. I saw an indent above the ridge of his nose as he lifted a hand to smooth his hair back. "I've noticed you before," he said, "always walking past me. Kinda reminds me of that Pharcyde song, 'Passin' Me By.' You know the Pharcyde?"

I flipped my Cindy Crawford hair and nodded. "Yeah, totally." And that was no trying-to-be-cool lie.

DOOR # 1

Eon, January 1996
Homies: Brandon, Dana, Marku
Location: Somewhere in Oakland
Drugs: Acid, weed

My first rave and first time doing acid started at a donut shop with Brandon, my new boyfriend. Momentous. After a month of dating, I was still in an I-can't-believe-he-likes-me phase. My ego was slowly inflating into a red heart-shaped balloon. Free-spirited girl, stoner quarterback guy, we were both fire signs—Sagittarius here, Leo there. Our chemistry heated quickly. Brandon was fine and mine, and since we'd met, every day had been more exciting.

Dana had told me about underground illegal parties called raves, but given my midnight curfew, I hadn't been able to go to one yet. She'd been to a couple before and explained that the donut shop was the Map Point, a random place where you went to get directions for the party. She'd called a phone number earlier and a recording had given the location of the Map Point. The process had the curious spirit of a treasure hunt. It was the coolest.

I had no idea what to wear—something that wasn't usually a

problem for me, having read *Vogue* since I was eleven. I decided to take style notes from Dana and Deee-Lite's Lady Miss Kier, my fashion icon du jour.

Dana wore a shrunken vintage tee, bootcut jeans, and maroon New Balance sneakers. With her trademark hunter-green down jacket, she had a cool '70s vibe. I opted for glam and wore my black Betsey Johnson Mary Jane's, nude fishnets, denim short shorts, and a black spaghetti-strap camisole. The finishing touches were Dana's emerald-green Adidas track jacket and high pigtails twisted into bouncy ringlets.

The plan was simple: I called my parents from Dana's line when we were getting ready at her house to check in and say good night. She and her older sister had a private line because they were boy crazy and boys were crazy for them, and the never-ending calls were an annoyance to their parents. I also had a personal phone line, but it wasn't from too many boys calling; it was from my begging for one, to talk to my girlfriends about boys.

Then we did the ol' lights-out-sneak-out maneuver. We said good night to Dana's parents like we were going to sleep, took our acid, crept out of her house, and met our boyfriends down the block. We ran across the sepia-lit streets, ducking down, afraid someone would see us. I'd plotted this for weeks—it had to work out.

En route to the Map Point in Marku's vintage BMW, the music vibrating from the speakers was a new sound to me. I dug the continuous bouncy pulse. Cosmic spasms activated energy inside me rock and reggae and hip-hop never had. The four of us were talking nonstop when I noticed my pulse quicken, my vision sharpen. *Is it the music or the acid?* I wondered.

Dana was sitting shotgun, blowing a whistle to the beats. Brandon and I were in the back. The car paused. I focused on three red lights—shiny red ornaments dangling in the dark. Our words spiraled around us, trailing into tangents. High-pitched chirping noises pierced my ears, activating my anxiety about getting caught sneaking out. Dana rolled down her window, still blowing her whistle. The freezing breeze jolted me like a vampire slap to the face.

I blurted, "Dude, shut up!"

It came out sounding different to me than I expected, more shrill, like my voice in a tape recording.

"I'm sorry!" she yelled back, laughing. "I was doing it with the music!"

"It's annoying!"

"Want me to roll up the window?"

"No, I need it," I said, enjoying the invigorating air.

I sank back, curling into my seat, massaging my hands together to warm them. They were corpse cold, like that vampire's hand that had slapped me. I grabbed Brandon's leg for warmth and noticed a silver shimmer. I'd been unknowingly touching my face, spreading glitter from my eyes to my fingertips. My mouth and cheeks were sticky from kissing Brandon and reapplying my lip gloss. Kissing, reapplying, kissing, reapplying. I tried to put my seatbelt on and couldn't find the clip thingy. My fishnets were digging into my stomach. Glitter sparkled around my eyes as I blinked.

Blink. Silver.

Silver. Blink.

While I was mesmerized by my light show, I heard Brandon spit some rhymes: "Talking talking back and forth, where are we going, unless it's . . . south? Or east. Maybe west. West is the best, definitely."

My finger drummed my lips up and down, making baby noises. Silly, but it felt good. Brandon did it too. We laughed. Restlessness was building inside me. I couldn't sit still. I just wanted to get to the party.

Dana turned down the volume and over her shoulder said, "Guys, no matter what happens tonight, we have to have fun. Okay? And you guys, leave Marku alone because he's not very happy right now. He's trying to concentrate."

"Oh, it's cold!" Brandon yelped. "Why is it so cold?"

My body shivered in agreement.

"I turned on the heater, guys. Quit your whining," Marku yelled back. "Ah! There's the donut shop. We're here."

I couldn't stop shivering as we parked on San Pablo Avenue. We untangled ourselves from the car and walked toward the unassuming donut shop. Blinded by the bright fluorescent lighting, once I saw the rows and rows (and rows and rows) of glistening dough puffs, my mouth watered. I wasn't hungry—it was a feast for the eyes. Dana and I oohed and aahed at the beautiful pastries spilling over the edges of the pans. The guy behind the counter watched us in silent amusement. He was probably used to stoners coming in for a late-night fix.

"Ladies!" Brandon called from beyond. "Over here."

Two dudes were sitting in a corner with a cash box and a box half full of donuts. We shuffled over.

One of them said, "Hey, guys, it's five dollars each." He looked like an ostrich.

Brandon paid for me while the ostrich handed him a piece of brown paper. "And here's the directions to the party," the ostrich said, flapping his flat mouth. "It's, like, seven minutes away."

The other guy looked more like a bear in his shaggy brown fur vest. I wanted to pet it. He asked me and Dana, "Want a donut?" his narrowed, velvet brown eyes smiling. We dove in like kids after a piñata rips open.

It was a dramatic effort getting back into Marku's Rubik's Cube of a car. It was the donuts' fault: we didn't want to harm them by crushing or dropping them. When I sat back in my seat, I took the first bite of that donut—chocolate glazed with chocolate sprinkles—and found that it was too sticky, too sweet. I could barely swallow one bite. I threw it out the window.

Electronic music vibrated from the speakers as we drove to the rave. I battled thoughts of my parents catching me. I'd already been grounded after breaking my curfew hanging out with Brandon one night. To pull this off, I'd been on my best behavior.

I was nervous, but getting caught was a risk I was willing to take for Brandon. And for a rave. And trying acid, a hallucinogen my brother Justin had told me all about. There was always a thrill in breaking the rules, but this party—illegal, underground, experimental—was totally intriguing. I had to know what I'd been missing.

After some rights and lefts, we approached a dark block of warehouses.

"There's some people," Marku said. "That must be it. I'm taking my acid."

We parked and approached the short line. Dana and Marku lit their cigarettes. Thudding bass coming from inside the building distracted me from the conversation. I popped a piece of gum and looked at the people in line with us. A couple of geeky guys. A petite girl with long raven hair, sucking on a lollipop while rapidly speaking to a guy in overalls. A barrel-chested guy with a baseball cap worn backward, leaning against the wall. He was solo, hard and cool; I thought maybe he was a drug dealer. There was an antsy feeling in the cold air. Everyone was eager to see what was behind Door #1.

We made it through the door and followed a narrow, glowing hallway to a room where yellow, green, and blue lasers bounced off the walls. The place reeked of cigarettes and sweat. People were fluttering about, quick and slow. The room vibrated electric music more alive than anything I'd known was possible. The crowd was dancing, smiling, welcoming us. I'd entered a disco inside a spaceship inside an enigma. It was way more than a mixtape—it was a movement.

Disco ball sparkles reflected off huge black speakers alongside a table where a guy with cascading dreads was wearing oversized headphones. He held a headphone with one hand while the other played with a spinning record. His head bobbed to the beats. He was totally into it. Everyone was into it.

Dance. Drink water. Kiss Brandon. Breathe. Pee. Dance. Talk to her. Smile. Watch the lights. Take off my shoes. Apply lip gloss. Dance. Smoke a cigarette. Talk to him. Talk to her. Laugh. Sit. Stand. Sit. Stand. Dance. I didn't know what I wanted to do first. I wanted to do everything at once.

My shoulders did their sassy thing and my feet kicked side to side. Slow. Slow. Quick quick. Slow. It felt so good letting go go go after the previous hours leading up to now now now. Simmering down, pumping faster, my superstar self emerged. Weightless, boundless, happiness, I surrendered to the beat. All worries and insecurities vanished. I looked at my friends and the fascinating strangers around me and sensed that we were all feeling the exact. same. way.

Brandon grabbed my hand and pulled me after him.

He led me down another hallway to the Chill Room, the raver's refuge for when you wanted to, well, chill. A haven where water, fruit, and new friends abounded. This room was different from the first room. Quieter, spa-like music played, and mattresses that looked like Legos covered the ground. A blue glow soothed the space. People sat together in small groups, chatting and laughing. Colorful rave flyers and empty water bottles littered the floor.

We sat down on a mattress. My skintight outfit was suffocating me. I looked around and envied the girls in baggy pants, baby tees, and sneakers, so casual cute. I tried taking off my shoes but couldn't undo the buckle puzzle. Brandon ran a feather up my leg, an amplified tickle. I tensed and shooed his hand away.

"That felt sooo weird," I said. "Seriously, it did."

He smiled. "I think acid is a sexual drug, don't you?"

"Uh, I think it's the music," I said, looking away. The glorious underworld overshadowed my beautiful boyfriend. Everything was a discovery, endlessly fascinating. I wanted to know everyone in the room. Bubblegum ice cream, My Little Pony, sunflowers—I studied the prismatic visions on the walls.

"We should have an orgy," Marku blurted, his dirty-blond hair thick like a mushroom top on his head. That's who he looked like—the mushroom from Super Mario Brothers. "Or at the very least, you girls should kiss."

Dana and I exchanged glances, silently communicating that it was no big deal.

"We will if you guys will," she countered.

The boys exchanged a big-deal glance.

"You girls first," Marku said.

"Oh no, you first," Dana flirted, luminous like She-Ra, Princess of Power. "Don't worry, we will."

"Work up to it," I said. "First the cheek, then the mouth, then tongue."

"Hell no!"

"Bad idea!"

We all laughed, then Brandon stopped abruptly to say, "That reminds me of that movie *KIDS*. Did you guys see it? The first scene, when the guy and girl are making out, like, hella hard. It's close up, and their tongues are all over each other and you can hear the sucking sounds. It was hot."

Inspired, I grabbed Brandon and consumed him. The kiss was extra slippery. Then Brandon pecked Marku on the cheek.

"Awww," Dana and I said in unison.

The pumping music from the large room called to me. I got a second, third, fourth wind of energy.

"Let's go dance!"

We spent the next few hours dancing, chilling in the Chill Room, and meeting new people. There were teenagers like us, and also twenty-somethings, from all over the Bay Area. The conversations we had were more interesting than daily chatter with friends at high school. Some examples:

"What is that? A roach on a bicycle?"

"I'm trying to squint my eyes to see, but I can't because of the ecstasy."

"I'm slowly going insane. I knew this would happen."

I kept going back to the dance floor for one more song. Were they even songs? They seemed to go on forever. And I would dance to them forever. The steady pulse of the music becoming my pulse, hypnotizing me.

The dance floor eventually cleared out. I had no idea what time it was. My legs felt like Jell-O and my energy was fading. Exhaustion washed over me. I was sobering up.

Brandon emerged out of the glow again, his sexy smile comforting me. He grabbed my hand and we headed out Door #1—a door it felt like we'd entered eons ago.

It was still dark out. A studied glance at my pager told me it was about 5:00 a.m. I rested my head against the back seat as we coasted home, buildings wavering, knowing the sun would soon rise. We were calm and quiet, satisfied with the night's events. Sensations left us, out the exhaust, into the morning.

Dana flipped around on the radio. It only took a few chords for me to protest, "Yuck! We're not listening to Hootie and the Blow-my-penis-fish!"

She clicked to the classical music station, which, wordless and melodic, was just right.

My head rocked toward Brandon. "My toes, they're so squished," I said, freeing them from my shoes, stretching one leg across the console between Marku and Dana.

"You have diamonds on your toes," Dana said, marveling at the diamond-shaped impressions on my skin.

"If you're that uncomfortable, you should just take your clothes off," Brandon mumbled, half smiling, sleepy-eyed.

I was too tired to laugh. "Tell me some words of wisdom," I said.

"Words of wisdom?"

"Brandon, can we smoke a bowl at your house?" Dana called back.

The night ending meant Sunday was next. Normal, boring Sunday. I didn't want the night to end. The need to go back, to go to another rave, was building strongly inside me, like water against a dam. The music, the lights, the people, even the dirty warehouse resonated with something inside me. A yearning to belong to something secret and different. Raves were a place I could let my weird, sassy, ugly, and beautiful emotions dance together. I'd found my tribe. I was turned on emotionally, physically, and spiritually. I was whole.

Before that night, I'd lived in a snow globe of emotional confusion. Behind Door #1, I could dance in the middle of that blizzard—now rainbow-colored glitter—embracing it, flowing in life.

Experimenting with acid had shown me a creative dimension inside my mind, and raves were my playground within that dimension. Some people say they're never the same after doing LSD. I can say that too. More in a positive than negative way; it was mind-opening, perception-changing, self-realizing. I'd learned there was potential for a deeper level of understanding and creativity. Self-expression was part of the raver ethos, and I wanted to be a part of that.

I warmed up to Brandon in the back seat, exhausted, content, confident I'd go to another rave. I tried not to think about the reality of going home to nosy parents in the morning. I just needed a few hours of sleep to recharge.

6

MIND MELT

Area 51, February 1996
Homies: Johanna, Jamie, Brandon, and some other girls
Location: Santa Cruz Civic Auditorium
Drugs: Acid

My second rave seemed like a simple plan. In my dad's Honda Prelude, I would drive myself and two of my friends, Johanna and Jamie, to Santa Cruz. I was sixteen, and I'd only had my driver's license a few months. In another car were three rave-curious friends. We all told our parents we were going to a reggae show at Ashkenaz, an all-ages club in Berkeley. After the show, I was sleeping at Johanna's house, Johanna was sleeping at Jamie's, Jamie was sleeping at her other friend's house, and so on.

A few weeks had passed since my first rave. I was jonesing for another one. The music, lights, energy, freedom—I'd found a special place where I felt like I could be myself. The problem was, my newfound creative outlet wasn't exactly parent approved. It wasn't police approved either. But that wasn't so much my issue yet.

I assumed my parents wouldn't let me go to raves. My curfew

was midnight, and most raves didn't go off until at least 1:00 a.m., when people's drugs kicked in—and I didn't dare ask. I'd gotten away with it once, and when Brandon heard about a rave in Santa Cruz, a coastal town south of San Francisco, I wanted to try my party luck again.

Brandon and I decided to meet at the party. Of my gaggle of teenage girls, I was the only one who'd been to a rave before. When I'd told my friends about that life-changing night, they'd decided they all wanted to go to one too—and try acid. Johanna had dropped acid before and said she could get some. Party on.

That night served up the most wicked storm of the winter, which tested my driving skills during the two-hour drive. In the whipping wind and rain, the blurry red taillights of the cars in front of me were bullseyes I tried to focus on.

We caravanned with the other car, them following me. By the time I reached the venue, my body was stiff with the tension I'd been squeezing into the steering wheel, and my eyes were dry and tired from straining to see the road. I needed a pick-me-up, stat.

I pulled into an expansive outdoor parking lot and, between swipes of the windshield wipers, saw a white amphitheater. It looked more like we were going to a rock concert than an underground party. After parking, I squinted at the monster building, raindrops squiggling on my windshield, and held out my palm. "Jo, acid, por favor?"

We downed our blotters, fixed our makeup in the visor mirrors, and then ran with the other girls toward the amphitheater, weaving through parked cars, laughing while trying to stay dry. Johanna slipped the other girls their acid while we waited in a short line at a side entrance.

Upon entering, the thudding bass permeating from the center of the building rocked my core. Like a zombie sensing a room full of fresh brains, I fixated on a closed orange door down a cement hallway. My heartbeat became the pulse of the bass. I raced toward the door, leaving my friends in my glitter dust. I reached for the thick metal handle, holding my breath, opening the door.

White spotlights darted around illuminated grandeur. Rainbow-colored lights highlighted large canvases suspended above the dance floor center where the DJ and his tables were. People danced or sat in groups, neon green glow sticks bobbing. Incense and musk charged me. My friends stood in awe, smiling.

"This is so dope!" Johanna yelled. Her wavy brown hair was pulled tight into a high ponytail. Her silver hoop earrings shined like mirrors. Bursts of iridescent glitter made the apples of her cheeks pop above a confident smile (thanks to junior high braces).

"Wow" was all Jamie could say.

"I know!" I yelled. "Let's go dance!"

I was weightless, flying down stairs and stairs and stairs toward the center of the universe. Finally, I stood in the middle of the pulsating crowd.

"Look out for Brandon," I yelled to my friends over the music.

Bobbing my head, dipping my shoulders, I smiled at anyone who looked at me. Guys wore white visors and super-wide baggy jeans—the widest jeans I'd ever seen. Girls wore sports bras and pony bead necklaces with pacifier pendants. Moving, swaying, feeling, everyone was dancing in an energy force.

The lights brightened. The music got louder. Foot-stomping, heart-pounding, core-shaking music. I was turned on and tuned in. Next up: dropping out.

Someone tapped my shoulder. I spun around and jumped at

the sight of my sexy boyfriend. Brandon hugged me and picked me up, my feet kicking in the air. I would have stayed in his arms with that wondrous world revolving around us forever.

"Hey, Sparkles." He smiled. "I found you."

Johanna and Jamie watched him with googly eyes, as if he were Leonardo DiCaprio—no, Johnny Depp. (Although if he resembled any actor, it was Keanu Reeves.) His brown eyes fixed on me, and as usual I noticed his enviably long eyelashes, always flirting. I stroked his black hair, my fingers lost in a nest of velvet feathers. We started dancing together.

"Where are your friends?" I yelled over the music.

"Oh, around." He shrugged.

"Are you high?" I asked.

"Hell yeah." He nodded. "We dropped like an hour ago."

"Cool." I nodded back.

"You?"

Purple orchids graced his face. "Yeahhh," I smiled, "I'm definitely feeling something."

"I have to pee!" Jamie yelled.

I looked at Brandon, grabbed his hand, warm and sweaty, and pulled him back up the stairs and stairs and stairs.

We exited through another heavy orange door. In the hallway, a cute, stout guy with an eyebrow ring and buzzed haircut wearing a T-shirt that read "Aliens suck" walked by, smiling. Two girls in matching Adidas tracksuits held hands and skipped through the crowd in chunky platform sneakers. A guy wearing a surgical mask sat with his back against the wall, his eyes rolling back into his head like he was drunk.

After the bathroom, I skipped into the hallway and saw my friends standing together, Jamie and Johanna looking at their pagers. They looked up at me with worried expressions as I approached. I looked at Brandon, and his smile had turned into a frown.

"What's going on?" I asked.

"Have you looked at your pager?" Jamie asked, her blue eyes bulging like an iguana's.

I hadn't checked mine for a couple of hours. I lowered the strap of my red Jansport backpack to find my pager and held it up to look at it, struggling to read numbers that looked like gray sprinkles doing cartwheels. But I knew what had happened in my twisting gut—my pager showed multiple pages from my home phone number.

The thudding bass fell far away, and the amphitheater opened up to the sky. Meteors started shooting down, exploding onto my perfect world, setting everything on fire. My heartbeat bounced in my temples. My friends were watching me while I watched the party kids passing by, smiling and swooning, having the time of their lives.

My bag fell on my foot, and its contents spilled onto the floor. I felt dizzy from the intense pressure between my eyes. My fingertips tingled. I wished I could stop time.

I looked at Brandon, pleading. "What should we do?"

He raised his baby caterpillar eyebrows. "Uh, you guys need to find a payphone and call your parents."

We hustled, frantically searching for a payphone. Thoughts spun around. *How long have my parents been paging me and what do they know and where are the other girls and are their parents trying to reach them?*

I followed Brandon to the entrance, where he asked a guy if there was a payphone inside. He said something to Brandon, but

I couldn't hear because the voices in my head were yelling at me. Brandon said there was one outside. We ran out the entry door.

Johanna, Jamie, and I followed Brandon outside in the rain, looking for the payphone. A blast of wet air forced me to stop and catch my breath. Raindrops ran down my forehead, tickling me. I swatted them away. Jamie stopped too, repeatedly tucking her blond hair behind her ears, chanting like a crazy person, "Is that a phone? Wait, that looks like a phone. Shit, that's not a phone. I can't tell. . . . Is that a phone? Where is a fucking phone?!"

Johanna was standing with us, her jaw clenched, eyes darting around. Black mascara had started circling her blue eyes. Raccoon eyes. She appeared more in control of herself, which was helping me to stay calm. Freezing rain was pouring down, soaking us.

"There!" Brandon yelled, pointing to something at the bottom of some M.C. Escher stairs. The blue metal box looked like a Ms. Pac-Man arcade game. A streetlight formed a sepia glow around it. Raindrops were falling stars bursting into shiny pieces of confetti hitting the ground. They vanished into black pudding pouring into the gutter.

"I'll call first," I said, running toward the phone.

I'd never talked to my parents on acid before. I couldn't imagine anything worse. I was panting like I'd just run a marathon in the storm of the century. It was the end for us all, and the absolute end of my rave adventures. And they'd only just begun!

Jamie and I huddled in the phone booth while Johanna stood in the rain talking to Brandon. They were using their jackets as umbrellas held over their heads, waterfalls dripping down their shoulders.

I hesitated before dialing, knowing I was about to have one of the weirdest conversations of my life. Weird bad, not weird good. Defending shoplifting or sneaking out to meet boys was cake compared to this drama. If we'd waited an hour to take our acid, it all would have been easier to manage. Trying to come up with believable lies while tripping amidst glitter rain bombs while my friends and boyfriend watched me, relying on me, while my heart ached for the magic inside the building, was mind-boggling. My stomach was in knots. I couldn't feel my legs, but I wouldn't let myself fall. *Stay calm*, I told myself.

Brandon handed me a quarter, and his eyes locked with mine, sending me positive vibes. "You can do this," he said.

I waited for my breathing to slow down. *You can do this.* I slipped the quarter in the slot and tuned into a distant ring.

"Sam?" My dad's voice was familiar but frightening.

"Yes." My voice was familiar but shaky.

"Are you in Santa Cruz with Jamie?"

"Yes."

"Are you at some illegal party?" he asked, agitated.

Three sentences formed in tomato soup like SpaghettiOs. "It's one of these rave parties. We heard about it from some friends. I'm not sure if it's illegal."

"Are drugs involved?" he drilled.

"What?" Meteors blasted down again, splashing puddles. I wanted to drop the phone and run. I watched Jamie twisting and untwisting and twisting her ratty ponytail.

"Are drugs involved?" I repeated.

Jamie's jaw dropped.

Brandon whispered, "Fuuuck."

Johanna watched the ground, unblinking.

"Not that I know of," I said. It sounded believable in my head—but was it?

"All the parents have talked to each other. We know you're not where you said you'd be tonight," he said. "And even worse, you drove to Santa Cruz in this horrible weather. Samantha, you weren't thinking!"

I imagined the tendons in his neck behind his salt-and-pepper beard popping out. They stretched like the roots of a tree when he was explosively mad.

My chest heated up. "Dad, I'm sorry. I wasn't thinking."

"And one of the girls—Sonia, I think—told her mother she was scared because she was high on LSD."

Sonia! The name flashed before me in pink neon. She was the driver of the other car and a friend of Jamie's. She always played cool and wasn't particularly friendly to me. I thought she was tough like me. She was the last girl I thought would fess up to her parents.

Jamie whispered, "What?"

"Are you on LSD?!" My dad yelled through the hard plastic.

"No!" I lied, nervously laughing it off. "LSD? What? Really?"

He paused, then said, "Have you been drinking?"

"No, they don't serve here, or I mean, at the rave party they don't serve alcohol." *That was the truth. And it sounded believable. I can do this.*

"What about Jamie and Johanna?"

"They were in my car," I said, steadying my tone, my palms leaking sweat. Or was that moisture from the rain? The plastic phone slipped. I clutched it tighter. "I don't really know the other girls and what they're doing. We haven't seen them since we got here."

My dad told me to find the rest of the girls and then call him back. I agreed, said goodbye, and slammed the phone down.

I updated my friends. We were stumped by the curveball Sonia had thrown. But that's because we were oblivious to the truth-serum effect of acid.

The sweet freedom inside the amphitheater was on the tip of my tongue, but the positive vibrations from the music were leaving me. I could feel fear crawling on my skin, forcing its darkness into me—lifeless, sober, stuck.

Stay calm, I told myself. There was still a chance I could pull this night off and get back to the rave, I just had to ignore my hallucinations and tangents and buzzing body while we sorted this mess out. Focus blew into me with the next gust of wind: *Find Sonia, the snitch.*

"We need to find them," I blurted.

My friends stared at me, their eyes growing smaller and larger, closer and farther, swaying as if we were on a boat.

"Maybe they're by the cars," I said.

The rain let up. We charged on slick ground to find the rest of the girls. They were standing around Sonia's car, and they turned to look at us in unison, their baby faces distorted like reflections in a carnival mirror. I asked who had already talked to their parents and what exactly they'd said. No one else had called their parents except Sonia.

I didn't see Sonia. I walked around her car and saw her through the open window, sitting in the back seat with another girl holding her hand. Her reddened eyes met mine. With her streaked mascara and blotchy cheeks, she looked like a sad mime.

I leaned down to talk to her.

"All our parents are talking to each other and looking for us."

"Yeah," she whimpered, "I talked to my parents."

"Well, my parents know I'm in Santa Cruz, and they're pissed," I said, struggling to keep my tone level.

She was looking at something behind me.

Annoyed, I said, "So why did you tell your mom you were on acid?"

Her eyes bulged, then welled up. "Because I didn't know what else to say."

My face inched closer to hers. "Why did you say everyone else was on acid too?" I whispered, and then barked, "You can't bring the rest of us down with you!"

Sonia's car wasn't a car anymore, it was a spaceship, and she was an alien attacking my perfect world. I was enraged, entering a full fury flurry.

Next thing I knew, my hands were orbiting around in the air and I was shouting at Sonia through the window. "That was totally unnecessary! How come you didn't come find the rest of us? What's your problem?" The words tasted sour coming out of my mouth.

Bitch Alert! I felt like we were Brenda and Kelly fighting on an episode of *Beverly Hills 90210*—and I was Brenda, the meaner one. I couldn't help myself. I'd never been upset on acid before. A rage wave had taken over, everything was out of control, and it was Sonia's fault. I had to blame someone. I'd lost my calm.

A sharp pain zapped my left temple, bringing me back into my body. I stood up, pressing my fingers into the pain, and looked back at my friends.

A disheveled audience stared at me. Brandon's face was stunned; this was way more drama than he'd signed up for that night. Nothing like that first rave, when we were high, dry, and carefree.

Sonia didn't answer me. She stared out the window, looking past me, her eyes searching. Was that what regret looked like? Or fear? Or amazement? She looked lost. I realized it must be her first time doing acid. I struggled to find balance between calm and chaos, heaven and hell.

Focus.

I attempted being nice to Sonia. "I said I would call my parents back after we found everyone. Can I use your cellular phone?"

She handed over the phone, which looked like a Transformer, and I turned to the group. "Sonia told her parents that she's at a rave in Santa Cruz on acid," I said. "Who wants to admit that same thing to their parents? I for one don't, so I'm going to stick to my story of not knowing she was on it." Then I pulled Brandon aside and told him I was scared.

He hugged me and gave me a pep talk, reassuring me I was right by not confessing to being on acid. We agreed that I shouldn't mention him either, since that would irk my parents more. I hoped that already admitting to some of the lies would mean my parents would let up.

I stepped away from the group, took a deep breath, and dialed. My dad picked up after one ring.

"Hi, Dad," I said, calm.

"Did you find the other girls?"

"Yes, we're all here. I'm using Sonia's cellular phone."

"Is she all right?" he asked. "Do you think she needs to go to a hospital?"

Glancing at her holed up in her car, I considered it. "No. I'm pretty sure she's okay now. But she definitely shouldn't drive."

My dad sighed. "We talked to the other parents, and we don't want you driving back tonight. We have arranged for a room at the Motel 6 off the Shoreline exit, where you and Jamie and Johanna will spend the night. Sonia's parents are coming to get her. You're sure you're okay to drive to the hotel?"

"Yes," I said. "Motel 6, Shoreline exit—got it."

"Call us when you get there. And tell Jamie and Johanna to call their parents. They're worried sick. Okay?"

Smoke-tailed ghosts drifted off glistening cement.

"Okay?!" he repeated.

"Okay!" I yelled back. (I thought I'd said the word already, but it must have been stuck in my brain.)

I hung up. The rain had stopped. Everything was still. The storm had passed. Reviewing the new plan in my head—*Shoreline exit*—I couldn't believe I'd convinced my parents I was sober. They trusted me. Denial was the only way.

I handed my friends the phone and told them to call their parents. Jamie was spitting excuses. Brandon and I calmed her down, convincing her she could do it. Johanna also resisted, and I said, "Dude, what if your parents knew you were the one who got the acid?"

Her nostrils flared.

"You might want to make sure Sonia didn't tell them that too." I didn't mean to scare her. The manipulation just came out. I was trying to cover all our bases.

"Fine, yeah, okay," Johanna said, turning toward Sonia's car.

Standing in the cold with Jamie and Brandon, I felt some relief knowing I had friends in my corner. Between every blink, I saw glow-in-the-dark spirographs. Every moment, I wished it all wasn't happening.

Johanna appeared and exhaled. "All good. Sonia didn't tell her parents who got the acid. And she promised me she wouldn't tell them."

We relaxed after the calls to our parents, thinking we'd convinced them we were more innocent than we were. We separated from the other girls while they waited for Sonia's parents. We'd become cliques with judging eyes and nothing to say to each other.

Brandon told me to try to sleep at the hotel and that everything would work out. After a sloppy kiss, he jokingly patted my ass goodbye, then turned away. I envied him as he walked back toward the amphitheater.

Shoreline exit. Somehow, I safely drove us to the Motel 6 in the middle of the night. I was still tripping but all the drama had erased some of the high. When we entered the plain, quiet hotel room I sat on one of the beds to call my dad and let him know we were at the hotel.

I rubbed my hands together to warm them, took a deep breath, and picked up the phone to dial home. When my dad answered, he told me to get some sleep and to call him in the morning if we wanted to get picked up. Zoning out, watching the fibers of the blanket form fleur-de-lis patterns, I agreed to everything.

After hanging up, I took off my soggy shoes and socks. The bottoms of my black stretchy pants were drenched. I stripped down to my top and underwear and got under the covers. My feet were corpse cold. I didn't speak much with Jamie and Johanna. We were too out of it. The pitter-patter of rain hitting the windows made me want to sink into the bed deep, deeper, deepest, farthest away from the real world outside.

Jamie lay in bed next to me, flipping through the TV channels. Actors' faces were distorted and ugly. I couldn't follow storylines. Things weren't making sense. I just wanted to watch pretty things. We found some cartoons. Perfect.

My eyes were heavy. When I closed them, I saw blobs of mud. Where did the glow-in-the-dark spirographs go? Gone—washed down the gutters. My mouth was raw, my throat scratchy.

A glow emerged from under the curtains, waking me from a wavering sleep. I slowly sat up on the bed. The TV volume was low, and Jamie was lying beside me, tossing and turning. Irritating commercials were playing, flashing and fluorescent. I reached for the remote to turn everything off.

The rain had started up again and was hitting the windows outside. Inside, I was obsessing. *Maybe it didn't happen. Then how did we end up in a hotel room? Because it was raining too hard after the rave and I didn't want to drive. Then why did you call your parents? Because they paged you, but then I convinced them I was at a reggae show in Berkeley and everything was fine—see, listen to the music in the background. Then where were Sonia and the other girls? I don't know, we didn't end up hanging out with them. You aren't with Brandon, are you? No, he's camping with his family. Camping in the rain?*

Lies spun around. Excuses and rationalizations. I was still wired, and so tired. The clock on the nightstand said 6:24 a.m.

The number was clear, unmoving—the acid was nearly gone.

A shower, I thought. Wash away the acid, the anxiety.

I avoided looking at my lizard skin in the shower under the bathroom's bright light. Hot water was the opposite to the cold, violent water that had attacked me the night before, almost as wonderful as those happy moments at the rave. The water massaged my shoulders as I swiveled my body until I felt the peace I needed to carry on.

Steam fogged up the bathroom mirror above the sink. I slathered the hotel's honeysuckle lotion all over my flushed legs and arms and ran my fingers through my wetted hair to brush it.

When I came out of the bathroom, the curtains were partially drawn. Overcast light filled the room. Johanna and Jamie were awake, sitting on the beds talking.

"Let's go," I said.

They agreed and didn't ask if I was okay to drive. They trusted my judgment. But did I trust myself?

The shower had rejuvenated me, and the acid had faded, but my mind wasn't sharp. It was like those commercials I'd grown up watching. My brain was a fried egg with a broken yolk running along the sides of a greasy pan.

Speaking of eggs—no, I wasn't hungry. Food was the last thing on my mind.

One step outside the hotel room and the wind slapped my hair across my face. The storm was back on. Juicy raindrops hit us as we ran to my dad's car.

I was wide awake when I sat in the driver's seat. I turned the key and started the drive back to Oakland. Drops of water danced on the windshield, in sync with Jamiroquai's funky beats playing from the stereo. Johanna, sitting in the front passenger seat, promised to stay awake with me. Jamie quietly looked out the window in the back seat.

A car passed, splattering water all over us. Blinded, I slowed down. The white lines on the sides of the road blurred. Growing puddles surrounded us. A thicket of trees bounced along the winding two-lane highway. My heart pounded as if I'd just downed too much coffee. I broke into a cold sweat and wiped my wet palms on my thighs to dry them, afraid they'd slip on the wheel and send us spinning out of control and off the road, killing my friends in an instant and leaving me to die in a slow, gurgling bloodbath.

"You're doing great," Johanna said. "Once we get over the hill, it will be easier."

I clenched the wheel. "I can't see shit!"

"I know," she said, white-knuckling the handle over her window. "This must be really hard. I'm seeing everything you're seeing."

"Am I going too slow?"

"No—go as slow as you need to."

It was easier when we reached the freeway. Soothed by Jay Kay's soulful voice, I powered us home. My eyes rested on the road ahead, occasionally glancing at the rearview mirror to see Jamie passed out. She'd always liked the rain growing up. I wondered if she still would after this saga. Cold, slippery, heavy—I was sick of it.

After dropping Johanna and Jamie off at their houses and arriving at mine, my pulse quickened again. I hovered in neutral, watching the gate open to my house, then drove in at a turtle's pace. I entered the house through a side door that led to the quickest route up to my room.

Tiptoeing in, I heard the TV playing in the eating nook next to the kitchen and saw my mom there, reading a newspaper.

"Honey," she said, quickly standing up.

I didn't have the energy to speak and forced a smile.

She came over and hugged me. "Are you okay?"

Warmed by her love, I nodded yes. She pulled back and studied my eyes for something—reassurance, maybe.

"We're so relieved you're safe," she said, holding my shoulders. "But you know we need to talk to you."

An urge to cry tickled my throat. "Can we talk about this later? I'm exhausted."

"Go upstairs and change. Your dad wants to talk now."

I wondered where my dad was as I walked up the staircase and ducked into the first door at the top to cut through the guest room that connected to my bathroom and bedroom. It was a shortcut to my room—an annex, if you will.

I peeled off my second rave outfit. I'd been so excited about it, but now my white tank top was more sticky than sporty, and the rest of it was waterlogged. I threw my navy Adidas track jacket, which had protected me from the storm all night, at a chair. I kicked off my baby-blue KangaROOS sneakers, now a shade darker. All the pieces of my outfit flew around my bedroom in a clothing tornado, clearing a path to my terrycloth robe adorned with bananas, cherries, and lemons.

Lying on my bed in my delicious robe, I closed my eyes, sinking into luxury. The rain was still pitter-pattering. I hoped I would fall asleep fast and dream the previous night away.

Then a jarring knock assaulted my bedroom door. My stomach flip-turned and I yelled, "What?!"

"Samantha?" my dad asked from the other side of the door.

"Yes?"

"Can we talk?"

I sat up, sulking, tightened the belt of my robe, and walked toward the door. As I reached to turn the doorknob, another bang jolted my nerves.

I pulled the door open, roaring, "Could you knock any harder?"

"Well," my dad said, looking at me severely through his black-rimmed glasses, "I didn't know if you were going to open the door."

His brown eyes looked black in the shadows of the doorway. His mouth was buried in the full beard he'd always had, except for the one time he shaved it, per my request, when I was little. My family agreed he looked like the actor Alan Alda without it, but it was too weird—we loved the man with the beard—so he grew it back.

"Yes, fine!" I said, pushing past him and strutting down the hall. "Let's talk."

"Can you stand still?" he asked from behind me.

I didn't know where I was going, but talking to him in my room, where he might see a rave flyer or something private, wasn't happening. I stopped at the front of the house, where a balcony overlooked Oakland and the Bay Bridge. San Francisco hid behind fog in the distance.

"Okay." I held on to the railing that curved down the stairs. "I'm really tired. The hotel bed was so uncomfortable and I—"

"No, Samantha," he interrupted. "No more lies."

"I wasn't lying. I was just saying I didn't get much sleep last night."

"Yeah, well, neither did we," he scoffed.

I felt a tug of guilt. We had a staring contest. He won when my eyes broke away to look at the dollhouse he'd made me propped on a table in front of the windows, filling space, collecting dust.

"Can you tell me what happened last night?"

I threw my arms up, going sassy hands on him. "I told you on the phone, remember? Yes, I stupidly drove Jamie and Jo to a party in Santa Cruz and lied about where I was. You caught me. I'm sorry. It was irresponsible and stupid, and I'll never do it again."

He quietly asked, "Were you drunk driving?"

I got a whiff of his bitter three-cups-of-coffee morning breath.

"No, I didn't have the chance to."

His lips tightened.

"I mean, no," I said.

He started shaking his head. "Do I have to remind you that that's how my brother died? You can't, can't drive drunk!"

"I know not to drive drunk! I don't know what else to say. You've told me a thousand times. I know!"

"I've also told you not to lie a thousand times. I just can't believe anything coming out of your mouth," he yelled, gripping my arms tight, shaking me. "Don't you get it? How can we trust you when you keep lying to us?"

I stared into his bloodshot eyes and then pulled myself out of his straightjacket grip. Drained by the past twelve hours, and afraid my dad was going to hit me, I ran down the stairs.

My mom had been standing at the bottom listening to our conversation.

"Mom!" I grabbed at her, looking back to see my dad chasing me down the stairs.

"James!" she yelled, crying. "Calm down!"

51

I ran through the dining room and pushed through a swing door into the kitchen, fire spreading through my chest. My mouth was desert dry. I filled a glass of water as my mom and dad walked into the kitchen. I gulped it down, and then tears poured out of me. My dad's eyes were as red as my mom's. He was crying too. He stepped toward me. I tensed and shifted backward. My mom sobbed. I resisted hugging her.

"Sam," my dad said, facing his palms against an invisible wall between us. "It hurts so much when you lie. The truth. That's all we want."

My lips were sewn together. I couldn't say anything, truth or lie. I'd just survived the most stressful night of my life and was having the worst fight with my dad yet. I wanted the floor to swallow me and spit me out somewhere else. Preferably somewhere like my cozy bed. Or a rave.

I set my glass down and took a deep breath. "Here's what happened. Johanna told me about a rave party in Santa Cruz. Jamie told some of her friends at her school about it, and they wanted to go too. We knew you guys wouldn't let us go, so we all said we were going to a show at Ashkenaz. We'd only been at the rave, I don't know, about an hour when we got your pages. I left the rave to find a payphone to call you."

My dad looked at my mom, who had stopped crying for my spiel.

"How does the LSD fit into this?" he asked.

I shook my head, looking at the empty glass on the counter. "That was news to me. I had no idea they were doing that."

I let my tears go. My dad forced me into a tight hug. He was trembling, his body odor thick in my nose. My mom overflowed with tears.

Why was telling the truth so hard? Was the truth that scary?

Short answer, yes. My parents had already caught me sneaking out, shoplifting, lying—all of which I'd gotten grounded for. If they knew about my elaborate scheme to see my older boyfriend at an illegal rave and drop acid, they would take my freedom away. I would be grounded forever, I'd never get to go to a rave again, and I'd have to surrender to a normal high school existence. So yeah, telling the truth was scary, and I didn't care what toll it took on my family.

I needed to rave. It was where I could be myself. It was where I belonged. And unlike Sonia, I could handle my drugs.

7

I FEEL LOVE,
DONNA SUMMER REMIX

Before I'd started dating Brandon, being grounded had been a trend. After I met him, it became the norm.

My parents were usually cheerful, laidback folks. They had a thriving social life—my mom loved to cook and host dinner parties on the weekends, enjoying my dad being home, since he traveled for work often during the week. And they weren't super strict; they wanted to trust their kids. But when our parents gave us some freedom, we often abused it, leaving them anxious and untrusting. It was a constant emotional tug-of-war.

I'd never played hooky before I met Brandon. What we did was only mildly rebellious: we left campus after lunch to see the movie *Seven*. After the movie, we went to a park and lazed around in the grass. I arrived home around my usual after-school time, and my mom questioned me about a call she'd received from school earlier that day. I guess Naomi pretending to be my mom and excusing me for a doctor's appointment hadn't been as believable as we'd thought it would be.

She sighed. "We have to tell your father about this."

I nodded.

"It's probably better that you tell him first," she continued. "When he gets home tonight."

I frowned.

When I confessed later, my dad hastily asked, "Were you having sex with him today?!"

I scowled at the accusation. "No! Dad! We just went to the movies and then hung out in a park. Geez."

He demanded details and I supplied them, along with a ticket stub. I was grounded for two weeks.

One weekend, I asked my mom to go shopping with me to buy a lava lamp.

She chuckled. "You know, your father and I had one of those in our first apartment."

Theirs had been the typical 1960s gold and red. Mine was black and purple—the '90s version.

My bedroom was a breeding ground for all things trippy. It became my personal Chill Room. An inflatable Gumby stood in a corner next to the stuffed Ren & Stimpy dolls perched on my burgundy dresser. Magazine tears of Linda, Claudia, and Naomi vogued on my walls. I draped purple netted fabric around my black wrought iron bed, creating a whimsical nest.

The Area 51 Santa Cruz disaster happened on my first free weekend after being grounded for playing hooky with Brandon. For that, I was grounded for a month. No overnights, and I had to be home right after school. Major downer.

When my dad told me what my sentence was, he led with,

"Your mother and I think you may benefit from speaking to someone. A professional. A therapist."

I considered it. I knew I was breaking the rules, but I couldn't help it. I was a girl who just wanted to have fun. If I couldn't speak to my parents, I thought it might be helpful to talk to an older person other than my brothers.

Justin was going through his own stoner stuff, and we mostly talked about weed. I wasn't very close with Reed. He had graduated from college and was living in a loft in Oakland. I only saw him for family stuff. When we talked, it was about him and his busboy job at a local restaurant that required him to keep his wavy brown hair short, which he didn't like. He had a sociology degree from a reputable college and was whip smart, always kept up with Mom and Dad's political conversations. He rarely asked what was going on with me, and I didn't think he wanted to hear about raves and my boyfriend.

I missed the days we lived in the same house and I would listen to his music through his door at the end of the hallway. Sophisticated, melancholy Morrissey. Dark, intense Depeche Mode. Reed and I couldn't connect through conversation, but I felt connected to him through his music. He was my mysterious older brother with Luke Perry hair and a red Swatch guard on his watch. I looked up to him and hoped one day we'd be friends.

Therapy was more my dad's idea. A self-made technology entrepreneur, he grew up in Oakland with a brother, homemaker mother, and police officer father. Both his mother and father were drinkers. Living in the volatile throes of alcoholism created a divisive environment. Then my grandfather lost his job. Home life got worse, and my dad couldn't stand living with his parents anymore.

He moved out of his parent's house at sixteen and was on his own.

He applied for college at UC Berkeley and was accepted. Tuition for California residents was free then, and he slept on a friend's living room floor in his sleeping bag during his first semester. Unable to afford an apartment, he eventually dropped out of school to find full-time work.

His first job was a posting machine operator at a diamond sales company in Oakland. He worked there while he took a data processing class, hoping it would land him a better job that would pay for school. He soon got a software job at Wells Fargo Bank that proved to be more lucrative than he'd imagined. He got an apartment and a girlfriend he would marry too soon. After two years of marriage, he and his first wife called it quits. He refocused on his career but was lost as to why his relationship had crashed and burned.

One stoned night, a friend suggested that my dad seek the help of a therapist. Communicating feelings didn't come naturally to my father, due mostly to his closed-off parents. Therapy was a foreign concept. And a luxury. But he could afford it, so he decided to give it a try.

With the help of therapy and a little medicinal marijuana, my dad worked out his relationship issues. He continued college at a different school in 1963—the year John F. Kennedy was assassinated.

Around 1965, my father became buddies with an interesting character in Berkeley named Owsley Stanley. Another Berkeley dropout, he was a chemist involved in the college's psychoactive drug scene. By the time my dad rubbed elbows with him, Owsley was creating some of the cleanest LSD in the Bay Area. The first LSD millionaire, Stanley manufactured mass quantities of acid out of his private lab and supplied the author and psychedelic activist Ken Kesey, the Grateful Dead, and my dad.

After a few busy years working a day job, resisting the draft, and weekend acid trips, my dad met my mom in 1968 at his first consulting gig, where my mom was a secretary. Long legs, dimples, a sweet disposition—he asked her out right away. Their first date was a Janis Joplin and Jimi Hendrix concert at The Fillmore in San Francisco. They married seven months later.

My parents often reminded us kids growing up that they were working-class folks who'd had to make money and hold down real jobs in the '60s. Although I didn't know about the extent of my dad's drug use until way after my teen years, I knew both my parents had smoked weed—or "pot," as they called it—in their youth, and that at one point in time, they'd been kinda cool.

Fast-forward to me being grounded in the '90s. As long as I did my chores around the house, I received a monthly allowance. Loophole: I could still shop during my groundings.

I reorganized my closet and began planning my next rave outfit. A flash to the hallway at Area 51 and the shoes the guy with the surgical mask was wearing: white Adidas shell toes with black stripes.

Found.

I bought a furry Dalmatian backpack. I would have preferred a pug, like our dog, Sunny, but it would do. I also found a vintage red, white, and blue colorblock Adidas jacket on Telegraph Ave. I spent the rest of my allowance on Make Up For Ever glitter.

School was way more interesting knowing Brandon would be there. Most mornings, I would sit on the same bench where I first spotted him, waiting for his vintage white Chevy Malibu to roll across the parking lot. Because he was a senior, and the quarterback, he had one of the best parking spots on campus, steps away from the quad.

After he parked, he would walk up to me, say, "Hey, Sparkles," and hug me. He smelled like incense and Old Spice deodorant—woodsy, sporty. Sometimes he tried to kiss me, and I awkwardly kissed him back. Kissing in front of everyone made me self-conscious. And when he tried to hold my hand, I tensed, checking to see if anyone was looking at us. Hand-holding felt very intimate to me. I hadn't done it very much with guys before.

Foxy Lady—

I am so glad that there is no school tomorrow. I'm about to go get some new shoes. You may come if you like. "I Got a Girl" was on the radio this morning and I thought of only you. You got to come see me during class sometime, it's been a while. How come I never see you at practice and where were you after school yesterday? What's going on! Well, I hope the rest of your day goes well and I'll talk to you later.

—Jimi

Brandon's letters made me feel more special than a good grade ever could. When he passed me one in the quad or the hallway, I hurried out of his sight to read the words scribbled in pencil on notebook paper.

And why didn't he see me at practice and where was I after school? I was grounded, and too embarrassed to remind him. I didn't want to appear young and immature, even though that's what I was. So I was acting cool, or what I thought was cool. The weeks after Area 51, I felt like Brandon had been distant, but it was me who was acting distant. I wasn't able to spend any time with him outside of school. Maybe it was all in my head, but after our few special dates, I was feeling like our sizzle had fizzled.

And someone was always watching us. The girl Brandon had gone to the dance with, Kimberly, gave me the hairy eyeball at every chance. She was part of a clique of intimidating girls we called the "Senior Bitches," like from the movie *Dazed and Confused*. And as much as I loved Parker Posey's character's fierceness in the film, I didn't like having one stalking me.

I first caught her staring when Naomi and I were splitting our daily order of cafeteria French fries. Between chews, I said, "Dude, I think that Senior Bitch is watching me."

Naomi lifted a fry, her maroon nails shining, and said, "Yeah, well, that's because you got Brandon and she didn't."

The week of Valentine's Day was a mixed chocolate box of emotions. My girlfriends were sending their crushes Valentine-grams, candy presents delivered in class. I ordered one for Brandon but regretted it soon after—what if he didn't send me one? It was the first time I'd ever had a Valentine. My mom giving me cards and chocolates on February 14 wasn't exactly what I'd fantasized about when I became a teenager.

And then it came: 2/14/96. Judgment day. All morning, I watched as my classmates received Valentine-grams. I didn't get one. By lunch, I was irritable, wondering if he'd gotten mine yet. Anger was brewing inside me. I took it out on my cuticles, picking and pulling at sore fingers, trying to hide my compulsion under my desk. I was unfocused the rest of the day.

My last class was geometry, a challenging subject for me. When the door opened with fifteen minutes of class left, half of my classmates—including me—inched forward on their seats in hopes of getting something special, while the other half rolled their eyes in disgust (or jealousy).

A junior girl plopped something red on my desk. Pretending not to be ecstatic, I opened a silk pouch filled with Hershey kisses, heart candies, and a handwritten note:

HAPPY VALENTINE'S DAY, SPARKLES. I CAN'T WAIT TO KISS YOU
AGAIN AND AGAIN.

LOVE, BRANDON

Screw class—I wanted to leave right then to find him and melt inside his mouth like an M&M, kissing him again and again, in front of the whole school. Especially in front of Kimberly, that Senior Bitch. I was so relieved. He was mine. Was it love? I couldn't wait to find out.

When my grounding was over, my parents let me go to a Lenny Kravitz concert with Brandon. We dropped acid and found ourselves on a good vibe at The Warfield in San Francisco. Blinding spotlights, roaring rock, animated faces—it was sensory overload. Whenever it felt overwhelming, I nestled into Brandon, feeling fine.

As we stood close to the stage, Brandon hugging me from

behind, his body locked with mine, I looked up at Lenny, his dreadlocks flying around like octopus tentacles, his abs like Moroccan tiles, and I had an Adonis moment. He was the most beautiful man I'd ever seen. I turned around to see Brandon, a dopey smile on his face. It was the one time he'd paled compared to another man.

"Come on and love me," Lenny sang.

Come on and love me, I repeated in my head, hoping Brandon would.

8

GLITTER GIRL
NEXT DOOR

Gaia, March 1996
Homies: Dana
Location: Somewhere in Alameda
Drugs: Weed

I learned a lesson about glitter when Dana and I went to a rave in Alameda, an island city near Oakland. We had ambitious face glitter plans. Think Ziggy Stardust NEON. We spent hours getting ready at her house and then snuck out.

I'd just parked my dad's Honda Prelude at a hidden spot in Dana's neighborhood so we could get high when we realized we'd forgotten something to smoke with. We hurried to make a J with Post-its we found inside a textbook in my car.

Yellow Post-its are a poor substitute for rolling paper, but they fire a quick blaze. Burning chunks of herb blew into the air like fireflies. We swatted them away, squirming and laughing at our desperate attempt to get stoned.

"We can do this!" Dana exclaimed, rolling another one. I knew I was somewhat high when I caught myself admiring her shimmering mermaid face every time we relit our makeshift joints.

☺

There had been no Map Point for this rave, and there was no line when we walked up to the single-story warehouse around 1:00 a.m. It was practically deserted inside. There were two dance rooms, and hardly anyone was dancing in the louder, larger one. There was no Chill Room. And we couldn't thoroughly enjoy the lights because we'd only smoked weed that night, sorta. The multicolored prisms didn't come to life when I wasn't in acid trip-out mode.

Lively techno music accompanied our search for acid, but we didn't come across anyone friendly. As I was admiring a table lined with lighted toys for sale—glow jewelry, wands with snow globe tops, sparkly bubble rings—I smiled at the guy in a white visor next to me. In a snarky tone and with a whip of his hand, he said, "Whoa, someone likes glitter a little too much."

I grabbed Dana and sheepishly walked into the darkness. I was offended and I wasn't having fun—it wasn't the same vibe as the other raves I'd gone to. There was hardly a vibe at all. And people were mean. I took a few rave flyers from people handing them out, and we left.

The night was a dud. We'd had high expectations, but nothing eventful happened.

Better nothing than stressy drama, though, right?

Where were all the friendly party people tonight? I wondered. *And doesn't every rave have a dreamy Chill Room?*

We snuck back into Dana's house and whispered in the bathroom while scrubbing our faces to get all the glitter off. As I slept, I think a couple pores swallowed some glitter that resurfaced as vengeful pimples weeks later.

That night made me think about always being prepared. We'd had our acid for Eon ahead of time; Marku had hooked us up. And Johanna had gotten it for Santa Cruz. Would Gaia have been so disappointing if we'd found a mind-altering party favor? Did I need drugs to have fun at a rave?

The next week at school Brandon asked me, "You're always sparkling, aren't you?" and reached a finger to my cheek to brush away a lingering metallic fleck.

He noticed the details I worked hard to perfect. He complimented my outfits and different makeup looks. He commented about my body often, all positive, like when he said, "Man, your legs go on forever" while caressing them.

His ego-boosting comments increased after I went to the *Rocky Horror Picture Show* and showed up at school with massive hickeys that looked like splattered tomatoes on both sides of my neck. He wasn't familiar with the cult musical, and I told him getting hickeys on your neck from strangers was a deflowering ritual. Or at least it was in Berkeley. Or at least it was a sneaky way for older guys to suck on younger girls' necks.

"If you were there, *you* could have given me the hickeys," I flirted.

He laughed, then teased me for wearing a turtleneck.

A couple of weeks later, I suggested that Dana, Marku, Brandon, and I trip out one night in my Chill Bedroom. I thought having Brandon at my house more would make my parents like him. When the guys showed up after dinner on a Friday night, they smiled big and greeted my parents.

"We're just gonna hang out in my room tonight," I said, whisking the four of us up the stairs.

We dropped acid and listened to an evolving electronica mix. DJ Keoki's uppity house to get our private party started. Deee-Lite's playful tunes to trip out and dance. Bjork's experimental art-pop for sitting around and playing with stuffed animals. Then, eventually, Enya's new age sound for winding down, ogling my lava lamp, and watching Marku create a feathers-dancing-on-pillows show.

A knock on my door startled me. Something was penetrating our cocoon. Someone. I told everyone to shush and act normal and slowly opened the door to see my mom standing in the hallway. The pores on her face looked like snowflakes. A halo of light glowed around her. Her aura was a warm sunshine yellow.

She said she and my dad were going to sleep and asked if I could turn the music down. I agreed, and then she was gone. She had no idea I was frying balls. I had no idea what time it was. I wasn't weirded out by the encounter; it left me with a satisfied feeling of being safe.

The four of us danced, laughed, and kissed one another for hours around my room, bathroom, the guest room, and the outdoor patio, channeling the same escapist vibe from that special first night at Eon. The boys left at some late-night hour, and my parents never brought it up. They trusted that since I was home, everything was fine. And it was.

My favorite thing to do with Brandon after school was get stoned, kick back, and listen to music together. Brandon's room was a converted guest bedroom, and it had a separate side entrance from his family's house.

His bed was on a raised wooden platform to the right of the entrance. At the foot of his bed was a TV with built-in VCR. Down some stairs was a living area with a futon and an oblong coffee table. A stereo sat on his desk, along with racks of CDs and loose papers. His closet was built underneath the bed platform above. A couple of lamps kept the lighting dim.

One Saturday night, we smoked a couple bowls and, happily mellowed, sat on his teal futon listening to Maxwell's smooth-talking, body-swaying R&B. I was leaning into Brandon, and his arm was wrapped around my shoulder. Incense smoke wafted above the coffee table, snakes turning into clouds.

He ran a hand up my thigh over my jeans, up my chest, and pulled me toward him for a kiss. We melted into every suck and swirl of our tongues. He felt my breasts inside my shirt. Then his hand reached for between my legs. I sank back to get more comfortable. He undid my jeans.

"Take off your shirt," I said, eager to watch him undress.

He sat up and lifted his green V-neck tee over his head, tousling his black hair. Sex oozed out of him. His hairless skin radiated heat. I wiggled against the cushion to push my pants down, kicking them off. I kept my black lace underwear on.

He shifted to lie on his side, sliding one arm under my neck while his other hand roamed my body. We kissed hard, competing for who could kiss the hardest. Cottonmouth from being stoned was long gone; we were drooling for each other.

Brandon's fingers found the warmth inside my underwear. I raised my hips up as his fingertips gently traced circles around my most sensitive layers. My tongue flexed with every pulse of his touch, encouraging him to keep going.

After stirring me up, Brandon stopped to take a breath, then slid a finger inside me. My body agreed with a sharp undulation. His finger glided back and forth inside me, slowly, knowingly, building me up for two fingers, three, and maybe something bigger and better than fingers. Maybe. Rousing sensations flowed inside me. I squinted for a peek at my sexy man. His eyes were closed as he kissed me.

"Let's go to the bed," I whispered.

He stood up quickly, leaving me breathless on the futon. He extended a hand and led me up the stairs to his bed. Then, facing the bed, he undid his belt buckle.

"Whoa! Leave your underwear on!" I spazzed.

He chuckled. "I will. I just wanted to get comfortable."

I jumped onto his bed playfully, trying to make up for my outburst. He jumped after me, landed in the covers, and rolled into my arms.

"Where were we?" he asked, sliding his hand inside my underwear.

I wanted to get comfortable too, so I pulled my underwear off. We started kissing again. Brandon slid two powerful fingers back inside me, forcing my body into a convulsion. I squeezed the stiff mound under his boxers. I wanted him inside me.

I opened my legs for him to go harder, better, faster. Lips, fingers, tongues, nipples . . .

"You can take off your underwear now," I breathed.

"Wow," he said, "you're getting so wet."

Surprised, I sat up abruptly. Brandon's fingers fell out of me. He raised his hand from under the sheet. Bright red blood covered his fingers. I was warm and wet between my legs, and I threw the sheet off to see a crimson mess.

"Oh my god!" I blurted, covering my face with my hands.

"Shit," he sat up, keeping his hand raised.

"Oh my god, this is so embarrassing," I said through my hands. "I got my period all over your bed."

"Uh, maybe. I think I just popped your cherry, babe."

I wailed a dramatic sigh. Brandon leaned over to grab some tissues and started wiping his hand.

"Really, it's okay," he said, cocking his head to the side. "Nothing to be ashamed of."

"Yes, it is!" I yelled. "What time is it?" I grabbed for my stuff, searching for a clock.

He looked at his watch and winced. "11:55."

"Fuck, I have to go!"

I threw my clothes on. Brandon kissed me and reassured me it was all right. I jumped into my car and zagged up, down, and around the hills to get home.

Brandon and I lived close to each other. His house was by the 7-Eleven where Tommy and I would get Slurpees after getting stoned. I would have made my midnight curfew if it weren't for that stupid stoplight—that was my excuse when I got home late to find my dad waiting for me.

"You should just plan for that long light," he said, stomping up the stairs toward his bedroom.

"I can't control these things," I said. "Cut me some slack, Dad."

9

LOVED UP

My dad did cut me some slack, and I wasn't grounded for that night. Soon after, I was with friends heading to a rave in San Francisco.

After a fun hot box, Dana drove me, Johanna, Tommy, and Val, another friend from school, across the Bay Bridge. To avoid drama, I'd made sure the attendees had either already been to a rave or had experience with drugs. Preferably both.

With the exception of Tommy, who crossed his fingers hoping his parents wouldn't track him down that night. He'd listened, wide-eyed, when I'd told him how earthshaking Eon was. He'd been dying to go to a rave, but his parents were stricter than mine. So we'd both been on our best behavior for weeks, getting home before curfew and doing extra chores to make nice with our parents, and now it was finally happening.

We drove by an industrial building downtown with no sign and a few people lingering by a closed door. I'd expected a warehouse-type space—a place that could go unnoticed. While hunting the dimly lit parking lot for a spot, a couple of dudes in baggy pants and bucket hats shambled away from the venue, yelling to us, "The party just broke up, don't bother!"

"What?!" we yelled back, rolling down our windows.

One guy stopped. "They shut the music off about thirty minutes ago. And turned on the lights. That's usually a sign the party's over. You might want to bounce before the cops show up."

After hearing us wail like kittens, the guy's friend leaned into our car. "Do you guys need any Ecstasy?"

I'd heard of it and was curious to try it. We took him up on his offer. Dana was the only one who'd done ecstasy before, and since we couldn't go back to anyone's house without creating a stir, she suggested going somewhere in nature. After a brief exchange, we decided to create our own rave closer to home.

We stopped at a liquor store to get water, something Dana said we needed lots of. I grabbed some gum. My stomach was aflutter with nerves. We were getting back into the car when Tommy announced, "I'm taking mine now. Dana, is that cool with you? I mean, you've already done it, and you're driving."

"Yeah," she said. "Go ahead. I'll take mine when we get closer to the place."

I inspected the mystery pill before putting it in my mouth. It looked like a round white baby Tylenol, which it very well could have been since we'd bought it from a stranger. Tommy didn't savor the moment; he quickly swallowed his.

An anticipatory quiet consumed me as we drove back over the bridge we'd crossed just an hour before. The weed had made my eyes dry and heavy, and I closed them, opening my ears to the music coming out of the car speakers. Fast. Reverberating. Digital. Some kind of techno. Tuning in to the orbital sounds, I tuned out my friends' voices as the car rolled over slabs of steel on the bridge. The caged lights of the midway tunnel through Yerba Buena Island glowed golden through my eyelids.

When we reached the end of the tunnel, my eyes opened and . . .

OHHHHH MYYYYY GODDDDDD

PHASE 1

Sight and sound merged, bursting inside me. My senses ignited. A steam engine train, conga drum taps, stompy heavies—sounds bounced around me, and I was instantly uplifted. The flutter in my stomach turned into a flitter, a wiggle, a ripple of butterflies trapped inside me.

I was sitting between Tommy and Johanna in the back seat. My arms flew across their chests, bracing myself for 100 mph.

"Holy shit!" I yelled. "Do you feel what I'm feeling?"

"Duuuuude." Tommy's voice echoed. "This is craaaazzzyyy."

"Oh my god!" I said under my breath. "I need to get out of the car."

"Hold on!" Johanna said, laughing.

"Uhhh, I don't know if I can," I said.

"Hold my hand," she said, her warm, soft skin becoming mine.

Dana yelled back to us, "Is it working?!"

Val was in the passenger seat. She turned around to face us, her blond curls wild in the wind. She reached her left arm out to us and let out a loud "whoaaa!"

My eyes were a different kind of heavy now. They wanted to roll up and back into my head. I couldn't focus. I was grabbing at Tommy's knee, kneading it, needing it. I couldn't feel my other hand. It had drifted off into space. Bright, dim, stars. Aliens! The blood in my veins bubbled. I rolled down the window. Take my breath awayyyyyy! I tried to focus on the glittering night horizon as new sensations exploded inside me.

I grabbed my water bottle and chugged and . . .

A freezing waterfall quenched a powerful thirst inside me.

"Oh my god oh my god oh my god."

"I know I know I know."

"Are you guys okay back there?" Dana asked.

"Yes! Holy shit. Dude!"

"Okay!" she yelled. "Where do you guys want to go?"

"I don't care, just get us there, I'm about to pop!" I yelled.

"Tiiillldddden?" Tommy suggested.

"Yes!" I agreed. "Anywhere. I just need to get out of this car."

"Me too!" Val squealed.

"We'll be there in, like, ten minutes," Dana said. "No unnecessary noises, please!"

We exited the freeway and headed into the Berkeley hills, swaying with the twists and turns. The streets were familiar but better, shimmering and vibrating, welcoming and soothing. It was hypnotic, mesmerizing, fabulous, amazing, beautiful, gorgeous—it was a lot of things. I was seeing, hearing, tasting, touching, and expanding all at once. It was wonderfully overwhelming.

I heard myself ask, "Tommy, how are you?"

"I'm great!"

"Fantastic!"

"Awesome!"

"Wonderful!"

Suddenly, I was super excited by the idea of applying lip balm. And smoking a cigarette! And kissing someone! I wanted to kiss someone ASAP. Just as I was about to grab Tommy and fulfill my desire, the car slowed and stopped.

PHASE 2

I pushed the car door open and ran into a midnight meadow of grass. I dropped down on my knees, ripped two fistfuls of grass out of the ground, shot up, and set the shards free into the sky. I stretched my arms up, over my head, reached for the stars, released. A chill gave me another rush.

Like sparks from a firework, the five of us dispersed, frolicking around the lawn, yelling and laughing. Waves of gold and red and blue circled us, illuminating us.

Though not the safest setting to take drugs in, or the warmest, you could count on the hills of Berkeley for an open range. The dense redwood and eucalyptus trees of Tilden Park muffled our rebel yells. We merged with nature, with each other. We danced, absorbing the music blasting from the open car windows.

"I'm going to climb that tree!" Val yelled.

Dipping my shoulders to the beats, my body loose as liquid, I watched as she ran toward the trees, her curls bouncing in the moonlight.

Dana's black Toyota Corolla became a car version of a Chill

Room. At one point, Tommy and I sat in the back seat for 3,600 seconds.

"Does my voice sound like a robot?" he asked me, his voice higher-pitched than I'd ever heard it.

Lost in my crystal ball ring, I replied, "My voice sounds like a fucking feather."

"I sound like a machine."

"No you don't."

"In my head I do."

Val poked her crazed face into the open car window. "Guys! I'm itchy and really dizzy. And I'm about to fall asleep. But I'm not. I don't know what I'm talking about." Poof! She was gone.

I craved another cigarette. I'd never enjoyed smoking cigarettes that much before. They fed me. It was like I was sucking energy in and blowing out all worry and negativity. A breeze swept over us. I shivered uncontrollably.

"Is everything blurry for you?"

"I'm hot I'm cold I'm hot I'm cold I'm hot I'm cold I'm hot, I can't decide right now!"

"Yo, hook me up with some water."

"Whoa—smoking weed just really enhanced the high."

"I'm so fucked up."

"I know, don't you love it?"

Regarded as a stabilizer rather than an upper, ecstasy breaks down emotional barriers and tames neurosis, allowing freedom of the spirit. It increases the brain's dopamine and serotonin levels, releasing it into the nervous system. The result? Energy and euphoria, plus sensory overload, sometimes laced with hallucinations. And, when you're in a group: bonding.

Arousal swelled inside me, reaching a boiling point. The

only male body available was Tommy. I wanted him. Bad. So bad. Soooooooo baaaaaaaad.

He was sitting on the curb between the grassy lawn and parking lot when I approached him and Johanna.

I placed my hands on my hips, trying not to fall over, and said, "Tommy, I need you. I need to kiss someone right now."

He looked up at me with rolling eyes and said, "Oh shit. Samantha, I can't."

"Tommy! C'mon, aren't you horny?"

"I am! But I can't. I'm sorry. I can't even stand up right now."

He was too high and too gay to kiss me.

Johanna looked up at me. "I'll kiss you."

"Oooooh shit," Tommy said, giggling.

Johanna stood up, took my hand, and led me to the Chill Car. We closed the doors and pounced on each other in the back seat. It was my first time kissing a girl. She was incredibly soft. We pawed at each other like wildcats, catching our fingers in each other's hair, circling our tongues.

She had large breasts, and my average 34B self had always been curious to see them. I smoothed my hands over her chest, and she removed her shirt in a flash. I took mine off too. I kissed her neck, and she tossed her head back in pleasure. This revved me up, and I licked her like ice cream.

Lustrous flesh spilled out of her bra. I teased her tight nipples with my tongue. Moonlight shone through the window, illuminating Johanna's slender wrists and tender lips, and I realized I was hooking up with a girl. With my best friend. But I didn't care. She made me feel sensual and safe.

I was stroking her breast when she ran her hand down between my legs. Her blurred smile reassured me. My pants evaporated as her fingers found my core, where I'd been tingly all night. Her touch was gentle. It reminded me of mine, when I would explore myself in my bed, lights out, doors locked, Sneaker Pimps singing low. She caressed me with rhythmic strokes as our mouths found each other again. She dominated me, insinuating her fingers into all my slippery entrances. It was naughty. New.

She stopped kissing me to grab the lever on the passenger seat in front of us, folding and sliding it forward so we had more space. She pulled my underwear off and crouched down in front of me so she could get a better angle to consume me. Then her tongue spun around, a tornado on my most private place. I ignored any second thoughts and surrendered.

PHASE 3

Moonlit mania gave way to early dawn. Morning emerged. The comedown was subtle and gentle, tapering into an afterglow phase. The brightness in my mind dimmed and my body felt weighted. My fingers tingled. I was relaxed inside my snow globe, lying in a hammock covered in a blanket of gold.

We gathered together to keep warm in Dana's car as our extreme high faded into an overcast Sunday. Even though my head was foggy, my soul was awake, mystified by the release of ecstasy. Among the five of us, there was no shame regarding our exploits, sexual or otherwise. It had been a night that could never be repeated, spiced with details that wouldn't be explained; we had experienced something extraordinary together.

"Does anyone else feel like a bagel?" Tommy asked.

Growls had replaced the butterflies in my stomach. After all, sustained hours of ultimate bliss can leave one famished. It was 7:00 a.m., too early to go home. With smudged makeup and matted hair, we breezed down the hills toward Noah's Bagels on Solano Avenue.

It was awkward between me and Johanna in the following weeks. We couldn't look at each other without blushing. Our friends had their ideas of what had happened in the back seat, but only Johanna and I knew. When the blushing faded, I felt closer to her. Bonded. I knew her intimately. We trusted each other. And ecstasy had created an unquenchable curiosity for both of us.

Magical rainbows and forever friendships aside, one question remained: *Did I just cheat on my boyfriend?*

10 / BAD VIBES

"There's something I think you should know," Dana said, holding a pillow in her lap.

We were hanging out at her house after school. Her tone was serious.

"Okay," I said as I stopped flipping through her closet.

"It's about Brandon. I wasn't sure if I should tell you or not, but I found out something about him and his ex. Marku told me. It just came out, and well, I guess I'd want to know...."

My stomach clenched. "Something about him and his ex?"

I walked over to sit with her on her bed. Worn stuffed animals tumbled into her unmade bed as I mirrored her position. I sensed she didn't want to continue the conversation she'd started. I'd seen enough TV to know I was about to star in my own after-school special. I wanted her to go on; I wanted her to stop.

Her eyebrows dove into each other as she said, "I'm so sorry."

"What is it?!" I laughed nervously. "Come on, you have to tell me now."

"I know, I know." She sighed. "There are rumors that Brandon has been sleeping with his ex."

The room started closing in on me.

"There are also rumors he's messing around with Kim Shaps."

That stung like lemon on a fresh cut.

"What?!"

"I know, I'm sorry—it's like, a double shit whammy."

"Kimberly?" I spat. "That nasty Senior Bitch?!"

She nodded. "Apparently Brandon's ex has been after him all year to get back together. I think she's been, like, throwing herself at him."

I couldn't move; my body was frozen and burning at the same time.

"As for Kimberly, well, everyone knows she's a slut." Dana rolled her eyes.

"Wait!" I yelled, jumping off the bed. "He's cheating on me with *two girls*?"

Her fist slammed into a pillow. "I know! I'm sorry. He's such an asshole."

"I . . . really?" Tongue-tied, tummy-tied, I thought I was going to barf into Dana's face, *Exorcist*-style. This was the worst news possible—not what I was expecting, the last thing I wanted to hear. I needed confirmation it was true. I grabbed my backpack. "I'm going to talk to him," I said, dashing out the door.

It was early May, and my sophomore year was almost over. The fresh spring air I'd breathed that morning was replaced with shallow breaths of bitter fear as I drove toward Brandon's house. Vibrant orange poppies were wilted, dying.

I rolled my window down to cool my inflamed cheeks and chest. My head swirled with words of denial: *It can't be true. There's no way. He loves me. He hasn't said it yet, but I feel it, I know it.* My eyes burned as I fought back tears. I wouldn't let them go until I heard him deny it. What I really wanted to do was pull over and scream, but I gripped the steering wheel tight, determined to get the truth.

The closer I got to his house, the more anger edged in, pushing denial aside. *No wonder she always scowls when I look at her*, I thought. *Fat thighs, too much makeup, Senior Bitch. She hates me and she's fucking Brandon. And the ex? What the fuck? He dumped your ass, deal with it. But she's pretty. Beautiful, actually. More beautiful than me. Is this why he hasn't pressured me to sleep with him? Because he's getting it anyway? Fucker.*

As I swerved down his narrow hill, I saw his Chevy Malibu parked in the driveway. I jumped out of my car, ran down the wooden stairs to his room, and knocked on his door fast and strong, like a woodpecker.

"Hey!" He opened the door, surprised.

"Hey," I said, pushing him inside. "I need to talk to you."

"Uh, I was about to go meet Marku, but what's up?"

I turned around, put my hands on my hips, and asked, "Are you cheating on me?"

His baby caterpillar eyebrows rose. "Whoa! Wow. What?"

"Brandon, I need you to tell me the truth. You've been acting weird lately, and I just have this feeling."

He walked over to his futon. "Come over here," he beckoned.

The smell of patchouli lingered in his lair. He looked as cute as ever. But when I looked at the futon, I saw someone else's face. Long brown hair. Bright blue eyes. Freckles. His ex's face.

"No," I said, firm. I couldn't sit. I couldn't be near him. I needed an answer.

He sat down. "I don't know what to say."

"What the fuck does that mean?" I hissed. "Is that a yes?!"

"Did someone tell you something?"

"No. I just feel like something is off, and we haven't slept together yet, so I put two and two together. I'm not a fucking idiot. I'm not some stupid girl you can cheat on!"

"I know, I have a lot of respect for you. I just . . ." He averted his eyes to the floor, then the wall, then the table. "It's complicated."

"Yeah it's fucking complicated," I scoffed. "I would think having three girlfriends complicates things. What the fuck? How long has this been happening?"

"I'm sorry."

Rejected. I couldn't believe it. I thought he really liked me. Maybe loved me. I stared at his pretty face. He was frowning, ugly and pathetic. I wanted to choke him. Or, at the very least, kick him in the balls, which is what my brother Justin had always said I should do if I needed to defend myself against a guy.

"Thank you for not denying it," I said, trembling, as I turned for the door, blinking back tears.

He didn't call after me, which was what I wanted him to do.

I drove home through rapids, tears streaming down my face. My nose stuffed up as I blasted "In the Meantime" by Spacehog to comfort myself, singing along desperately. The song filled my head with lyrics that fought my swirling insecurities.

Was Eon and doing acid together one-sided? Did we have a connection or did I imagine it? But he accepted me for who I really am. Weird, silly, confused, I didn't scare him away. Was it all an act to get me to sleep with him? Was I that stupid?

I hastily cut corners and ran stop signs—I didn't care if I got in an accident.

When I got home, I burst into the kitchen, where my mom was preparing dinner, and before she had a chance to say anything, I announced, "You'll be happy to know that Brandon and I broke up, so I won't be getting into any more trouble."

As if!

I ran up the stairs, slamming doors behind me, and plunged my face into a pillow—you know, the whole dramatic scene.

Exactly 296 tears later, a gentle knock on the door accompanied a soft-spoken "Samantha?"

My mom opened the door and sat down on my bed next to me. She didn't say anything. She just hugged me as tears spilled out.

The rest of the week at school, I changed course, avoiding any places Brandon might be. But I wasn't dwelling on what he'd done. I couldn't. It was too hurtful. I was plotting instead. And venting to Johanna and Naomi. I'd never been hurt so badly by a boy—by anyone. My feelings were too much to handle, and someone had to pay for my grief.

Kimberly. She was a slut who needed to know that she couldn't mess with me.

That Friday, Naomi, Johanna, and I went to the grocery store after school to pick up some things. The shopping list:

- Shaving cream
- Peanut butter
- Toilet paper
- Chocolate syrup
- Honey
- Shampoo
- Ketchup

- Marshmallows
- Dog food

We stashed the groceries in the trunk of Johanna's car and went to my house, where we waited for my parents to go to sleep. Late that night, the three of us snuck out of my house to her car.

It was a heart-pounding drive to Kimberly's home in the hills. When we approached her house, the lights were out. It didn't matter who was home; all that mattered was that her car was. And it was: her champagne VW Jetta shimmered like a rhinestone in the driveway.

We parked around a corner, grabbed the groceries, and Naomi instructed, "Keep it quiet, keep it swift."

We were wearing all black.

Enter stealth mode.

Red squirts of ketchup shot across her car like confetti party poppers. Marshmallows hailed on the windshield. Honey dripped into the ketchup, and we smeared them together to make diarrhea. Hershey's chocolate syrup slid down the car doors. We didn't have anything to get the peanut butter out with, so we left the jar on the roof of her car as a present. Pantene shampoo created an opalescent goo that filled in any blanks.

Naomi walked over to the wooden garage door. It was naked, begging to be decorated. She shook the shaving cream, pressing her finger into her lips to signal quiet, then turned around and started spelling something. Meanwhile, Johanna and I sprinkled dog food all over the car, topping our scandalous sundae with brown sprinkles.

A light in the house flickered. I flinched. That was our signal to wrap up. Naomi shushed us. We hurried to pick up any empty containers and started running away, bursting with laughter. I paused in the street to take a mental picture of our handiwork. Kimberly's car looked like an automotive interpretation of a Jackson Pollock. But the garage door was the masterpiece. In bloated white letters, Naomi had written "BITCH" across the brown canvas.

"We fucked her shit up!" Johanna yelled as we sped away, lauding one another and laughing.

I slept soundly that night. A noticeable weight had been lifted.

The next Monday at school, I basked in empowerment. The three of us had agreed to keep our stunt a secret. I checked to see if Brandon's car was in his parking spot. It was. If it weren't, I would have wondered where he was. As much as I wanted to, I couldn't get him out of my head.

Another car I was curious to see was Kimberly's Jetta. At lunch, we snuck away to find it to see if there were any remains. There weren't, but knowing her parents had a bitch revenge for breakfast felt devilishly good.

Tuesday was ho-hum.

Wednesday, I wondered why Kimberly was approaching me. It was lunch, and I was sitting with friends at our regular spot on the quad.

"Hi." Kimberly stood in front of me, one hand on her hip. "Can I talk to you?" She sneered at Naomi. "In private."

My jaw clenched. I nodded, stood up, and followed her to a

grassy corner where everyone could see us. Kimberly and me. Senior and Sophomore. Slut and vigilante.

"It's obvious that you know about Brandon and me, and actually, the whole school knows about it, and I'm not exactly proud of it," she said. I studied her plain face as she talked, trying to find a flaw—a pimple, maybe, or a hairy mole. "But last weekend someone messed with my car and my house, and that is not cool. If someone has a problem with me, they should confront me and not mess with my family's property."

She spoke quickly. *Is she nervous too?* My face warmed.

"Did you do it?" she asked, her heavily eye-lined eyes looking through me.

I bit my lip, didn't answer.

She continued, "Well, when my dad washed our garage door, what you spelled with the shaving cream burned through the wood. We need to paint it over."

"Seriously?" I said, hoping my blushing didn't give me away.

"Yeah," she said, attempting her ice stare again.

Cue my mom's voice in my head reminding me, "If you're in trouble, it's better to tell the truth; that way, the consequences won't be as bad."

She asked me again if I'd done it. Caught off guard by the garage door news, I said yes. We hadn't meant to cause any lasting damage. Whoops. She said her parents would contact mine and walked away.

I went back to my friends, who were anticipating hot gossip. I didn't say anything, just pulled Naomi and Johanna aside. They gave me grief for confessing, and I explained that we'd damaged the garage door, which was messed up. I'd already resigned myself to the fact that we'd probably have to pay for the damages.

I spent the rest of the day feeling defeated, dreading going home to make my second confession of the day, to an even harsher audience. I knew it would be better to tell my parents before they received the phone call from Kimberly's parents, though, so I told my mom straight after I got home.

"Your dad's going to be pretty mad about this," she said, shaking her head after I explained everything. I told her that the whole school knew Brandon had cheated on me and I was stupid for thinking he really liked me.

"I'm sure he did truly like you. He just sounds like a jerk," she said in a tone that was more like a best friend's than a mom's. She hugged me, then stepped back, holding my hands loosely in hers. "I understand your anger. Remember my boyfriend before I dated your father? Even though he's the reason I came to California, we were on and off for years because he was a huge jerk that I was stupid enough to keep going back to. And I never got to tell him that to his face. I've always regretted that. If anyone deserves your anger, it's Brandon, not the other girl."

It made sense, and yet I hadn't thought of it. Brandon was the one who'd been dishonest—leading me on, lying. He was the one who deserved to get his precious car messed up like my heart was.

My mom added, "But that doesn't mean you should go vandalize his garage door too."

After all was revealed, my parents paid Kimberly's parents to fix the garage. I was grounded for two weeks. My relationship with Brandon was over, the thrill of revenge gone, the damage done.

Before Brandon, I was in love with the idea of finding love. Then I fell in love. I'd only had a brief taste of that natural euphoria, but it had tasted divine. I knew how to achieve drug-induced euphoria, but love was magnitudes better. I'd been waiting for Brandon to tell me he loved me before I told him. But I'd never gotten the chance. *Was it really love if he didn't love me back?* I wondered, feeling an emptiness inside my chest, a little to the left. It made my entire body ache. I tried to ignore that pain as I yearned for his look, his touch, him.

Looking back, I considered my hypocrisy: How could I be pissed at Brandon for cheating on me when I'd cheated on him that loved-up night with Johanna? Truth is, it hadn't occurred to me to tell him. Because it was with a girl, because I was on ecstasy, it hadn't felt like cheating—I'd felt zero guilt about it. That night had been mythical. Besides, I was sure that if I'd told Brandon about it, he wouldn't have minded; he probably would have thought it was hot.

It was the last week of school and I was in the girls' bathroom doing my midday check. Nadia, one of the coolest (read: nicest) and prettiest senior girls came out of a stall, washed her hands, and stood beside me, looking at herself in the mirror.

"Hey, girl," she said to me in the reflection. She'd never talked to me before, but she always smiled at me in the hallways.

"Oh." I smiled. "Hey!"

She smoothed her black hair pulled into a high ponytail. "I just want to say, speaking for many girls in this school, that what you did to Kimberly was totally warranted. It sucks that everyone knows about what happened with you and Brandon, but we're so glad she got a taste of her own medicine."

Her comforting words were unexpected. Parched for positivity, I soaked them up like aloe vera on a sunburn.

Nadia continued talking through the looking glass. "I'm sorry about what Brandon did to you. He's so full of himself."

Touched by her sympathy and revived by her validation, I said what had been stuck in my head: "Thanks, Nadia. I'm just really glad I never slept with that asshole."

She raised an eyebrow and then, with a knowing smile, said, "See ya," and turned to leave.

"See ya," I said, looking back at my reflection.

It felt good knowing that I wasn't the only one who thought Kimberly deserved a message in a ketchup bottle. Nadia had just picked me up after my fall, when I was feeling bad about pushing another girl down, and created momentary balance in my life.

There weren't any mascara clumps to fix. I looked ready. I turned to leave, ready to release myself into my first summer of rave.

Join us in this journey to a deeper state of consciousness. Experience the joys of peace, freedom, love, and truth as your submerge your mind, body, and soul in the waves of our underground river of sound.

—*Intoxication flyer*

11

GOOD VIBES

Second Chakra, June 1996
Homies: Tommy
Location: The Victorian, San Francisco
Drugs: Acid, nitrous, weed

Inhale and hold it in," the girl told me as she handed me a full yellow balloon. With two hair buns twisted atop her head, she looked like Sailor Moon.

Tommy and I were on acid in a Chill Room, sitting on a scratchy sofa. We'd been tripping out watching people inhaling balloons. Enormous balloons. Carnival-sized. We figured at first that they must be sucking helium and laughing at silly chipmunk voices. But they were laughing so hard, some falling over onto the floor. And they weren't speaking very much. They were definitely high on something.

I put the balloon opening to my mouth, holding the gummy piece tight with my fingers and cupping my other hand around the balloon. I slowly released my grip to suck in the cold air. A cooling sensation filled my lungs. The balloon was so big I could only inhale half of it. I held my breath.

The room narrowed, lengthening like a tunnel. I sank into

the sofa—cushy now, not scratchy, tucking me in like my dad did after reading me a bedtime story when I was a little girl. My cheeks tightened and my mouth opened. I was laughing uncontrollably. Deliciously. I let it out. Everything was hilarious. The room, the rave, the world had just told me the funniest joke I'd ever heard.

I opened my eyes. Sailor Moon was looking at me with an O-shaped mouth, saying, "Wah WAH wah WAH wah WAH." The sound echoed inside my head.

I'd been transported into a tunnel where I was levitating, swimming in happiness. Freestyle first, then slowing into breaststroke, in sync with my laughter vibrations. I was synchronized swimming—dancing and swimming—my two favorite sports growing up. The temperature was perfect inside my tunnel—seventies and sunny—and the air was crystalline clean. When I reached for another stroke, my body stretched and strengthened, opened and received. I was by myself but didn't feel alone.

It started fading away. The giggles drifted out of my body like bubbles floating into the air. I was leaving the tunnel of happiness. I tried to hold on, but there was nothing to grab on to. Just air. I absolutely loved that warm, glowing, otherworldly place I'd just left. I wanted to go back there immediately.

Arriving back to the ambient sounds of the Chill Room, back to semi-reality, I found Tommy smiling sedately next to me. Green moonbeams flashed across him as he sat back on the sofa with half a balloon clenched in one hand.

"Duuuuude" was all he could muster.

I realized I was still holding the rest of the sunshine in my hand too. I put the wetted opening between my lips and inhaled. This time, I sucked in and out, making the balloon smaller like an orange, larger like a watermelon. I knew I could replicate the joy I'd just experienced, maybe make it more intense.

Funny, warm, brilliant—the good vibrations welcomed me as I freestyled back into the tunnel.

Finally, Tommy had made it to his first rave, and he and I were having a fabu time. I'd told my parents I was sleeping at his house and vice versa. I was surprised when my parents allowed me to sleep over at Tommy's. That was pretty cool. They must have been relieved my newest boyfriend was gay, a non-threat. But still, like sleeping at a girlfriend's house, all it took was one phone call to each other's parents and we were screwed.

But so far, so good. Whip-it good.

I wanted more. Like, right then and there. Sailor Moon said another tank was in her friend's car parked outside the party. Tommy and I followed her down the stairs, leaving the party for a dark alley outside.

I didn't waste any time once I had my next balloon in hand, and I attempted to suck the entire thing down in one go. I was trying to stand up, but it's hard to stand still while laughing uncontrollably, on acid, with less oxygen reaching your brain. I was running around like a chicken with its head cut off. I leaned over and saw my knees, cars orbiting around me, and then I heard a loud "BAM!" and the tunnel of happiness went black.

Where did everything go? What happened? Did something hit me?

"Samantha, are you okay? Samantha, are you okay? Samantha, are you okay?" I heard someone say at the end of the tunnel.

Tommy, is that you?

Tommy's voice was getting closer and closer, clearer and clearer. I opened my eyes. I was lying on the ground outside.

Grayish buildings with fire escapes looked down on me. People with worried looks on their faces leaned over me. Tommy and Sailor Moon were among them.

"Samantha, are you okay?" Tommy asked, close and clear.

I muttered, "I think so."

"Dude." He was kneeling next to me. "Thank god. We were about to take you to a hospital."

"Hey, hun," Sailor Moon said gently. "Maybe take it slower next time."

The high on nitrous was short-lived, only lasting seconds, so really, you could do it again and again and recover quickly. Unless you did it for hours—which made you turn into a purple couch potato—or ran into an open car door head-first and passed out, like I just had. It's best to take oxygen breaks between balloons. Your brain needs oxygen. Duh.

I slowly sat up, still piecing together what happened. I looked at the parked cars in the shady alley, dull and dirty. The blow to my head had knocked some of my acid high out of me. A lightning zap of pain through my right temple reminded me of my party foul.

People peeled away and went back to the party, including Sailor Moon. I stood up and dusted off my fall, reassuring Tommy I was okay. We checked our pagers when we got to his car: 4:55 a.m. Tommy and I had seemingly pulled off the night, but we hadn't thought about where we would go post-rave. It was too early to go home.

On the drive back to Oakland, the constant hum of the car's engine was calming, but whenever I moved my head, pain zapped my skull. I cracked my window, hoping the bay breeze would blow the pain away.

Tommy exited the freeway and drove up into the Oakland hills.

"How are you feeling?" he asked.

"Fine," I whispered. "Better."

He parked in front of a hill before a neighborhood. The sky was the cobalt blue it turns before sunrise.

"Can you hike?" he asked.

"Are you kidding?"

"It's really not a hike," he said. "Just up this hill. Have you been here before?"

A chill sent goosebumps up my arms. I zipped my vintage navy-blue Adidas jacket up as far as I could before stepping out of the car. I followed Tommy, watching my steps up the narrow dirt trail in the dawn light.

We were out of breath when we reached the top. After standing together and admiring the twinkling city lights for a minute, we sat down in the damp grass. No one around, everyone below, we smoked a bowl.

Fiery golden rays ascended from the horizon. Zap. Seconds later, it was blindingly bright. Zap. Sequins flickered between my eyelashes as I blinked, struggling to witness the spectacular. After a few minutes, golden turned into apricot. My migraine was gone.

That sunrise—that moment—was perfect, being there with Tommy. It hadn't been my most graceful rave, but the warmth of the sun made it a perfect morning after.

"How are you doing with the whole Brandon thing?" Tommy asked, blowing out smoke and handing his glass pipe to me.

"Ugh, so over him." I rolled my eyes.

"Nice. Fuck that guy."

"Yeah! Thank god I didn't!" Inhale.

"Really? I totally thought you did," he said. "I would have."

Exhale. "I wanted to. We almost did. Luckily it never happened."

"Dude, we are lucky our parents didn't call each other tonight, last night, whatever," he said, inhaling.

"Totally. That rave was fun, before the—ugh, incident," I said, rubbing my temple, still sensitive to the touch. "I'm sorry, so embarrassing."

Exhale. "Don't trip, dude. I had the best time. Seriously—it was the best night of my life."

"Really?"

"Yes! Everyone was so cool. And the music was amazing. I loved it. I want to go to another one next weekend."

"Me too! I'm so glad." I smiled.

"I can't wait." Inhale.

As we talked, I admired Tommy's apple-green eyes, his winning smile, his giggle. I felt a love for him I'd never felt for a guy. I wasn't attracted to him sexually, but I felt we were deeply connected, in sync, and I knew he felt the same way.

"So where can I find those dope-ass baggy jeans everyone was wearing?" Tommy asked. Exhale.

12 / CREATURE OF THE NIGHT

saw things at raves I'd never seen before—some real, some hallucinations—but one thing was a specific part of the scene's aesthetic: excessively large pants. They floated through the laser-lit rooms, skimming dirty floors, animating the wearer. Phat pants, or phatties, as ravers called them, were more dramatic than the popular baggy jean style of the '90s.

Our go-to brands were LA-based JNCO, an acronym that stands for "Judge None, Choose One," and Kikwear. These pants had wide hems that ranged from 23" to 69" with openings often broader than shoes, sometimes covering shoes. Phatties created an androgynous look worn by boys and girls—at least, that's how it was in the Bay Area scene. Boys wore them with baggy tees and sporty jackets; girls paired them with sports bras or baby tees.

Phatties were to ravers what bellbottoms were to hippies of the '60s, though they never became as mainstream. They were comfortable, allowing a full range of motion for dancing, and had ample pockets for holding lip balm, gum, water bottles, cigarettes, drugs, and the like. Comfort was key when you partied all night, pumped full of drugs, then wanted to feel cozy in the AM when you were knackered. Phatties made me feel more secure. They were my rave armor.

When Tommy and I set out to find phatties, we could only find Tommy Hilfiger jeans that were more baggy than phattie. We bought matching blue denim pairs that didn't quite cover our sneakers, but they did swish with my steps as I walked. With one pair of jeans, my style evolved from vintage skater chick to raver girl.

Life, June 1996
Homies: Johanna
Location: The Deli, San Francisco
Drugs: Ecstasy, weed

Soon after Second Chakra, I was kissing a new friend named Jack I'd met at a rave in the city. It was a birthday party for a local DJ named Carlos. Johanna wore a neon green feather boa. You could spot her under the black lights that made everything glow. We dropped ecstasy—it was my first rave on E—and fluttered around the party, spending hours apart without even realizing it. We always reunited on the dance floor.

I wore my wannabe phatties with a black camisole, X-Large belt, and black-and-white Adidas shell toes. I was spellbound dancing with my new glow wand, silver sparkles swimming inside an orb of water. Johanna danced with her boa, a neon snake circling her moves.

"Hey!" I yelled at her. "What do you want to do?!"

"I don't know. . . . It's too loud in here, dude!"

"Word. I can't see straight right now. Let's go make friends."

That was when I met Jack. He was from Monterey and had slicked-back black hair (not unlike Brandon's) that framed strong, masculine facial features (not unlike Brandon's). He looked like a prince out of a Disney movie, except he was wearing a teddy bear backpack. I had my Dalmatian backpack. He also had a light toy—a mini Star Wars lightsaber that glowed red. We had so much in common.

We found each other on the balcony of the cube-shaped venue and started talking as we leaned over the railing, looking down at the dance floor.

He wore a pacifier pendant around his neck, and I asked, "What's up with the pacifiers?"

"Oooh, you don't know?"

"I mean, it's obviously to suck on," I said, putting my cherry Blow Pop back in my mouth.

"You suck," he flirted.

"You suck!"

We sat down on the carpeted floor, playing with our illuminated toys, giggling. Jack started rubbing my thighs. The hairs on my arms saluted his touch. I'd always been self-conscious that my arms were hairy for a girl, but Jack didn't notice.

He slipped his pacifier into my mouth. Chewing on the gummy delight, I understood: it released tension I'd been holding in my jaw from the amphetamine in the ecstasy. He pulled it out, a juicy loop of drool coming out with it. He started kissing me. Something was wonderfully different about his tongue. At first I thought I was extra sensitive because of the E; then I was sure something hard was swirling around my mouth—and yessss, his tongue was pierced.

A lusty surge came over me. I pulled him in, kissing him harder, lapping up the new sensations. House music bounced up through the floor, into my body, igniting energy. I opened my eyes, looking around to see if anyone was watching us. No one was. No one cared. The party was one big PDA fest anyway. Everyone was there with us, feeling the music, letting go. So that's what I did.

Jack got onto his knees, pushing his chest onto mine, tipping me onto my back. He adorned my neck with kisses while I grabbed his back and sides, massaging him. He lifted up my top, pulled my bra down, and thrust his magnificent tongue at my nipples. They were so hard I thought they might shoot off and hit somebody in the eye.

Then he stopped abruptly, pulling my shirt down, smiling. "Let's get back to the party," he said.

I wanted more, but it was all good because I wanted to get back to the party too. We kissed and exchanged numbers.

I found Johanna and we decided to leave; our E was fading. We headed to her house. Johanna didn't really have a curfew. It was amazing. She was my only best friend with lenient parents, therefore she was an ideal rave best friend.

Remembering Jack's pierced tongue, I asked my parents if I could get mine pierced. They laughed.

"That is the weirdest thing to get pierced," my mom said.

"Actually, Mom, it's not the weirdest. What if I wanted to get my nipple pierced?"

"Ouch!" she exclaimed.

"How about I get my tongue pierced and I start therapy?"

"I don't think so," my dad said, ending that. "But I do think it's time we find you a shrink."

I went with Johanna to get her tongue pierced at a tattoo place on Haight Street in the city. I forged my parent's signature and got mine done too. It didn't hurt that badly. It was fast, and the adrenaline rush was fantastic. The aftercare was a bitch, however. I had to rinse with mouthwash constantly and could only eat macaroni and cheese for days because of my swollen, sore tongue.

The levity of summertime put my whole family in a better mood. I wasn't the friendliest daughter, but I wasn't frightful; most days we were cordial.

My tactic was simple: I didn't speak to them very much. Especially after getting my tongue pierced, for fear they would see the metal in my mouth. I often hung out with Justin, smoking weed with him on his balcony at night after our parents went to bed. At raves, I was an extrovert. At home, an introvert.

And a thief. I took to stealing twenty-dollar bills from my parents' wallets.

Twenty dollars = one hit of ecstasy.

My parents suggested I meet with a few therapists to make sure I found the right fit. They went on about how important it was to really feel comfortable with the person. The idea of being in therapy got me thinking: *Am I imbalanced?* A suppressed part of me was afraid something could be wrong on a chemical level. Maybe that was why I was impulsive and took drugs to cope with my tumultuous feelings.

My grandma on my mom's side was addicted to gambling and cigarettes. As kids, Justin and I summered in Vegas and stayed with her and her roommate, my aunt Diane (my mom's sister). Aunt Diane also smoked and was a junk food junkie.

Their kitchen was stocked with Entenmann's and Twinkies, and they let us rent any scary movie we wanted.

My grandma used to take Justin and me to the casino where my aunt worked. We would spend hours playing in the arcade while my grandma played the slots. Quarters were candy for us. My aunt worked the graveyard shift, starting work at midnight, so Justin and I never saw her working.

One night I grew tired, so I curled up on the gaudy carpeting next to the Skee-ball machines, blings and dings singing me to sleep. Justin realized it was past midnight, and our grandma hadn't come to get us at our usual 8:00 p.m. meeting spot. He woke me up and took me to find our aunt. She was sitting inside a brass bar cage, her hair nested in an Aqua Net helmet hairdo, a lit cigarette stuck between her red-painted fingernails. My grandma had lost track of time playing the slots. She'd forgotten about us.

We didn't summer in Vegas anymore after my mom found out about that.

I never met my other grandma, my dad's mom. Before I was born, she passed out drunk in her house holding a lit cigarette. She'd left an oven burner on, and it caught fire and burned down the house with her in it. I also never met my dad's brother, who killed himself in a car accident driving drunk.

Depression and addiction ran in my family, and because of that my dad was fearful about alcoholism. He'd told me enough for me to know why he was sensitive about these things, but I was a half-listening teen who didn't comprehend the depths of his traumas. I didn't think I'd ever become addicted to slot machines or junk food like my grandma or auntie, and besides, those didn't seem like vices to me then.

I was the happiest I'd been in a long time that summer. I was sixteen, my heart was healing, and raving and taking ecstasy was my fuel, as was knowing I had a family safety net in case something bad happened. About once a month, my moods swung, and I was definitely hormonal. But maybe I acted the way I did because of something predetermined. Was I out of control because of something out of my control?

I flipped through a magazine, waiting to meet with Karen Masters, a psychologist who specialized in teenagers. Sitting in the white-walled waiting area, I noticed that all the doors down the hallway were closed. Uncomfortable silence. I didn't want to be alone with my sober thoughts; music playing in the background always kept me even-keeled.

The sound of a door clicking open echoed down the hallway. A tall, slim woman stepped out. She was wearing a mid-calf skirt that was as stiff and brown as cardboard.

She cocked her head. "Samantha?"

I half smiled and stood up to walk into her office.

After Karen closed the door behind me, she sat down in an upholstered chair with a high back and smoothed her hands over her cardboard skirt.

"It's nice to meet you," she said, smiling with horsey teeth. "Have a seat."

I walked toward the moss-green couch across from her. A large window lit her office. A mahogany wooden desk with an accordion cover was against the wall behind her. The cover was closed. A wheeled chair was tucked in under the desk. After sit-

ting down, I watched a eucalyptus tree sway over some tele-
phone wires out the window.

"How are you today?" she asked.

"Um." I tugged at my hoop earring. "Good, I guess."

She nodded. "What did you do today?"

"Most of the day I was at work. I work at the nail salon in
Montclair, Amie's Creations," I said, glancing at her unpolished
nails. I continued telling her about how I was a receptionist at the
salon and it was pretty easy. I was in it for the discounted manicures.

After more small talk, she asked me, "Have you ever seen a
therapist before?"

"No," I said. "I promised my parents. I mean, I'm here because my parents thought I should talk to someone. A professional." I looked back out the window. Blue sky peeked through
drifting clouds. "I guess because we're not communicating much
these days."

She nodded.

"Like, there's lots of things," I said, not sure where to start.

"Mmmhmm." She uncrossed and crossed her legs. She was
wearing pantyhose. Gross. "Lots of things? Like what?"

I looked at her straight on. A thick row of bangs framed
her face. Her nose was narrow and angular. She wasn't wearing
any makeup, or if she was, it was natural-looking. Her straight
light brown hair was pulled into a low ponytail. Gold ball stud
earrings and a simple gold band on her left hand were her only
jewelry. Everything about her and her office were understated.

"You're not going to tell my parents any of this, are you?" I
asked.

"No." She smiled. "I am obligated to tell your parents something if I think you're in danger of hurting yourself."

A suicide gesture when I was fourteen came to mind. After being grounded for getting caught shoplifting at Macy's with Johanna, I wanted to spend the night at her house. My dad said no, he thought she and I should take a break from each other. Fuming, I ran upstairs into my parent's bathroom and swallowed a bunch of Tylenol. An emergency room visit and two cups of activated charcoal later, I was in my bathroom barfing up black paint. I was trying to send my parents a message: Listen to me. Let me be me. Let me be free!

I was too ashamed to bring that up, so I said something I would have liked to tell my parents but didn't dare to. "Well, I'm going to raves, like, every weekend. My parents don't know about that, really."

She nodded.

"I'm doing some drugs."

Nod.

I sighed. "They kind of caught me once, but that was a big mess I don't want to talk about."

"What drugs have you done?" she asked casually.

I reached for my Polo Ralph Lauren purse next to me to get my raspberry Lip Smackers. I applied the waxy balm while deciding how honest I should be.

"They know I'm smoking weed, but I'm pretty sure they don't know about the acid or ecstasy, which I've only done once," I lied, ready for her to raise an eyebrow of judgment. "And I got my tongue pierced after they said no, so I'm hiding that from them too."

I tried to find something interesting to look at besides a yellow book spine. In the painting above the desk, a girl in a dress sat in a field of golden grass, looking back at a house, desolate. *Christina's World* by Andrew Wyeth. A small brass clock was on a table under the window. I had forty-five minutes to go.

I exhaled. "I wish I could tell them more about what I'm doing, but they won't get it. And they definitely won't let me go to raves, so it's just easier not to get into it. My dad, he's so stubborn, and he would freak if he knew what went on at them. There's no way they'd be cool with all the drugs." I crossed my ankles, and a pain below my stomach reminded me of the horrible menstrual cramps I'd been having all week. "Do you know about raves?"

"I do." She nodded.

"Really? Well, it's all about the music. And dancing. At least, that's why I started going. There's also drugs. And there are so many fun people. It's just so much more interesting than school."

"Tell me about school." She uncrossed and crossed her legs again. She was wearing loafers. Loafers with pantyhose and a cardboard skirt, she was like a paper doll.

Since summer had started, I'd enjoyed not thinking or talking about school. But now I found myself venting to Karen about how much I hated taking tests and how I wasn't into normal school activities like going to football games. That led to telling her about Brandon.

Before I knew it, she was glancing at the antique clock and saying, "Well, our time is up."

I'd told her more than I thought I would. And I wanted to go on. She'd listened quietly and validated my feelings, even the ones I wasn't able to name. We agreed to meet every Wednesday. I hadn't had a breakthrough at my first therapy session, but I did feel better, lighter, as I walked back through the silent hallway.

6.29.96

Dear Me:

Dude I'm so bad. Johanna is going to NYC for a month so we X-d today on Haight. Wooooooooooo. I'm still feelin' yo. I apologized to the girl at the drag queen store about the boa and Johanna apologized to the little boy she ran into and dropped all his flyers. Right now, I can't remember anything from what I was doing just four hours ago. Dude, I was so high, water didn't even taste like water and I couldn't even eat a lollipop. I love ecstasy. I'm going to research it on Monday to see what the hell it does.

Outtie 5000,

-Me

13 / FREEDOM '96

Freedom, July 1996
Homies: Tommy
Location: Outdoor venue near Livermore
Drugs: Acid + ecstasy = candy flipping, weed

t was a Saturday night, and I was having dinner with Tommy, his sister, and his parents at his house. It was all surface talk about Tommy's job as a camp counselor and his sister's latest sport activity. Keeping my elbows off the table, whenever I answered his parents, I smiled, presenting myself as a responsible young lady their son should be friends with.

When I first met his parents, they were serious and untouchable, like the ivory leather couches in their living room no one ever sat on. It struck me as odd that someone as free-spirited, funny, and open about his sexuality as Tommy had been raised by such reserved parents.

"What are you guys up to tonight?" Tommy's mom asked as we cleaned the dishes after dinner. Her ash-blond hair rested above her shoulders in nearly the same hairstyle as my mom, who was in her early fifties. Barbara Walters hair.

"We're thinking a movie and then sleeping at Samantha's," Tommy replied.

"What are you going to see?"

I glanced at Tommy. He hadn't planned the lie that far.

"Not sure," he said. "I guess we should look at the paper."

His mother was curious—not a good trait for Tommy's raving future. I'd told my parents Tommy and I were having dinner and then watching a *Sleepaway Camp* marathon at his house. There were three, so we'd probably get tired, too tired to drive home. A movie and sleeping at each other's houses was our go-to scheme. Nothing elaborate. Keep it simple. Movie nights were what we mostly did between raves after smoking bowls at one of our secret spots around Oakland anyway.

Antsy to get ready, I thanked Tommy's mom for dinner and bolted to his room. A few minutes later, he came in with a newspaper, which he threw on his neatly made bed before closing the door behind him.

He raised his eyebrows. "Mark Farina?"

I nodded yes and plopped my Adidas duffel bag full of clothes onto his bed.

Tommy put the mixtape on. Cue the music video montage.

We mixed and matched Adidas shirts and track jackets. Tommy humored me by trying on a baby tee. Even though he looked super cute, he said, "Way too gay," pulled the shirt off, and threw it at me. We shimmied around his room, booty bumping, looking at ourselves in the mirror, laughing and whispering about the night ahead.

We coordinated outfits inspired by the rave's Fourth of July freedom theme—bright and brighter. Tommy wore a red vintage Adidas tee with a white flower logo front, a blue-and-gray puffer vest, and my red bucket hat. I wore a cobalt baby tee and red Polo vest topped by a furry black Kangol bucket hat. We wore similar pairs of blue jean JNCOs we'd found at a record-slash-clothing store on Telegraph. We may have looked more like kindergartners than sixteen-year-olds, but once we got to the party, we knew we'd fit right in.

Tommy hurried back into the bedroom after calling the rave hotline as I broke into a frantic sweat attempting French braid pigtails.

"Dude," he whispered, "this party is going to be so dope. It's, like, hella far out in the boonies n' shit. Hurry up, sugar tits!"

We told Tommy's mom we were going to see *Independence Day* and then sleep at my house. She seemed to buy it.

What had caught our attention about this rave was the outdoor festival part. We'd been to a handful of raves at warehouses or run-down buildings in the Bay Area, but al fresco seemed the ideal place to candy flip for the first time—that is, take acid and ecstasy together.

"I hear you get the trippy visuals of frying and the body high of E," I said through chewing gum.

"Yeahhh," Tommy said, "but, dude, sometimes I get visuals from E, don't you? So the visuals must be crazy."

"I wonder if acid makes the E high last longer since acid lasts hella long, you know?"

"Ooooh, maybe, hopefully," Tommy said, turning off the freeway to get gas.

He pumped while I looked at myself in the visor mirror,

adding gold glitter bursts around my eyes. Shiny happy me.

We went into the store and grabbed Snapple iced teas, water, gum, and two packs of Marlboro Ultra Lights. Walking back to Tommy's car, I stopped to speak into my latest accessory: a black dictaphone. I don't know what had compelled me to grab the mini tape recorder sitting on my dad's office shelf one day. Something to record my rave adventures just seemed like a fun idea.

"Yo yo!" I said into the recorder. "It is 9:58 on a Saturday, June . . . July—"

"July 6!" Tommy yelled.

"July 6, 1996," I continued, "I'm standing here at a gas station with Tommy, and we're prepping to go to Freedom."

Tommy wagged a leg in anticipation. He pulled my hand holding the recorder toward him. "This is how I sound when I'm sober. Just wait—it gets worse." He was referring to his impending turn into his flamboyant rave alter ego.

We got back onto the freeway. Tommy turned up the volume. I tried to enjoy the energetic beats, but the unspoken fear that our parents would call each other still nagged at me. We both had pagers, but I worried there wouldn't be a payphone anywhere at this venue if it was in the boonies. *How will we call our parents back if they page?* I distracted myself from my thoughts by rechecking my backpack to make sure I had all my supplies.

We approached where the 580 freeway collides with Interstate 5, and I told Tommy, "Turn off the freeway up here, I think. What does this say, Regent Road?"

"That sign says Royalton Road."

"That's probably it," I said. "Your handwriting's messy. Are you a leftie?"

"Shut up, dude. I had to write it down quick so my mom

couldn't see," he said, exiting the freeway. "I think it's just straight from here."

"Yeah, fifteen minutes according to your chicken scratch."

"Cool. Let's drop our acid."

I was thinking the same thing, already holding the little plastic baggy containing two pencil-eraser-sized blotters. I handed him his hit and then put mine on my tongue and swallowed.

A pit of light surrounded by hilly shadows appeared in the distance. We slowed down. No signs, no people, we turned into a dirt parking lot half full of cars.

When we stepped out of Tommy's car, a pulsating beat greeted us, luring us as we walked through the car maze toward the pit of light. Red laser beams danced on the hills, in sync with the music. My pulse quickened and my tummy fluttered as I followed Tommy, who was three steps ahead of me.

I looked past the short line of people at the entrance. All I could see was a dirt ground, camping tents, and a table with large yellow Igloo water coolers on it.

"When should we take our E?" Tommy asked, adjusting his hat. "Should I wear this lower?"

"I don't know. Maybe when we start feeling our acid. Hat's good," I said, adjusting my hat to make sure it was in the exact right place.

"Roger that."

We paid ten dollars to a bronzed man wearing a navy-blue bandana headband and then walked through a patch of orange, green, and brown tents. Some zipper doors hung half open, and I saw elbows and knees moving inside them. People stood around the tents and walked around them like us, heading toward the party's heartbeat.

We approached a dance area where bodies spazzed around a dusty bowl. Now the lasers were massive beams shooting up from all sides, illuminating the air electric, masking any stars above. My body swayed, the upbeat sounds infusing me.

Tommy wasn't dancing. He was standing with his excited leg wagging to the beat, looking like he was about to blast off. But his expression was worried; he looked like a little boy who'd lost his parents in a crowd.

I stopped dancing. "Dude, are you okay?"

His forehead flexed. "I can't dance. I don't know what's wrong with me, dude. I think I've lost my groove."

"Let's take our E," I said.

We walked to find a water station. I got out my Little Twin Stars pill holder containing two light blue pills I'd bought at the last rave. We downed them and went back to the dance area. I clicked on my recorder.

"He-he-hello, double agent Durbin reporting in at—"

"Can I give you a little message?" Tommy interrupted.

"Hold on, what time is it?"

"Time is no factor here!" Tommy yelled, squinting at something across the dust bowl. "Is that Marku?!"

Short, mushroom top—my vision was morphing, but it was definitely my ex-boyfriend's friend. Tommy, who'd always had a crush on him, went straight toward him.

"Wait!" I yelled, trying to see who Marku was with, hoping it wasn't Brandon.

When he saw us approaching, he smiled. "Hey, guys!"

We hugged hellos, and I blurted, "Is Brandon here with you?"

"What?" He cupped his hand to his ear.

"Is Brandon here?!"

"Brandon? Nah."

Relieved, I was about to introduce myself to the girl standing next to him wearing denim Bermuda shorts when I recognized her from a grade ahead of me.

She grabbed my arm. "I have so much energy right now! I feel so good, feeling the good vibes, enjoying all these good people!"

Marku leaned into us. "She's E-ing for the first time."

Tommy laughed obnoxiously loud, like Marku had said the funniest thing.

"Wanna smoke a bowl?" Marku asked.

"Hell yeah," we answered.

We followed Marku through tent city. I was light and loose. Joy was bubbling through my body. Marku looked ordinary in his high school uniform of baggy jeans, hoodie, and Chucks. He'd been raving longer than me but hadn't adopted the style. Nothing about him was colorful or glowing.

"I never want to do acid again! I just want to do this!" Bermuda shorts girl was going off, stumbling over the cords pegged to the ground. "I want to do this, like, every weekend! Every day!"

Marku ducked into a brown tent where a couple of guys were sitting. Awestruck by the most beautiful man I'd ever seen, I nearly fell over sitting down. His blond hair was neatly gelled. Iridescent glitter made his crystal-blue eyes pop. Underneath the sparkling layer was the face of a male supermodel. His prominent cheekbones sat above pillowy lips. He had some stubble on his chin and a silver nose ring.

A brilliant smile revealed straight white teeth, and he gracefully extended his hand. "I'm Luca."

Tommy told him what I was thinking. "Wooow, you're sooo pretty."

Luca's friend beside him was Angel, who was more cute than pretty. He had jet-black hair and eyes. Same silver nose ring. More facial hair. Less glitter.

"This party blows bubblesss," Luca said, his voice trailing off into soft sibilance.

My first gay crush emerged. I loved Tommy and all, but he was buddy love. Luca was too beautiful not to fall for.

"How old are you? Where are you guys from? How long have you been partying? Who are your favorite DJs? What are you on?" I asked and asked and asked.

Eighteen. Martinez. About a year. Jim Hopkins, Donald Glaude, Jeno. They'd taken ecstasy that hadn't kicked in yet, hence why the party blew bubblesss. They were a duo, but I couldn't tell if they were a couple.

Marku handed me a glass pipe loaded with a fresh bowl and flicked a light. I sucked in and then blew out quickly, eager to speak. I passed the pipe to Tommy, clicked on my recorder, and began interviewing Marku.

"What's your name?"

"Marku."

"Last name?"

"Simon."

"What's your middle initial?"

"T."

"What does that stand for?"

"Terrible."

"Occupation?"

"Pizza delivery."

Tommy leaned over. "What's this party called?"

"Freedom."

"I am feeling quite free right now," I said.

Bermuda shorts gushed, "You are all so beautiful! Can I hug you guys? All of you? All at once?"

Luca gave her a dirty look. He was probably jealous she was high and he wasn't. I wanted to cheer him up, so I reached into my bag to get my glow wand.

"Hey, girl, want to see something else beautiful?" I asked Bermuda shorts, turning on my light.

"OoooOooooOoooh." Her eyes and mouth animated with pleasure.

"Ooooh, I love that," Luca said. "I think I need to smoke another bowl. Always helps, you know?"

Oh, I knew.

"Want a lollipop?" I asked him.

I handed Bermuda shorts my glow wand and gave Luca a cherry Blow Pop. The fabric on my thigh was neon green because of a glow stick lantern hanging from the ceiling of the tent. White dots moved through the denim like a river, flowing closer and farther, forming crosshatch patterns I'd never seen in my pants before. Never seen anywhere before.

"I'm going to describe what my body feels like right now," I told my recorder. "My feet are tingling. I can't feel my legs. My butt is rather heavy. My hands are clammy. I'm sitting cross-legged, and so are you and you and you."

Tommy looked at me. "Let's walk."

We said bye to our new friends—we'd see them on the dance floor.

"Can we meet up with you guys later?" Bermuda shorts asked, wild-eyed.

"Yes," I said.

But you never knew. . . .

Pre-smartphones, trying to find friends at a rave could turn into a three-hour expedition. But that search was one of the best parts. Chance meetings around every corner led to discoveries, new friendships, and bizarro conversations. Walking around a party aimlessly when most people were high and more social was one of the ways raves created a sense of community.

When we stepped outside the tent, a rattling sound in the music alerted me to the full-on carnival happening around us. The dance floor had grown. Dusty air transported us into the chaos of a desert sandstorm not unlike Burning Man. People moved faster, flickering past me, carrying light toys, sucking on pacifiers. The lasers had changed to a white spotlight that swerved through the crowd and across tents. An elaborate light show projected on a hillside. People whistled and whooped.

Far away from my real world, thriving inside my rave world, I inhaled my cigarette. Exhale. "Hello, hello, I'm really fucking high right now," I told my recorder. "I'd say on a scale of one to ten of being high, I'm a fifteen."

"Fifteen or sixteen." Tommy exhaled smoke into the dust.

"Let's walk."

"I can't walk."

"Actually, I can't either."

"I need water."

"Ooooooh water."

We soldiered through the dust to reach the outer edge of the party where the hills began. There was a line of porta-potties and another water station there. As we downed cups of intensely refreshing water, Tommy's face blurred and animated, like the ghost face from *The Scream*, but friendly. My vision was dicey, Missoni zigzags bursting through every blink. My bladder throbbed.

I gripped Tommy's arm. "I'm going to need you in the bathroom."

"I feel you, dude."

We smoked another cigarette as we waited in line for a porta-potty.

"What was that girl's name with Marku? I don't even remember her name...."

"Potato."

"Her name was not Potato."

"It was something like that."

The slap of a plastic door and I pulled off my Dalmatian backpack, securing it around my front, ready to enter the green bathroom box.

Breathe in, step in.

Breathe out, step out.

A light source captivated me: a jumbo table lamp. Or a life-size flashlight. There was a messy tangle of red squids swimming around it.

Tommy was talking to two people, so I spoke to my recorder: "We were just in a porta-potty, and it was scary. Scary Larry. I'm so high right now I don't know what to do with my life. I'm having too much fun. Is it possible to have too much fun? I think I'm higher than Tommy."

"What?" Tommy asked. "Are you talking shit about me to your recorder?"

"If my parents ever found this tape, they would trip out. They would trip ooooouuuttt. They would trip ooooouuuuuttttt," I repeated myself, marveling at the echo of my voice. "I have so much energy right now dude I don't even know I'm just feeling the good vibes with these good people it's all so good!" Was that me talking or Bermuda shorts girl?

"I wonder where Marku is?" Tommy wondered. "Should we go back to the tent?"

"Dude! Potato has my wand!" I remembered. "We have to find them! I'll be really mad if they take it away. But, anywho, I don't know what time it is, and you know what? I really don't care. However, I would like to find my wand—is that the sun starting to come out?"

"Are you recording this?" a girl who sounded like a squirrel asked me.

"I like you. You're cool," Tommy said to her. "Whoa. I am so high."

"Are you taping? This is the funniest thing I've ever seen," Squirrel Girl continued. She looked like a squirrel too, with a button nose and fluffy ponytail. "I am so awed by the fucking expression of your creativity. Wow!"

"Whoa," I said. "I am so high. I need to sit down."

"What's your name again?" Tommy asked Squirrel Girl.

"Wildflower."

We sat down with our new friends at the bottom of the hill.

"You better watch what you say to that thing, girl," Wildflower warned me. "Remember what happened to Nixon?"

Her friend, a scrawny dude with a backward baseball cap, said, "I can't believe you guys have a tape recorder! Let's just have ourselves a phil-go-sophical conversay-tional," he muttered. "Dude, I want to fuckin' just have that shit, dude! I'll have the tightest conversation with someone and then, yeah, can't remember shit the next day. Man, I never thought I could just record it."

I didn't think much of their astonishment at the time, but Squirrel Girl wasn't blowing sunshine up my ass—she was insightful. According to myself on one of the tapes, I had a few reasons for recording. A bullshit one is that I had "a bad memory." I was in excellent health when I started raving. My memory was fine, save for some short-term marijuana-induced memory loss. But can you remember that deep (or not so deep) conversation you had that time on liquid acid? Probably not.

Recording gave me something to do while walking and talking and tripping all night. Tommy was usually there, but when he wasn't, my recorder was my invisible friend I could say anything to. I also interviewed people, capturing their musings and forgettable moments too. Sometimes I forgot I was recording, and muffled conversations played back. Or the music in the background. Hearing that comforting bass always took me back when I heard it. Sometimes Tommy and I would get stoned and listen to the tapes, months or years after a party, reliving the moments, laughing at ourselves.

"Some guy thought I was a cop earlier, and I was like, do I look like a cop to you?" I said. There was always one person who would joke I was a narc because of my tape recorder. It was usually a guy. Paranoid Android.

"You'd be a pretty go-getter cop!" Wildflower yipped.

"Dude, you would get so sexually harassed if you were a cop," the guy said. "I was watching fuckin' *60 Minutes* or some shit, and they were talking about the army and how it's, like, 75 percent of women in the army or police force get sexually harassed or raped or whatever."

I tuned them out as they continued this serious talk. I liked them because they were friendly and fascinated by my recorder.

And Wildflower spoke with amusing exuberance. But the conversation was getting too real. Raves were a place I could escape reality. I didn't want to be reminded of abused women when I was high.

I focused on the laser show on the hill: "It's a big person . . . then . . . ooh, shit, it keeps changing. A spiraling galaxy. Spiral galaxy. Spiral galaxy. Wait, wait, wait . . . it's a BIG star. A red-and-blue spirograph. Spirograph. Spirograph. A robot that explodes into a growing cluster of meteoroids that bursts into millions of trickling stars that whirl into a big planet Earth that spins and slows to a hovering halt."

Wildflower handed us each a bracelet she'd made from colorful beads. I'd noticed these pony bead bracelets on the arms of ravers before—rainbow-colored jewelry glowing under the blacklight. Mine was a cotton candy swirl of pink beads. Tommy's was blue, green, and white beads with an airplane centerpiece.

"Getting back to all this hysteria. My foot is, you know, just chillin' in my shoe. But it's got a little tingle in the toes. I don't know what time it is, but the sun is, in fact, starting to come out." My vampire instincts kicked in, and I clicked off the recorder. I leaned into Tommy. "It's time to disappear."

We set off for our last lap around the party. I pulled Tommy's hand through the crowd, air thicker, bodies funkier. I was doing my walking-dancing moves through the undulating crowd, swinging my shoulders to the playful beats, smiling through. The positive energy filled me up. I couldn't get enough of it. I wished I could bottle it and drink it anytime, until the next weekend, until I could fill myself up again at the next rave.

A woman's voice from the speakers sang out, commanding us all to throw our hands in the air air air, and everyone danced with tribal force, their hands waving in the air air air, yelling and whistling. People danced in front of the speakers, inside the speakers, becoming the music. A stompy bam. Spaceship blips. A cowbell.

Tommy busted a move. He kicked his Adidas around, jerking his hips, swinging his arms. His eyes were near closed, his smile fluid. Tommy had gotten his groove back. He was free.

We left the party at dawn. With the car windows cracked, we smoked cigarettes and chugged raspberry Snapple iced teas, tuning into Everything But The Girl's trip-hoppy sounds. Our acid lingered, magnifying surfaces and twisting thoughts, but everything was positive. Just drifting by. The ecstasy energy boost was gone. A cellular buzz in our brains and dusty boogers in our noses remained.

Cool air whipped past me as I looked at the barren hills under the lightening blue sky. "What is that?" I said, pointing through the windshield. "It looks like giant stick figures."

"Whoa," Tommy said. "I think that's a windmill."

Three windmills. We were driving past Altamont Pass, one of the earliest wind farms in the country. The sky opened over the elegant fixtures, sunlight stretching across rolling golden hills. Ten windmills. As we continued driving, more windmills appeared. Fifty white aerodynamic windmills. Some slowly turning, most standing still.

"Wooooow," we said to each other, amazed.

I was relaxed by the satisfaction of another night filled with visions, friends, and music bringing me inner peace.

"We need nicknames," I said, blowing smoke out the window. "Like that girl, Wildflower. And Potato, even though her name wasn't Potato. Do you think Angel is his real name?"

"Hmmm." Tommy lit another cigarette.

A red car rounded the bend on the other side of the road. "I've got it!" I shouted. "Ferrari."

I was inspired by my dad's pride and joy: his '86 Ferrari Mondial.

"Tight." Tommy smiled. "I want to be Adidas."

"That's a brand. You can't be a brand."

"Um, what do you think Ferrari is?"

"Fine."

"I'm going to be Adidas. Just Adidas. Like Madonna."

"I'm going to be Ferrari Ravioli." It had a nice ring to it.

As I watched the windmills stand and whirl in the bright morning light, I eased back into my seat and rolled my window down all the way, releasing every last worry outside into the world to be blown away by the breeze.

14 / BLOW ME

A couple weeks after Freedom, I was having dinner with Justin and my mom when I announced, "Margot's coming over tonight."

"Oh," my brother said, rolling his eyes. "Great."

"She'll probably sleep over."

"Margot?" my mom asked. "It's been a while since you saw each other."

I knew Margot from going to camp in previous summers. The setting of s'mores, ghost stories, campfires, dances, and my first French kisses, I loved camp. It was more fun than school, plus I found it easier to answer to young camp counselors instead of parents. Tennis camp was cool, horseback riding camp was cooler, and scuba diving camp was the coolest. Bonus: Justin and I went together.

I'd met Margot at Cloverleaf Ranch, a horseback riding camp in Santa Rosa. The cabins were in the style of stables and old circus trailers. Justin and I went for a two-week session while my parents got a parenting break. I'd enjoyed the arts and crafts, riding horses, water activities, and choreographing dances for the talent show—most notably, a lip-synching trio to "Vogue" in 1990.

Margot was loud and promiscuous, and she'd been my guide to the complexities of boys. A year older and a few years more experienced than me, she'd taught me how to kiss by making out with her hand (only because I wouldn't let her kiss me). She'd licked and sucked her knuckles while closing her eyes and groaning, making me uncomfortable, albeit slightly turned on, as we sat on our beds.

One time post-camp she came over to my house, and when I told her I'd gotten my period, she taught me how to insert a tampon. This entailed her dropping her mom jeans and lace thong, propping her bright pink pussy up against my full-length mirror, and showing me with an OB tampon—which, she explained, didn't have an applicator, so you had to "finger yourself" to push the tampon inside. I stood from a distance, speechless and blushing, fascinated by her comfort with her body. Margot used her sexuality to get what she wanted. It was her modus operandi, and though I wasn't interested in adopting her style, it was fascinating.

"I think she may be bringing some friends with her," I told my mom. "We're just going to hang out upstairs."

I was a pretty good actress, because I was hiding my excitement for Margot's arrival well. And I was feverishly excited. Not only because she was a real card, but also because I wanted her to meet the stylish rebel Ferrari Ravioli. Plus, she was bringing coke. It would be my first time doing it.

The doorbell chimed.

"I got it," I said, popping up from the table, my chair squeaking on the floor.

My mom came with me to answer the door.

"Heyyyyyyyy, girlllllllll!" Margot yelled as she stepped inside, her butterscotch eyes radiating.

I knew Justin was cringing in the next room.

Margot's thick black hair was long and flowing, and her cheeks were flushed, as if she'd just orgasmed. She consumed me in an Estee Lauder Sunflowers hug and enthusiastically hugged my mom too. Her infectious charm made us laugh.

Two girls followed Margot inside.

"This is Kasie and Sarah," Margot introduced them. "They actually live pretty close to you. In Piedmont."

Sarah was almost as tall as me, though more waify, with a long, freckled face and strawberry-blond hair. Kasie had pixie-cut bleached-blond hair that was side-parted and secured with a studded barrette. She shot me a superstar smile when we made eye contact. Both girls were wearing phat pants. They were ravers. My kind.

We shot up the stairs to my room. I put on some house beats —DJ Jeno—and Margot went to my bathroom to set up. I showed my spread to the girls with the smile and grace of Vanna White turning her glittering *Wheel of Fortune* letters.

Kasie and Sarah were also sixteen and went to Piedmont High. They'd started raving that summer. We were surprised we hadn't met yet. They'd met Margot through some punk rock friends because she was dating an older (always older) guy in a local punk band.

Margot came into my bedroom and announced that "it" was ready. We followed her into my white-and-blue-tiled bathroom, gold chrome fixtures shiny in the bright light. My stomach flip-turned when I saw a black leather kit unfolded on my counter. It looked like a travel manicure set, but instead of nail clippers and cuticle scissors, four syringes lay across it.

"Uhhh," Kasie uttered.

"Dude. Needles?" I asked Margot, serious.

Where was the mirror with an elegant white line on it? That's what I'd seen in movies, and that's what I wanted. Needles were for junkies. Heroin addicts. A symbol of addiction. Needles outside of a hospital were nasty and scary. Then again, Margot was kinda nasty and scary.

"Can we snort it instead?" I asked.

"I don't have enough for lines," she said, flipping her hair. "It's better this way anyway. More intense."

I wasn't sure I could go along with Margot. It was her boldest move yet. Even bolder than when she told me to watch her throw up her lunch one day at camp. She was bulimic and proud of it. Pretty twisted. Sure, I'd been smoking weed, taking acid and E and nitrous, but shooting up was another level. A level down.

"Let me see your arms," Sarah said.

"Oh, I don't shoot in my arms. That's for junkies. If you shoot between your toes, no one can see." Margot stared at us. We stared back. "Am I seriously going to be the only one doing this?" she said, putting a hand on her hip, turning on the peer pressure.

"I don't think so," Kasie said.

Sarah shook her head in agreement.

Eyes were now on me.

"Are those needles clean?" I asked.

"Um, yes, of course," Margot scoffed. "I told you, I'm not a junkie. Only junkies share needles."

I wasn't afraid of medical needles like some people. When it was time for me to get vaccinations or shots, I didn't mind; I just stretched my arm out and looked the other way. I had more of an issue with blood being drawn. Especially after the time a nurse struggled to find a vein and ended up poking me repeatedly with sharp needles, nervously apologizing for her novice technique. The next day, the spot had been tender, bruised purple. I'd always bruised easily, and I thought that was what my arm would look like if I ever got into needles. So when I started doing drugs, I had a couple rules: no needles and no heroin. Ever. Never.

"Well, if you guys aren't doing it, that's more for us!" Margot yelled.

"Dude!" I snapped. "Shhh!"

Kasie and Sarah left to listen to music in my room, which I'd turned up before closing both the bathroom doors so we were sound-proof. Pointless, I now saw, since we weren't going to be loudly snorting anything like I'd imagined. I looked at the syringes. Sitting next to them was a mini plastic baggie with black skulls and crossbones on it and white powder inside it. There was also a spoon.

To coke or not to coke? Even though Margot was crazy, I trusted her. She hadn't ever misled me. Actually, she was one of my most honest friends. I believed the needles were clean because she was a snob from Mill Valley who would only be dirty in the bedroom. Or the car. Or on a pool table. I had to trust her, and I wanted to try coke. The situation felt taboo, and excitement rushed through my veins.

I put my hands on my hips and exhaled. "Let me see you do it first."

Clearly amused, she sat on my toilet seat, took off her Vans high-top sneakers, and flung her socks off, sending them flying around the bathroom like boomerangs. She stood up, turned on the water, and filled the spoon. She balanced the spoon on the counter and opened the baggie with her French-manicured nails, and out tumbled a crumb of the coke into the water.

She stopped to ask, "Do you have rubbing alcohol?"

I ducked out to get it. As I slithered through the hallway, I heard my dad's voice from downstairs. He was home from work. I raced into my parents' bathroom, grabbed the bottle, and tiptoed back into my bathroom, fired up.

Two syringes lay on the counter with a cloudy liquid inside the tubes.

"Cotton balls?" Margot asked.

Check. She soaked one in the alcohol and cleaned the firm flesh between her second and third toes. Her cleanliness put me at ease. This didn't seem "junkie"; it was more like a scene in some edgy teen movie.

She took a needle off the counter, held it up, and sent a spray into the air for drama. She spread her toes apart and plunged the needle into her skin. I winced, looking away.

I knew she'd finished when she set the syringe on the counter. She stood alert, smiling devilishly, her eyes wide open.

"Whooooo!" she blew through her lips. "Makes my nipples SO hard every goddamn time!"

I could see them poking through her black bra under her white T-shirt.

I'd seen enough. My turn.

"Here!" she said, handing me the baggie. "Lick your pinky and dip it in and then put it on your gums."

She was bouncing. I dipped my pinky in the baggie, then smoothed it along my gums. It was extremely bitter. I smacked my lips and swallowed, but the artificial flavor lingered.

"Are you ready?" she asked, amped up.

"Fuck it."

I pulled off my white Adidas socks and flung them around

the bathroom like Margot had. I sat down on my toilet seat. Margot cleaned the area between my toes. The steady, pounding house beats coming through the door from my bedroom soothed and excited me at the same time. I craved a new high.

Margot got down on her knees. "Rest your ankle on your knee and stay still."

I copied the position she'd sat in and whispered, "Just go, do it, before I change my mind."

I watched her face as she leaned toward me, her nostrils flaring. When the needle was almost there, I looked away.

A prick, a sting, and schwing! A jolt, a sizzle, a bolt! I jumped up, propelled by the lightning in my veins, heating my blood, activating my senses. I grew tall, taller, my tallest self. I wanted to run around in circles like a hamster on a wheel. My gums were numb—whoa! My body was electric—wheee!

The body high was familiar, like when I was energized rolling on E, but this was now right now so now! I needed to run. I needed water. I needed to go number two. I needed to move and talk and move and talk, and I burst into my bedroom, where Kasie and Sarah were sitting on my bed talking, not moving.

"Hey, guys! Want to see my glow wand?" I asked them, skipping over to my backpack to get my favorite toy. Margot talked fiercely to Sarah while Kasie marveled at my light force. I started dancing with it, and Kasie smiled, watching, as I put on a light show for her, spinning the glowing globe with the pounding music. Inside my Chill Bedroom, I felt the freeing feeling of being at a rave. A feeling I'd fallen madly in love with.

There was a knock on my bedroom door. I froze in a robot move, my arm bent in the air. My head whipped fast to look at my door.

"Who is it?!" I yelled.

"Justin."

I pulled open my door, relieved to see my brother.

"Can you guys turn the music down?" he asked, the whites of his eyes a stoned pink.

"Oh sure, sorry!"

Margot ran up behind me. "Hey, Justin! How are you?!" I could feel her boobs squished against my back.

"I'm cool," he said, turning away. So cool.

"Sorry, bro, we'll be quieter. Wanna hang?"

"Nah, I'm tired."

I closed the door, pushing in the lock on the knob.

"Good night!" Margot shouted through the door. Then she looked at me. "Are you ready for another one?!"

"Already?"

"Yeah, you want to keep it up."

"I think I'm good. I'm still hella hyper."

Margot turned to Kasie and Sarah, saying, "Last chance, girls." Their smiles withered.

"Honestly," she continued, "it's not that crazy of a high. It's like a shot of espresso."

"Um, more like three shots," I said, holding three fingers up.

I was happy but felt like I was already slowing down, coming down. *That was quick*, I thought. *Quick like nitrous. And not as fun.* Then it dawned on me that I'd just shot up cocaine in my bathroom with my parents only doors away. *Don't push it*, I told myself. I thought about the needle and felt gross, not glamorous. I decided against doing another one.

Margot dipped back into my bathroom for another shot while we danced around my bedroom. When she was hardnippled and bouncy again, we went onto the patio for some air.

"Can we smoke?" Margot asked.

"No way," I said.

"Psssh," she hissed. "Next time we're doing this at my house."

"Oh my god—is that a giant trampoline?!" Kasie yelled, pointing to our backyard. It was the perfect way to blow off excess energy. We smiled in agreement. I went back into the bathroom to put more coke on my gums; I'd liked the numbing sensation. Margot packed up her kit.

We rushed down the stairs and tore through the kitchen, where my mom and dad were talking.

"Hi, Dad!" I yelled, the most excited I'd been to see him since Christmas morning circa 1989. "We're going to jump on the trampoline!"

"Hi, Dad!"

"Hi, Dad!"

"Hi, Dad!"

Our stampede of teenage girls in baggy pants left my amused parents in a wake of floral perfume. We were out the back door before anyone could question us.

After I peed in my underwear from jumping and laughing hard, I stretched my body on the static surface, my arms and legs spread out like a doll's. The four of us crashed and lay down, panting, spent. My throat was dry, my armpits wet. A black night sprinkled with glitter stars twinkled over us.

We lazed for a while, stargazing, girl talking. The coke high had dissipated, and I was nearly sober, just light-headed. We rolled off the trampoline, tiptoeing on the damp grass back toward the house. I smoothed my hair, adjusted my bra.

When we entered the house, my mom was watching TV in

the breakfast nook and flipping through a cookbook. She suggested all the girls sleep over since it was late, and offered to make French toast in the morning. The girls thanked her, and we escaped upstairs.

Pajamas, clean teeth, pillows—that was all I wanted.

My body was tired, but my mind was wired. Margot and I talked for hours in the dark, lying in my bed. We reminisced about camp, and I asked her all my burning sexual questions: "How often do you orgasm? How does a sixty-nine work? What kind of birth control do you use?" She teased me for still being a virgin, and I told her what happened with Brandon.

"Lucky you didn't sleep with him," she said as I finally gave in to my heavy eyes, shutting everything out. "You'd be totally fucked up if you did."

I decided after that night that I would try coke again, but the old-fashioned, glamorous movie star way. That was the last time I ever saw Margot.

15

DOUBLE TROUBLE

Intoxication, July 1996
Homies: Tommy, Natalie
Location: San Francisco,
the blue warehouse by Illinois Street
Drugs: Ecstasy (two hits), weed

The venue for this Friday night party was sort of like the warehouse in the indie rave movie *Groove*. The blue warehouse had a fenced-in outside back area. Inside was a dance area, a Chill Room, and bathrooms. Like, real bathrooms, with doors and toilets and sinks. Luxury. There was also a random drummer dude who sat outside jamming with the house beats. He annoyed me; I didn't want to hear clink-clink clank-clank when I was feeling the boom-boom bam-bam.

"This isn't working!" I whined, shaking my tape recorder, the little red light flickering. "Oh wait, no, okay, it is working! Yo yo! This is Ferrari Ravioli reporting in. Natalie is really itchy—"

"Everrrryyywwwheeere," she slurred, her freckled face smiling as she rubbed herself sensually.

"And Adidas has wandered off," I continued. "Anyway, I

have, like, a piece of skin hanging from the roof of my mouth. I think that's from too many lollipops, but I could be wrong. . . . Most likely, I am!"

Natalie, a friend from school, and I were standing in the main room waiting for Tommy, who'd left us for the bathroom. The music was getting faster. My senses revved up. There was a minimal light show—just a few blue, green, and pink lasers darting around. Zero projections on the walls. A few sofas lined the perimeter. One water station. The room was half full of kids standing like us, the rest dancing facing the DJ.

Natalie and I were talking and itching. My E was slowly hitting me, I could *just* feel it. I wondered where Tommy had gone. When he disappeared for too long, I missed him.

"I'm about to fall asleep, but I'm not," Natalie said. "I don't know what I'm talking about. There's a burning sensation all over me. I'm so itchy! And really dizzy."

"Do you want me to scratch you?" I offered, swirling my fingertips in the air. "Because I've got long, long nails, and they're hot pink!"

It was Natalie's first rave and first time doing E. I had become an enabler. A rave advocate. I would tell all my friends how fun raves were, and then they wanted in. How could they not? Most of them didn't become ravers, but they seemed to enjoy a one-night stand with the rave world. And I liked seeing a friend's first time on E. I could never relive that uncontrollable euphoria, so I could either live vicariously through others or try new highs. (I opted for both, of course.)

And he's back—Tommy, with an update: "So I was walking, you know? And I was, like, is this the line for the bathroom or whatever, and these chicks were, like, this is a chick-only bathroom, so I was, like, whaaat, so I had to go piss, like, in the boondocks 'n' shit dude. That's my story." He giggled. "I'm starting to E and shit is all good in my 'hood, Bob! So anyways, so then I was walking you know with my shoes or whatever walk walk walk and then, like, wait, oh yeah, then I was like walk walk walk shake your head to the music la la la you know and then la la la ra ra ra and then there was this drummer and he was, like, fucking up the whole thing and so I was, like, what the fuck whatever la la la walk walk walk and then, hold on, I'm telling a story!"

I was grabbing my recorder from his hand.

"But it's mine!" I yelled.

We fought over it like siblings.

"Oh my god!" he yelled at me.

I got the recorder back and looped my arm through his.

"Ferrari Ravioli's a bitch!" he yelled into the mic.

"Anyway." I laughed. "Let's go outside and make new friends."

We did, within minutes. Their names were Evan and Julie, and they were from Pacifica, a coastal town south of San Francisco. Twinkle-eyed and acne-scarred, Julie acted as if we'd been friends for years. Evan was a doughy, blond gay guy wearing a high-shine shirt and beaded necklaces. They were super friendly, and also on E.

"Dude." Tommy pointed to a group next to us. "They're taking off their fucking underwear!"

"That's sooo fucking tight," Julie said, inhaling a cigarette. "Tricks are for kids! Even silly little rabbits."

"Can I kiss you?" Natalie asked me.

I obliged, and we French kissed in front of our new friends. No biggie. Apparently, I was feeling my E.

"Dude, we need to find Shay to get our E," I said.

"No, you don't need any more," Tommy warned.

"For tomorrow night."

"Oh yeah."

We left our new friends to find our drug dealer. We had one now. She was a female dealer, therefore I trusted her. We'd met her a few raves earlier and had been getting bomb E from her since.

We slunk through the party, looking out for Shay. I was dazzled by neon lights (more brilliant now), entrancing beats (whipping robo techno), and beautiful faces (previously average-looking people). We stopped for a dance break.

I was about to lose myself in the music when I looked over and saw a familiar face. I stared at her for a while before I realized it was a girl from my school named Cara. We said hellos and tried to talk, but that's not the thing to do on the dance floor—too loud, too high. When I asked her what she was on, she said she was sober because she was driving. Having driven stoned and on acid, that was a foreign idea to me. I said bye, moved on.

I looked at Natalie; she was stumbling, dancing, trancing.

"I cannot see straight right now, dude," I said. "Let's go make friends."

We went outside, where kids were standing and sitting around in clusters, smoking, joking, and posing. We spoke to anyone who looked friendly.

There were the girls named Iris and Anemone, who had done their hair up like Bjork's cool multi-bun style.

There was John from Pinole, whose voice was soprano because he was on E.

There was Jerry from Indiana, who was twenty and wished he was sixteen again, sigh.

There was Chris, wearing the same navy blue Adidas jacket with white stripes as me, who tipped us off to a store in the city called Harputs where they sold vintage Adidas gear.

There was Natalie, who was getting a shoulder massage from John while Jerry massaged my knee while I made out with Natalie while Tommy checked the Chill Room for our dealer.

There was Shay. We bought four hits of E called Blueberries and a ten-sack of weed from her.

There was our new friend Evan, who yelled, "I love you guys!" from across the spread. "PLUR!"

PLUR. The raver's credo, it stood for:

Peace – Letting go of fear and living at peace with oneself, one another, and the planet for a greater good.

Love – As one learns to love oneself, one is able to love everyone else unconditionally.

Unity – A mutual, corporate bond is formed resulting from the love and peace experienced with one another.

Respect – Because of peace, love, and unity, one can accept others regardless of their beliefs or background.

This acronym graced rave flyers and signage throughout the parties we attended.

DJ Frankie Bones had coined the term at a Brooklyn warehouse party in the early '90s when he stopped his records after noticing a fight break out. He stopped the music and told the crowd they better start bringing the peace, love, unity, and respect, or he would break their faces. Something like that. When you wandered a party aimlessly, out of your mind with a head full of acid or ecstasy or both, you could always say "PLUR" to someone and know you weren't alone.

"I'm going to be an engineer, and I'm going to go to space."

"Can I go?"

"I'm hella high."

"Can I kiss your tongue again?"

"Do you guys know some guys from Monterey?" (That was me, secretly hoping I'd run into Jack that night.)

Then a girl with a labret piercing and Cheshire cat grin stopped Tommy and me in our tracks. "Excuse me," I held my tape recorder up to her, gonzo style. "What's your name?"

"Dreya."

She was holding a stack of rave flyers. She was the coolest girl I'd ever seen. I wanted to be friends with her. I was going to ask for her number—then, poof! She was gone.

Then we got hella high.

"I'm so high right now I don't know what to do with my life," I told Tommy. "I'm having too much fun. I can't walk, I can't talk, I can't see. I'm feeling the wind rush through my body. I think I'm higher than you."

"No, dude—I'm sooooo high."

"Is everything blurry for you?"

"Yeah, it kinda sucks."

I started fanning myself. "My face is hot but my body is not, I'm scared to dance, I'm going to fall over."

"Goodness gracious."

"I can't do it, Captain!"

"Yo yo yo, time is going by so so slow."

"Let's smoke a bowl."

That bowl hit the spot, brought us back to Earth.

We left the rave before sunrise and agreed to meet up with Evan and Julie at another party Saturday night called Ground Zero. Tommy and I were in the midst of our first double-nighter.

Which was perfectly possible, because Tommy's parents were out of town that weekend—a rarity that had to be taken advantage of.

Saturday was a blur: We napped for a few hours, smoked bowls, watched scary movies, and ordered pizza. I ran home to show my parents I was alive and repacked my Adidas duffel full of outfit options. Around 9:00 p.m. we called the rave hotline and couldn't believe it when we heard the directions to the blue warehouse—where we had just partied the night before. Where we'd made so many new friends. And had so much fun. We could relive the night all, over, again.

> Ground Zero, July 1996
> Homies: Tommy, Steven
> Location: San Francisco,
> the blue warehouse by Illinois Street
> Drugs: Ecstasy (two hits), a bump of speed, weed

Another school friend of ours, Steven, a six-foot-four, gangly redhead, was along for the ride. He decided to do acid that night. Just as well, since Tommy and I were all ready to go with our Blueberries.

Around midnight, we entered the party like we owned it. Déjà vu.

We soon found Evan and Julie. We also ran into Jack, which was exciting since I'd told Tommy about him and hadn't seen him since we made out and he inspired me to get my tongue pierced. I proudly showed Jack my tongue, the silver ball float-ing on it like a pearl on an oyster. He didn't seem very im-pressed, which made me momentarily sad.

Tommy and I went to stand in line for the bathroom.

"Dude," he said. "He's hella gay." He was referring to Jack.

"What? No," I said, waving off the idea. "We totally made out. He kissed my boobs."

"Ew!"

"Shut up, it's true. Why do you think I got my tongue pierced? It felt hella good, dude."

"Maybe he's bi."

I realized he'd never paged me to hang out after that night. But I hadn't paged him either. Tommy was my main squeeze, and I wasn't looking for a boyfriend. I was enjoying being free, experimenting with everything and everyone. But Jack being gay or bi was beginning to make sense, since he wore a Smurfs back-pack. That thought bubble floated out of my head and burst when it was my turn to pee.

Tommy waited for me in the doorway between the bath-rooms and the main dance room. Prismatic lights flashed be-hind his silhouette.

"Dude, when you were in the bathroom, I thought of the coolest shit," he said.

"Wait." I clicked record and held my dictaphone up in front of him. "Go on."

Slowly, into the mic, he said, "Sextasy. That is what you say when you have sex on ecstasy. Example: We had sextasy last night."

It was clever, but I hadn't even had plain sex yet, so I changed the subject. "Let's go find Julie and Evan."

"Ugh, I can't stand him."

"What? Dude, he's so fun."

"Whatever. He's so annoying."

"Wait, where's Steven?"

We went outside and found Julie and Evan sitting in a circle with some kids we didn't know. We introduced ourselves, and they made room for us. They were holding marshmallows. My E was about to kick in—I could *just* feel it.

"I'm sitting here with some fresh cool people, and we're hand-dancing with marshmallows," I told my recorder.

"Round and round," Evan sang, smooth R&B style. "Round and round we go . . ."

"This is a bomb-ass night, yo," Tommy said to me, all-around smiling.

And so it began, again.

We saw Jerry, who still wished he was sixteen, sigh.

We saw Dreya, sporting flared pants and glittery lips. I was too high to ask for her number, but I took her flyer for an upcoming rave in August called Open.

We saw the beautiful Luca and Angel!

"Talking to you live, from this bullshit party at this fucked-up warehouse, I'm having a great time," Luca said in his sexy drawl.

We found our long-lost friend Steven, who was also having a great time frying balls.

And then I met Anjali. Curly brown pigtails, ingénue brown eyes. She reminded me of Punky Brewster, my idol growing up, and we shared the same favorite color: red. She wore a highly covetable black-and-white Adidas track jacket. She had a glow wand and a stuffed ghost named Casper the Unfriendly Ghost.

I asked her, "Was he in *Poltergeist*?"

She lifted an eyebrow. "Maybe."

"I knew he looked familiar. That's one of my favorites. What scene, what scene?"

She lifted her finger to her cheek, puckering her lips. "You know the scene with the closet?"

"Uh, yeah, ingrained in my membrane."

"That's the one." She giggled.

I turned to Tommy. "Tommy, meet Anjali, my soul mate. Anjali, meet Tommy, my other soul mate."

"What up?" he said.

"Do you guys want a bump?" she asked.

We didn't know what of, and it felt uncool to ask. After all, I trusted my soul sister. Huddled in a group of friends, she revealed a mini plastic baggie full of white powder. It looked just like Margot's baggie of coke, but plumper. She shook the baggie, and some trickled onto the back of her hand. She raised her hand up to her nose and sniffed it up. She did one more bump and then passed us the baggie. I mimicked her movements. No one seemed to notice what we were doing. Everyone continued to gab and smoke cigarettes.

It was the first time I'd snorted a drug up my nose. It burned like a motherfucker. I knew it had to be some form of amphetamine. Crystal meth, ice, crank—whichever it was, it was speedy. It blasted my brain with clarity, jolted me awake.

Ten minutes later, I was dancing with my soul mates on the dance floor.

A song took over: "Disco's Revenge." It starts as a faraway "boom, boom, boom, boom, boom, boom, boom, boom." Then builds to "BOOM, boom, BOOM, boom, BOOM, boom, BOOM, boom." And eventually becomes "BOOM, BOOM,

BOOM, BOOM, BOOM, BOOM, BOOM, BOOM." My body boomed right along with the music. My mind emptied as the song played forever.

I found myself with former soul mate, Jack, around 5:00 a.m., talking about the weather. The weather, really? I accepted that we were just friends.

The sky was lightening from party-time black to Pacific blue. Tommy and I preferred to leave parties before the sun came out. It wasn't something we decided to do for a specific reason. It was more a feeling that the party was over when the sun came up. If we saw a rave in the light of day, would it feel like mystical nightlife anymore? Would we still dance and play? Or would we be too busy noticing the flaws, the grim reality of everything?

Tommy and I interrupted our friends as they were singing the Mentos theme song to tell them we were leaving. Julie and Evan asked if we could give them a ride to BART. It took a while to find Steven, and by the time we left the party, the sun was rising.

After we all squeezed into my dad's car, I revved the engine and turned on the radio. Prince's purr welcomed us into the blissed-out morning. And then I went down a one-way street and almost ran us into a semi-truck. U-turn. Whoops.

Later that day, after a nap and smoking a bowl with Tommy, I examined Dreya's flyer as we lay together in the hammock in his backyard. It said "Admit Free One" across the inside in silver font. Dreya had given me a VIP flyer. I felt so special. It was like getting invited to the most popular girl in school's party.

16

RAVE TIP #1: DON'T PANIC

One weeknight in July, Johanna and I were making candy bracelets—the kind Wildflower had given Tommy and me at Freedom. I'd raced to the craft store soon after that, bought various color beads and elastic string, and got to making DIY rave jewelry.

The first candy bracelet I made was for myself. I alternated blue, orange, and glow-in-the-dark beads with letter beads that spelled "Ferari" to represent my (first) raver sobriquet, Ferrari Ravioli. (Yes, I spelled it wrong. I didn't notice my typo at the time.)

Side note: this is now referred to as "kandi" bracelets, but we spelled it the old-fashioned way.

Johanna was back from New York, where she'd been visiting family. We had some acid, so we took it, naturally.

"Dude, did you know that Beastie actually stands for something?" I asked her, referring to the Beastie Boys.

"Really?" Johanna said, sitting on the carpet in her Chill Basement.

"Yeah, it stands for Boys Entering Anarchistic States Towards Internal Excellence."

"Whoa. Dope."

My pager buzzed around 11:00 p.m. I grabbed it from the stool and recognized my home phone number across the little gray screen. My stomach clenched. The last time I'd seen those numbers on my pager while frying was the Santa Cruz night. I'd hoped to never see them in an altered state again.

Unsure what to do, I examined my pager. "Do you see 5-1-0-3-3-9-1-9-2-0?" I asked, facing it toward Johanna.

She squinted to study the numbers on my pager. "Uhhh, yeah."

I reminded myself that I wasn't doing anything wrong. *You're just hanging out at Johanna's making jewelry.* I took a deep breath and looked at the gray carpet. Fuzzy caterpillars were crawling on it. Blink. They were gone. It was just a carpet. A really trippy carpet.

"It's all good," Johanna reassured me, stringing some beads. She wasn't wearing any makeup, and her hair was in a messy bun atop her head. The stripes in her pajamas were wavy like Fruit Stripe gum.

Right, all good, I thought. I could speak to my parents on acid. After all, I was a seasoned acid freak.

I picked up the cordless phone in the corner of the room and dialed home.

"Hello?" my mom answered.

"Hey, Mom."

"Hi, honey, what are you up to?"

"Uh, I'm just hanging out with Jo. At, her, house."

"Well, I realize it's late, but we have a car situation. I forgot your brother has a dentist appointment tomorrow morning."

"What time?"

"Nine."

"So what's the problem?"

"I had to drop my car at the shop today—the brakes are squeaking—and your dad has an early morning."

"Uh-huhhh," I said, watching Johanna organize her beads into color piles on the carpet like a toddler. Fuzzy caterpillars crawled between them. "What's the problem?"

"There's no way Justin can get there. You have his car."

"Oh yeah, duh," I said. "Um . . . I'm super tired. Can I just come by in the morning and pick him up?"

"I don't think so, honey. I don't want him to be late. He can't miss this appointment before he leaves for Portland."

My bracelet inspired me, and I suggested, "What about the Ferrari? The Ferrari!"

"You know I don't drive that thing," she said, annoyed. "Why don't you just drive home now before it gets too late?"

Cringe. I'd just started tripping and had at least six hours to go. We were in our pajamas and bent on making bracelets that night, all night. Johanna was lost in her craft, sitting cross-legged behind shining piles of beads that looked like rock candy.

"Samantha? Are you there?"

"Yeah! Sorry, Jo was telling me something. Yeah, I'll be home soon."

I hung up and blurted, "Fuck, dude! I have to go home! Like, now."

Johanna's smile dripped into a frown. "Sucks."

"I know! Fuck. Did I sound normal?"

"Yeah, totally."

If I hadn't been on acid, I probably would have pushed back more, but because I could barely follow the conversation, I'd agreed to my mom's demands. Besides, it wasn't like we were at a rave that night. Even on acid, I realized this was a good opportunity to behave.

I put my jeans on and gathered my jewelry supplies and then chugged down the Berkeley hills in the Bubble, my brother's white '74 Super Beetle. I'd named it the Bubble because whenever I drove it, protected by its dome of windows, I felt like I was inside a bubble—especially when I was high, when I could drift away into the sky. That summer, I'd been switching between driving my dad's Honda Prelude and the Bubble, whichever was available, but when Justin went away to college, his car was going to be mine. All mine.

Cruising along to DJ Simon's boppity beats, streetlights twinkled, and buildings blew by me. When I noticed other cars on the road, I felt like I was inside a game of Tetris. We were all moving parts within an endless grid, maneuvering to fit in with each other. Excited by being inside a game, I shifted gears, turning corners with vigor, racing home.

Whiz! Whirl! Whoop! Firebird invasion!

A flurry of sirens surrounded me. White strobes flashed in my rearview mirrors. My pulse accelerated, but I slowed down. Uncertain whether the sirens were in the music or real life outside, I turned down the volume on the stereo. It was real life outside. I was being pulled over.

What did I do?! Was I speeding? What drugs do I have on me? Weed. My chest tightened. I came to a stop off a main road that ran through the UC Berkeley campus. I turned off the engine. Killed the music. The night silence grounded me.

normal. NoRMGL. NORMGL. normal. NORmal. normal. NoRMGL. NORMGL. Normal. NORmal.

I looked in my side mirror and saw a police officer walking toward me. It was hard not to be mesmerized by the brilliant lights. *You'll need your license. Wallet. Get your wallet out now.* I reached inside my Polo Sport purse on the passenger seat and felt slick plastic. I unzipped the gold zipper of my wallet and slid my driver's license out of the slot. A twenty-sack of weed was in my purse, so I threw it on the floor.

The clean-cut villain stood outside my window. I cranked the handle to unroll it.

"Hi," I said, smiling, squinting at the brightness of the lights.

"License and registration."

It was the first time I'd heard that in real life. The authoritative demand scared me. I knew the registration must be in the glove box (that's where my parents always said to keep it), so I reached over and pushed the silver latch. A bundle of white papers spilled out of the mailbox, paper airplanes entangled with origami. I grabbed a few papers. White papers, black lines, they all looked the same as I shuffled through them like a deck of cards. The letters blurred, shifting larger and smaller. *I can do this*, I told myself. *I have to identify it.*

One of the papers was a square shape, smaller than the rest. My gut told me: *Bingo!*

"Here you go," I said, handing the square paper out the window.

I avoided looking at him straight on for fear that my eyes were red and would give me away. *Wait—are they?* I hadn't smoked weed, and the whites of my eyes didn't usually get red from acid. But my pupils got big. Full moon big.

Mr. Po stood there. Waiting. "And your license?"

"Oh yeah." I giggled. *Didn't I already give it to him? Where did I put it? Retrace. I had it in my hand before I opened the glove box.* "It was right here. . . ." *Don't think out loud!* My eyes scanned the black dashboard, my purse, the passenger seat. *Where the fuck did it go? Be normal.* A glimmer of something reflected between my thighs. I gasped, grabbed the laminated card with my goofy photo on it, and handed it out the window.

"I see you're a new driver," he said.

"Mmmhmm," I hummed, peeking up at him. His Adam's apple looked less like an apple and more like a bulging third eye staring me down, judging me.

"Where are you headed tonight?"

"Home." The word reassured me, strangely, since home was the last place I thought I wanted to be that night.

"Do you know what you did back there?"

Back where? My throat tightened. My palms tingled. *You mean taking acid? Or driving on acid? Be normal. Normal! This can't be happening. I didn't do anything. I've become an expert driver on acid. I can see lights brighter and hear sounds clearer. A flurry of sirens. A red light . . .*

"Did I run a red light? Was I speeding? I just started driving this car. It's my brother's, it, I, was I speeding?"

"No, you weren't speeding," he said. "Have you had anything to drink tonight?"

"Oh, I'm sorry but I, I don't . . ." I looked at him straight on. "I don't drink."

It was kind of the truth. I hadn't had or wanted alcohol since I'd started raving six months before. Alcohol wasn't sold or offered at raves, and since I'd discovered hallucinogens, inhalants, ecstasy, and the like, getting drunk at a rave had never crossed my mind. Booze didn't go with the rave vibe.

"You rolled through the stop sign back there," he said, pointing back down the road.

"Really? I thought I stopped. At every sign," I said, struggling. *Think straight. Talk straight. Normal.*

"I'm going to let you off with a warning this time. But make sure you always make a full stop at stop signs," he said, nodding once like adults do when they're giving you advice.

"Of course," I said. "Thank you."

He handed everything back. "Drive safe," he said, turning to walk away.

It was only after he left my window that I realized what had almost happened. I'd nearly been caught by the police driving on acid—*and* with weed on me. Basically, my dad's worst nightmare. My scalp felt tight. My thoughts were so fast and garbled I couldn't keep up with them. My head was about to implode, and my heart explode. The acid-induced anxiety was too much—I was teetering on the blood-orange border of a red panic attack.

I reached for my purse and plopped it on my lap. I felt around for my LeSportSac makeup bag, where the weed was. I unzipped the bag and squeezed the plump plastic baggie with my fingers, debating if I should get rid of it, throw it out the window.

I wished I had Tommy or Johanna or Justin with me to talk it out and help calm me down. Waiting for the cop to drive away,

I sank into the cool black leather seat, my temples throbbing. I was parched. I reached down to the passenger-side floor, where I knew an almost-empty water bottle or two would be. Crackle. Clench. Chug. Hydration helped as I waited, watching, willing the flashing lights that had started this whole mess to stop.

Whiz. Whirl. Whoop.

Stop! Stop! Stop!

In my rearview mirror, I saw the cop's silhouette sitting in his car, which was still parked behind me. *He's waiting for me to go.* He thought I'd lied about drinking and driving and was going to follow me home. It wasn't over. I turned the key, powering up the Bubble's boisterous engine. *There's weed in your purse. Be normal. Don't fuck this up. You're so close.*

The flurry of sirens and white strobes stopped.

Exhale.

Relief trickled through me, beginning in my fried brain, trickling down my spine, cleansing every buzzing nerve, extending through my limbs. After minutes of being a fireball of fear, my body finally relaxed. My fingers were the last to feel calm; the tips, wrapped around the sticky leather of the steering wheel, were still tingling.

I adjusted my mirrors to check for any oncoming cars, exaggerating my motions so Mr. Po would see I was a good driver. Once the road was clear, I shifted into first and chugged forward. He followed me. I turned on the radio, hoping normal music would make me feel normal. I clicked to the classical station, where I'd found solace the morning after Eon.

After a couple of stoplights and long, complete stops at stop signs, the police car turned in a different direction behind me and disappeared.

Waving trees greeted me as I rolled into our driveway, scanning the house for lights. The overhead stove light in the kitchen was the only obvious one, which meant my parents were asleep. It was about 12:30 a.m. I parked in the driveway, entering through a side door into the laundry room. Stacks of folded clothes looked like giant vanilla wafers on the dryer. Tops on hangers teetered like scarecrows as I walked by them and crept up the stairs.

My mind was racing. Two opposing emotions zagged through me: fear and relief. I told myself I'd never drive on acid again. *Normal. Normal. Normal.* I went up to my room, put pajamas on, and decided to watch TV in our down-downstairs.

The down-downstairs was a basement kind of room in the lower, garage level of our house. It had windowed doors that opened onto the driveway, making it a perfect sneak-out spot for when I "accidentally" fell asleep watching TV down there. It was a storage and living space with sofas, a TV and VCR, and my mom's sewing machine. It was also the space in the house farthest away from our parents' eyes and ears.

I picked up Sunny, took her downstairs with me, and watched *Earth Girls Are Easy, Clueless,* and *Pretty Woman*—a mac n' cheese comfort movie marathon. I sat on the carpet making candy bracelets until the acid faded. Eyes heavy, pulse calm, I finally relaxed on the sofa and turned to lie on my side. Sunny snuggled into the nook behind my bent legs. I pulled the blanket up to my neck and finally fell asleep encased in a colorful cocoon of candy.

In the days that followed, I didn't think much more about

the incident other than feeling relieved I hadn't been caught. There was a lingering numbness, though. A darkness quickly buried. This time, it wasn't my parents I could have been caught by. It was the law. Of course, I had been fooling both for months.

Looking back, I understand that I got away with running that stop sign because I was a white girl. But could I see my position of privilege at the time? Not in the least. After every close call, I only felt grateful for getting away with it—and I had no intention of slowing down. Not yet.

17 / GOING NUTRAGEOUS

The fly ladies of the R&B group TLC wore Band-Aids as decorative accents, therefore Tommy was stuck on Band-Aids too. I had put a red, black, and white *101 Dalmatians* Band-Aid above the logo of my red Jansport backpack. Tommy liked the solid neon ones. He usually put one on the outer sleeve of his tee shirt or the back of his white Adidas visor—his signature hat.

One weeknight in August, Tommy and I had a special mushroom mission planned that didn't involve going to a rave. It was around 9:00 p.m., and we were sitting in his car under the amber glow of the CVS parking lot in Montclair, where we could be found on non-rave nights representing our gang, The Village Mafia. We had formed our two-person gang that summer. The Village was our territory. We had a gang sign we flashed in photos. Our gang colors were red and blue. No, we did not represent V-Mob lower than the 580 freeway in Oakland—we knew better than to do that.

We had an eighth of mushrooms to fuel our night, but first, we needed accompaniments. We entered the drug store, grabbed some water, and headed to the First Aid aisle, our giant pants audibly swishing. Tommy's newest accessory—a thick yellow plastic chain he'd fastened through his front belt loop, draped dramatically down his thigh, and attached to his wallet in his back pocket—swayed with every step. Like everything raver, it was rainbow bright.

Between Ace bandages and Neosporin, we eyed our adhesive strip options. We slyly looked to the left, to the right, then grabbed the paper boxes and stole a few Band-Aids from each one, slipping them into our roomy JNCO pockets. The most prized Band-Aids I'd ever found were Care Bear ones; I only shared those with best friends.

Our next stop was the candy aisle, where we considered our sugary options.

"Hmmm," Tommy said, holding his finger to his chin, pressing it into the small dimple in the middle. "Maybe Snickers."

A red package with blue block lettering called to me. I reached for it. "I'm going Nutrageous," I said. It was the divine Hershey's candy bar loaded with chocolate, peanut butter, and peanuts—an amped-up bar version of the unparalleled Reese's Peanut Butter Cup.

"Good call," Tommy said, grabbing two. "I'm going Nutrageous too."

Back in Tommy's car in the parking lot, ready to eat our psychedelic dessert, we inspected the bag half full of dehydrated mushrooms.

"How many should we do?" I wondered aloud.

"All of them?" Tommy shrugged.

We divided up the caps and stems. Brittle in texture, curvy in silhouette, some of the caramel-colored caps were broken off from the stems; some were as big as quarters, some smaller, more dime-sized. The stems were stiff with brown threads that looked like dirt, a reminder that this drug was au naturel, grown and plucked from the earth. If you looked carefully, blue undertones laced the stems. They were probably *Psilocybe cyanescens*—the most potent, most popular psilocybin mushroom in the Pacific Northwest.

I held the pieces in my palm and put them in my mouth one at a time. The woodsy taste was strong. It nearly made me gag. I'd been accustomed to the refreshing taste of gum or sweet lollipops to chase drugs. The bitter taste lingered like a fart inside my mouth. The consistency was dry and coarse—it was like eating twigs. I followed every piece with a bite of my Nutrageous bar and had to drink water after every swallow to wash it all down. Little mushies, along with peanut chunks, got stuck in my teeth like popcorn. I dug my nails around my teeth to pry them out, then winced swallowing them. My jaw was sore from so much chewing. Eating mushrooms was a lot of work.

"Ew, dude, I always forget how nasty shrooms are," Tommy said, smacking his lips.

"I know," I said through a mouthful. "Maybe it would have been better to just dip the pieces in peanut butter. I remember someone saying that."

"I can't do this anymore." Tommy threw the remains in his mouth, chased them with water, swallowed them like pills. Then he belched and started the car.

"Should we pick out the meter?" he asked with one hand on the wheel, the other digging shroom pieces out of his teeth. "I wish we had floss."

Unable to reply because my tongue was busy vacuuming my mouth, I gave him a thumbs-up.

"Sweet." He drove us out of the parking lot.

Montclair spans about five blocks of retail stores and restaurants. The only bars are within restaurants, and the action there dies down early, around 10:00 p.m. Slow riding into the Montclair late night, there was a weight in my stomach like I'd just overeaten a pasta dinner. I felt unsettled, and I couldn't tell if it was from excitement or indigestion. A few burps relieved me.

As we rolled along, DJ Donald Glaude's house beats energized our mission. Peering past empty parking spots, I considered our options: The meter in front of the video store where we'd rented countless '80s scary movies? What about in front of Noah's Bagels, where we'd noshed on doughy goodness so many stoned times after school? Or the smoothie shop where we got our wheatgrass shots? We circled the streets, waiting for the mushrooms to kick in.

"That one?" I pointed, suggesting one in front of a jewelry store.

"Yeahhh." Tommy slowed the car.

And with that "yeahhh," I started giggling uncontrollably. Nothing funny had happened, but how he said the word—excitedly and slowly—and how his eyes had bulged like a fish's when he said it, was for some reason hilarious. I was overcome with the giggles. Spontaneous, wild, uncontrollable giggles.

Tommy giggled with me, "W-w-what?"

"I don't know, dude!" I yelled between giggles. "You just sounded hella funny!"

Tommy was cracking up. His giggles got louder and stronger, crescendoing into a full-on laughing fit. I held my thighs to brace myself as my eyes poured out happiness. Lost in the hilarity, my giggles catapulted into gut-busting laughter. My cheeks were warm and wet; tears blurred my vision. Tommy rocked himself back and forth in his seat, knocking his visor on the steering wheel, making him laugh even harder. We were caricature versions of ourselves, experiencing a sudden shift to silliness, and then—

"HONK!"

We jumped in our seats.

Tommy had accidentally hit his horn.

"Shhhhh!" I giggled, breathing hard. I broke from laughing to wipe my cheeks with my sleeves, caught my breath, then glanced out the window.

Double take. I rolled down my window to have another look. Shadows from the trees under the streetlights made intricate vibrational patterns. Snowflakes, spirographs, cobwebs— beautiful geometric forms jumped out of the sidewalk. A streetlight had golden halos around it, warm and vibrant. It was the prettiest streetlight I'd ever seen. The sparkling branches of a tree waved at me as if it knew me. An old friend, inviting and comforting. Everything pulsed. Alive.

Tommy was looking around in awe too. He sat back in his seat. "Whoaaaa, duuuude."

I was breathing rapidly. My toes were tingling. I couldn't stop smiling. The little red lights on the stereo, the plastic air vents, the silver shine of the rearview mirror—ordinary things were so interesting. Alive. The weight in my stomach had turned into crampy bloating, but a fuzzy buzz permeated through me. I told myself to belly breathe, thinking that if I made some space, I'd feel better. A gust of restlessness washed over me. I couldn't sit anymore. I needed air. I needed out.

I grabbed the door handle. "Let's do this!"

Then a spaceship approached from around a corner, flashing a spotlight at us. My stomach twisted. The bright light triggered a fear inside me that was too recent, too real.

"Shit!" Tommy exhaled.

We ducked down—not the slickest of moves. I peeked out the back windshield after the lights passed over us. It was only a Bay Alarm security truck doing its nightly rounds. Relief rippled through me as I looked at Tommy crouched down in his seat, his limbs curved. He looked like a fortune cookie. He started giggling, and another round of giggles rescued me from anxiety. I covered my mouth, fearful the security truck would hear me, but I couldn't bottle up the laughter.

"Is, he, gone?" I asked, chuckling.

Tommy sat up, his giggling subsiding. "Coast is clear!"

I sat up, cleared my throat, smoothed my ponytail. Burp. Sour peanut spit-up filled my mouth. I swallowed, cleared my throat again, pretended it hadn't happened. Gross.

I looked at Tommy. "Band-Aids?"

"Check!"

"It's now or never."

"Now!" he blurted.

I sprang out of the car. The cold air invigorated me as we dashed toward the parking meter. Tommy backed up against a storefront, looking side to side, checking for interlopers, his fingers held up in a pretend gun. Nervously giggling, we got to the meter and got to work.

We ripped Band-Aids out of their wrappers in a hurry, waxy paper falling onto the ground in a flurry, and stuck them to the hard metal—Tommy with speed, me with precision. We covered the whole thing with Daffy Duck, Barbie, Kermit the Frog, Scooby-Doo, and NASCAR racecars, from the scratched glass window in the front all the way down the stand.

The meter became fully animated in seconds. *The Little Mermaid's* Ariel smiled at me, surrounded by her colorful friends. We stopped to admire it. The Band-Aids grew bigger, got smaller.

"We have to get a picture!" I whisper-yelled as I ran to Tommy's car to get my camera.

I captured a photo of Tommy with our V-Mob meter, then we ran to his car and sped off, heading into the hills. Satisfied and safe in the passenger seat, I felt lifted by the throbbing bass.

"Fog around the lights and stuff, wow."

"That tree right there, wow."

"Wow, okay, well, yeah, um, sure, okay, yeah."

"I don't know where I am, like, inside my head."

"Wow, wow, shrooms, wow. What are . . . what is . . . that? Wow."

When we reached the middle of nowhere and everywhere, we got out of the car and stepped into an enchanted redwood forest. Crystals crackled under our footsteps. I stretched my arms up, extending my branches toward the sky, opening my chest and stomach. I shook my limbs and blew raspberries out of my mouth, releasing energy, expelling tension. My stomach felt lighter. Our energy was mellow.

Tommy turned up the volume on his car's stereo, and we left the car windows open so we could hear the music. We danced among grand trees and strange creatures, our minds roaming the infinite, surrendering to universal magic. A rocket, a shooting star, I was riding a rainbow within a dark tunnel. Fascinating, freeing, fantasy. I'd found the dark side of the moon.

The music got redundant. We got cold. And after about five hours of shrooming, we cozied up in Tommy's Chill Car. The magic had faded, and I was left with a body buzz that was less electric and more exhausted. But my senses were still heightened. I blinked and saw zebras prancing across my fleece sleeve. My sinuses were irritated from cry-laughing; my nose was runny. Tommy was funny, but not that funny. And unlike other comedowns, I was hungry and sleepy. All I wanted to do was change into my pj's and drink a smoothie in bed.

Our Band-Aids stayed on the V-Mob meter for months. I knew no one else would understand it—it was the work of weirdos— but I hoped people would at least notice and wonder, maybe even smile. Every time I walked or drove by it, I looked to see what remained. The colors and characters disappeared with the passing of time. People picked them away. But the memory of the shroom adventure remained, always making me smile when I thought about it.

18 / THVRZDAZE

"Okay, let's discuss the scenario," I said from Tommy's passenger car seat. We were parked in his car at 5:00 a.m. on a Friday morning after going to a Thurzdaze in the city the night before. Somebody had graffitied one of the interior walls, and the DJ stopped the music. Some guy announced this, asking that someone come forward and report anything they saw. No one had, so the party had broken up early.

"We just bought water from the 7-Eleven in Montclair," Tommy said, discussing the scenario.

"No—it's water from heaven," I said. "That's some holy water, dude."

"Actually"—Tommy paused to inspect the burgundy label—"it's Arrowhead Natural Spring Water. That's 1 quart and 1 pint and 2.7 full ounces."

"Wow, it says from 1894. It's almost a hundred years old."

"It's 1994! It *is* a hundred years old!"

"No, it's 1996, so it's 104 years old."

We were both wrong, clearly. Too much mental math.

Thurzdaze was pretty fun before the party ended early. It was at Maritime Hall, a historic art deco music venue in San Francisco perched atop a downtown corner. It had a ballroom and second-level perimeter overlooking the dance floor.

Tommy and Johanna were there, as was the Pacifica crew. We took two hits of E (called Playboys) because one just wasn't enough anymore. The music was the highlight. To Tommy's chagrin, Evan and I beatboxed together during a Blondie "Rapture" remix. After that, I danced with myself to the Donna Summer "I Feel Love" remix—a popular track I'd heard at nearly every rave that summer. Everyone got down during "Funk Phenomenon."

The dance floor got too sweaty, and we went to the mint green ladies' bathroom. Tommy always came with me into the girls' bathroom at parties, and I don't recall anyone ever having a problem with that. Probably because he entertained everyone.

When the party ended, we went outside to the parking lot to loiter since we were too high to drive, and we found Julie and Evan standing with some dudes we hadn't met yet. There were two Mikes. One was tall, lanky, and smiley—he was Julie's boyfriend. The other Mike was baby-faced and rocking some serious dreadlocks. So as not to confuse them, everyone called them Mike and Mike With The Dreads.

The two other guys were more skater than raver. One of them caught my eye in his Etnies sneakers and backward baseball cap. He was about an inch taller than me, with scruffy sideburns and strong eyebrows. I pretended not to notice him as we all hung around, sitting, standing, drinking water, smoking cigarettes, and slyly smoking bowls.

Post-party chatter commenced, and eventually the cute skater boy looked my way. "What's your name?" he asked me.

"Ferrari Ravioli."

"Ferrari what?"

"Ravioli."

"I'm Clayton," he said, inhaling a cigarette, holding it like a joint between his thumb and pointer.

"And this is Cesar," I said, lifting up my stuffed caterpillar to meet him.

Clayton gave me a confused look.

Cesar was the newest addition to my raver toy box. After meeting various stuffed animals at raves, Tommy and I had set out to find ones that inspired us. Cesar, a rattling, rainbow-colored caterpillar with red tentacles, was my guy. Tommy had Bubba, a little yellow duckling.

"Hey, you guys," Mike With The Dreads said, pointing to something in the sky. "Check out that billboard."

It read: "*Drug-impaired driving can be hazardous to your health. Medications can affect your ability to drive. Drive carefully.*"

We laughed at the irony of it. Were we being responsible riding out our highs in the parking lot rather than while driving in our cars? That night, I guess we were. But most of us were guilty of drug-impaired driving or "drugged driving," as we called it. We shrugged it off, ignoring the reality of how dangerous it was.

A wave of yawns swept over us. Tommy and I hugged everyone goodbye, which included a yummy hug from Clayton. When he pulled back, he looked at me intensely, his eyes shining copper in the shadows.

"Maybe I'll see you around. Bye, Cesar," he said, waving at the stuffed animal in my hand.

Clayton wasn't tall, or a pretty boy, or flashy. But he was ruggedly handsome, and I had an affinity for skater boys.

Johanna had been chatting up Clayton's friend, and she left with the Pacifica crew.

Tommy and I, meanwhile, glided across the street to a gas station to get cigarettes and water. Then I got in the passenger seat of Tommy's car and hit play on DJ Dan's latest mixtape. We had nowhere to go and decided to buy time at 7-Eleven.

And that's when we found ourselves sobering up sitting in Tommy's car, examining water bottles and rave flyers, planning our near weekend.

"I much prefer parties with outsides," I said, reapplying Watermelon Lip Smackers for the fiftieth time that night/morning. "We met so many people at all the outside parties this summer. Flyers should really say 'inside' or 'outside,' because when it's only inside it's so loud and you can't talk to people."

"Word," Tommy agreed. He was down to one-word responses. We needed a scene change. We'd been hanging out in the 7-Eleven parking lot for about an hour. I scoured the depths of my brain for a creative solution of where to go next, how to keep the fun going.

After a minute, an epiphany: There was somewhere we could go. Where we could shower. And swim in a twenty-five-yard heated lap pool. And relax in an outdoor hot tub. We could even play tennis. And grab some of my favorite cinnamon bread at the bakery down the street (if we ever got our appetites back). We could go to the Claremont Hotel and Spa in Berkeley. My family had a membership. Why hadn't I thought of that sooner?

We parked on the street by the stately white hotel around 6:00 a.m., when the navy sky was making way for teal blue. We traipsed in pretending we were there for an early-morning workout. We weren't in workout clothes per se, but we were pretty sporty in our track jackets and Adidas kicks.

It was one woman's bathroom Tommy didn't follow me into.

The dense steam and gardenia scent melted me as I walked in. It was the opposite of entering a rave, where the scent of cigarette smoke and musky sweat—which also seduced me—was the standard. Light and dark. Clean and dirty.

I indulged in a luxurious shower, the water washing away the crusty party layer that seeps in as the late night ticks on. Then I wrapped myself in a plush white towel and looked at myself in the mirror while combing my hair. There were remnants of gold glitter from the night before sprinkled across my face. Light purple circles cradled my eyes. My complexion was noticeably pale; I lacked any California tan that summer.

I rinsed with mouthwash and noticed a white-haired woman eyeing my oversize pants. It may have been a combo of her disapproving look and my toxic diet, but my mouth quickly filled with salty saliva and my stomach lurched. I ran into a bathroom stall and barfed, twice.

After mouthwashing again, I met Tommy by the hot tub. Physically I felt refreshed, but mentally I was cracked out. Thoughts were slow and haphazard. We sat on the ledge, rolling up folds of denim as we dipped our bare feet. Massaged by bubbling hot water, my happy feet were the antidote to an uneasy stomach and foggy head. Relaxation washed away any discomfort.

"Dude, we really need to start remembering sunglasses," Tommy said, squinting.

"Amen to that."

"I can't believe we haven't been here yet—like, after a party, I mean."

"I know! Maybe I was afraid I'd run into someone my parents knew. Johanna's family belongs here too, you know," I said, scanning the area. A couple of folks were doing laps, and some people were on machines in the gym past the pool.

Tommy let out a scratchy giggle. "It would be hella funny if we ran into Jo's parents."

"Uh, maybe for you!"

Lying back onto his elbows, kicking his feet around the water, Tommy asked, "What did you think of that Clayton guy? He was cute."

"Yeah, he was cute. Kinda short. He probably thinks I'm weird." The bottom of my foot found a jet, sending tingles up the backs of my thighs.

"Dude, whatever, that whole crew is totally weird." Tommy lay back onto the ground, shading his eyes with a hand. "He probably wasn't on drugs."

"True. Maybe he was just stoned."

Tommy smiled. "He liked you."

"Well, he didn't ask for my number," I said, reaching an arm up, arching it up and over my head, stretching like a rainbow. "And anyway, I like Jack. And Luca."

Tommy scoffed. "Luca! Are you cereal? He is such a queen. Good luck with that one, sister. And Jack and I are, like, straight homies. They've both been blowing my shit up, calling me constantly. I'm like, get off my jock, okay? Seriously."

I sat still, disappointed, trying to accept what Tommy just told me. I knew I didn't have a chance at a sexual relationship with Luca. But I still had a crush on him. He was the prettiest man I'd ever known. I fantasized that one night he would be hella high and we'd make out or something. Like I had with Jack. And Jack, he was AC/DC, but he and I had already hooked up. *Is he into Tommy?* He'd called me that week to see what rave we were going to that weekend—had that been to find out where Tommy was going to be?

I reclined next to Tommy on the hard ground. "So are you into Luca or Jack?"

"Nah," he said with closed eyes, "they're too femme for me."

His response made me feel better, but then I wondered about my crushes. Brandon was a distant memory that still stung a little. Jack and Luca were fascinating creatures that weren't serious contenders. I'd kissed a few girls. And let's not forget about the erotic ecstasy session with Johanna. Was I experimenting, or was I also AC/DC?

19 / VERY IMPORTANT PEOPLE

Open, August 1996
Homies: Johanna, Clayton, Luca, Angel
Location: Roller rink in Pittsburg
Drugs: Ecstasy, weed

Tommy's parents were on to him. Rats. They'd pieced something together from the weekend they were out of town—our double-nighter weekend—after finding a makeshift ashtray he'd forgotten about in their backyard. He denied denied denied, but his parents said until he told them what he'd been up to he was semi-grounded, meaning no sleepovers. He could still go out, but he had to be home at midnight, every night. They also told him he wasn't returning to my school the next year. He was going to transfer to his local public high school.

This was all bad news bears. Especially since everyone was buzzing about a rave that was going to happen Labor Day weekend: Megga Buzz One.

The situation with Tommy's parents made me grateful my

parents hadn't caught on to my partying that summer. How had I gotten away with raving every weekend, and sometimes on Thursday nights too?

I later learned this was a really stressful time for my parents. My dad's new business wasn't yet lucrative, and my mom spent her days working part-time for one of the Oakland school board directors. She was also involved in the National Women's Political Caucus, an organization that helps support pro-choice female political leaders.

My mom spent most evenings at home cooking, reading cookbooks, watching cooking shows, and plucking out her hair —a bad anxiety habit. She was tense because Justin was leaving for an expensive private college and my dad's technology company might never reach fruition. But such is the life of an entrepreneur and his wife.

I got away with my shenanigans because I was coming home every Sunday night in time for dinner (though not eating much of it) and holding down my job at the nail salon while my parents tried to keep everything afloat. Plus, I had therapy every week, which gave me an angst outlet.

The only upside to Tommy being on lockdown was more hang time with Johanna. It was a Friday night, and we were headed to Open, a party in a city called Pittsburg. When we'd called the hotline and heard "roller skating rink," we'd gotten wildly excited. Plus, I had the silver Admit One Free flyer from Dreya and was feeling so very VIP.

Driving to the party in the Bubble, night lights zooming by, I told Johanna I'd tried coke. She said she'd tried it in New York, along with another drug called Special K.

"Like the cereal?" I asked.

"Yes, and no."

I didn't tell her that I did coke with a needle because I was ashamed—I still couldn't believe I'd done that, and denial was in full force. Instead, I asked her about Clayton's friend. His name was Paul.

"So what did you guys do after Thurzdaze?"

"Oh." She shuffled through her bag on her lap. "You know."

"Uh, no." I glanced at the rearview mirror, watching for flashing lights. "I don't know."

"Paul said he'll be there tonight. Clayton too, I think."

What a sneaky way to divert my attention. But it worked. Immediately, I was consumed by the possibility of seeing my new crush.

Johanna didn't divulge juicy details like some girlfriends. Maybe that was part of her allure; she was like the brooding, closed-off guy you can't fully connect with, and that just makes you want to connect more. So you keep asking questions, always giving them a chance to open up. Or give them a freeing hit of E.

Or, in the case of that night, a couple lines of Ecstasy, which Johanna proposed after we rolled into the roller rink's parking lot and applied our lip glosses.

There was hardly a line at the front door. We concluded that was because the party was way out in the 'burbs. I presented my VIP flyer, and we charmed the promoters into letting Johanna in for free too.

The venue was nothing special on the outside, but inside it was a magical space lit by a cool blue glow. There were puddles of people sitting on mattresses and bean bags spread around the smooth oval floor. The DJ booth was at the far end of the rink. Vanilla incense and mellow house beats permeated the air. Giant paper butterflies hung from the ceiling, gently swaying. A disco ball spun sparkles across the walls. The entire spread was one giant Chill Room.

Skates were off limits because you don't want to let drugged ravers loose on wheels (although that would have been thoroughly entertaining).

Getting high was always the first mission upon entering a party. Johanna led the way into the bathroom, her neon green boa flowing around her. We entered the largest stall. She dipped into her X-Large messenger bag and pulled out a square mirror and a mini plastic baggie with yellow smiley faces on it. Inside it were two gelatin capsules. I held the mirror open and flat on my palm while she carefully opened one capsule and tipped the white powder onto the mirror into a cloud-shaped mound, then took out a credit card and chopped up the powder with the edge of the card, forming two lines.

"Dude," I whispered, "those are hella big."

"They have to be with E," she said. "It's not like speed, where you only need a bump. You need fatties like coke."

Where did this prowess come from? *She must have learned it in New York.* If that's what the ravers in NYC did, I wanted to do it too.

She looked up from two perfectly formed lines of E the lengths of toothpicks. "Do you have a twenty?"

I reached for my backpack. I was still stealing money from my dad's money clip whenever possible and gave her one. She rolled it into a short tube (a tooter) to snort the E with.

She handed me the tooter, carefully took the mirror, and placed it on her palm.

"You first," she said.

I bent down, placed my index finger over my left nostril, and placed the tooter up my other nostril. With a swift sniff, I breathed one of the lines in, and YOWZA! My entire nose was ablaze with chemical firebolts shooting into my brain. I'd experienced the burn of speed bumps up my nose, but this was eyebrow-raising and eye-watering. I reflexively held my nose. The pain subsided some, but I was sure when I removed my hand, blood was going to pour out. As much as I loved the ecstasy high, I questioned if that shattering sting was worth the pain. Nothing burns as much as snorting E.

"I know," Johanna said, waiting for me to recover. "Burns like a bitch." After more sniffs and checking my nose for blood, I held the mirror for her. She snorted it and winced.

My entire release system activated. "I have to pee."

"Me too." She opened the stall door and left me to do my business.

I collected myself and left the stall to wash my hands. Icicles prickled my fingers. The silver faucet looked Salvador Dali drippy. I reached for a paper towel and noticed a paper clump on the floor that looked like a brown butterfly vibrating, ready for flight. It was like every object was greeting me.

So, snorting E burned like a bitch, but the high, which hit me much quicker than a pill, was phenomenal. A familiar energy ignited me. Johanna and I bolted out the bathroom door into our pretty playground.

Sometimes it was like as soon as I was high, I found all my raver friends. It was like I *had* to be high to see them. Would I not recognize them sober?

First, we found Luca and Angel, whom Johanna hadn't yet met. Luca looked beautiful in OshKosh B'gosh overalls and a baseball cap with a baby-blue boa lassoed around the top. We stopped to hug hellos.

"Are you feeling it?" Angel asked us, his eyes loopy.

"Oh oh yes yes" was all I could say.

"Oooooh oooh." Luca played along. "Yes yes yes."

"Yes yes yes," Johanna chimed in. "Oooooh oooooh oooooh."

"I just want to say that this party definitely does not blow bubblesss," Luca continued. "This party is sooo cool. And I have suuuch good E. And it's just the booomb."

We sat on a mattress and formed a cuddle puddle—arms and legs intertwined, conversations flowing, the bass in the music building. I met Domino, a pudgy guy with a slight pig nose who entertained us by dancing with glow sticks. He hung all over Johanna, who, even though she was having the time of her life, exuded an air of calm.

I was busy admiring Defne, a sassy girl of Turkish descent. Shimmering lime-green eyeshadow illuminated her big emerald eyes. Her kiss-me lips glistened bubblegum pink. She wore white-on-white Adidas shell toes. A teddy bear backpack.

"Want a bump, darling?" she asked me. "Or a lollipop?"

Yes to both.

She took a mini baggie out of a purple velvet coin purse and grabbed my hand. "Go like this." She made a fist, turning her wrist so her thumb was facing up. She tipped some white powder from the baggie onto the flat part between her wrist and the bulge of her thumb. She sniffed it elegantly, not covering a nostril. I mimicked her, using my left nostril since my right one was raw from the E. And voilà!

She introduced the guy sitting next to her. "This is Jarrett, known for his stacks."

Jarrett was waif petite with a Cesar haircut bleached platinum blond. Everything on him was skintight, from his ribbed, white, long-sleeve top to his silver metallic pants. He clicked the toes of his layered rainbow platform sneakers where they hung off the mattress.

"Yes!" I yelled, invigorated from the speed bump. "I've seen you before!"

Luca tugged me from the other side. "You know Ferrari, I am Italian, and I've been thinking: If you're Ferrari Ravioli, who am I?"

"Lamborghini?"

"Lamborghini who?" He flicked his cigarette.

"Fettuccine?"

Luca blew a poof and smiled seductively. "Lamborghini Fettuccine it is."

A girl floated by in a white nightgown.

"Is that an angel?" Luca asked.

"No," I said, "it's a Mexican jumping bean."

"I was at a restaurant with my grandma, and she calls hot dogs wieners. All of a sudden she busts out with, 'Luca, you know what I'm craving? A wiener! A good wiener. An all-beef wiener.' I told her I was craving one too." Luca giggled as he looked at the crowd. "What is that E-bunny wearing?" he snarked. (An E-bunny is a girl who dresses up in costume for raves.)

"Do you want a tattoo?" I asked him.

"Yes, I'm going to get a tattoo of a penis."

"I don't want one." I smacked on my cherry lolly. "You should get it on your inner thigh, anywhere in that general area."

"Genital area?"

Johanna tugged at me from another side. "Do you want another line?"

I hesitated. I was having the time of my life and didn't want to change a thing. And I didn't feel like standing up. I wanted Johanna to take care of me.

She knew. "Cover me," she said.

I shifted to face her and fanned out my elbows while she got out her kit to prep our lines. Our homies knew the drill, and everyone leaned in, pulsing toward Johanna like a jellyfish so no one could see what she was doing.

Overwhelmed by the burn, I spilled some powder on Johanna's thigh. Defne volunteered to snort it off her. When Johanna handed her the twenty tooter, Defne scoffed, "Oh, darling, I'm not sniffing with that dirty dollar," and pulled a white plastic tube out of her velvet pouch. She bent down and sniffed along Johanna's thigh.

New DIY project: make tooters by cutting the tubes of plastic pens, which is what Defne did.

"Dude." Johanna sniffed. "We are the shit."

"The shiggity shit," I agreed.

"We are a whole 'nother level of shit." She looked around the party, nodding, applying lip gloss, and then she jumped up and ran toward the crowd dancing in front of the DJ tables.

Restlessness prompted me to stand—better yet, dance. I stumbled off the mattress and noticed Luca swirling my glow wand around, creating a light show for Defne.

"Give it a good shake," I said.

"Ooooh!" Defne squealed. "Look how pretty it is!"

"I am well aware." I reached my hand out. "Give it back."

"Darling." Defne fluttered her fake eyelashes. "We just want to sit with it."

"I'm going to dance. Don't break it." With that, I left them

and sauntered through the party. After drinking a bottle of water that tasted like a milkshake, I spotted Johanna's dragon boa
in the crowd. She was talking to two guys. They looked like
skaters. My tummy fluttered. I reminded myself to be cool, which
was hard, because I was silly high.

"Hey, guys!"

"What it is?" Clayton asked, kinda smiling. I couldn't tell if
he was excited to see me, because my vision was blurred.

"This is Paul," Johanna said. "Remember him?"

"Yeah, totally." I smiled and hugged him hello.

Paul was shirtless, and his shoulders were sticky and sweaty
from dancing. He had a buzz cut and a silver ring through his lip.
He was cute in a little boy way.

"Remember me?" Clayton asked, his smile clearer.

"Yeah, totally." I hugged him. He smelled like weed.

"I think I'm going to see a little blue light wherever I go
now," I said. "You know, because of so many nights of seeing so
many. I'm going to have night vision."

"Like the Bionic Woman," Clayton said.

A slice of treble, a knock-knock pitter-patter, a clapping
beat . . . I heard it: the Sarah McLachlan "Possession" remix from
a mixtape I'd recently bought.

"Oh my god!" I bounced. "This is my new favorite song! I
was just listening to this earlier in my car and kept rewinding it
and playing it, like, a million times. It's so tight. Let's dance!"

I grabbed Clayton's hand and pulled him toward the jumbo
speakers. Orbital sounds absorbed me. My head bopped, my feet
kicked. I watched Clayton groove, his eyes half open, his smile a
trailing blur. He was totally into it.

"I can identify this method in the music," I yelled at him.

"It's called a build-up backbeat." He bobbed his head, saying, "Robotics... tripnotics... hypnotics."

I couldn't believe it—he was rapping. I danced harder, trying to contain my happiness. The music was so good, and I was so happy, and Clayton was so cute, and even though I missed Tommy, it was turning out to be a reallly gggreat nighttt.

"Entering the stratosphere," I rapped. "Where people dance and trance and move around the room with a boom!"

"What DJ is this?" he asked me.

"Essence."

Clayton and I danced together to fast beats with a hard-edged playfulness. Luca found us and gave me my glow wand back. He danced with us too. Happiness was dancing with myself, my friends, and my glow wand—that's what life was all about. That and Ecstasy with a side of speed.

Mid-shimmy, the top of my wand flew off into dance floor oblivion. "Fuck!" I yelled. Clayton dove into the crowd after it. He quickly emerged with my globe and held it up to me like a bouquet of flowers, a proud smile across his face. I screwed it back onto the wand, but it didn't fire up.

"Can I have it?" he asked me.

"What are you going to use it for? It's broken."

"I don't know. Maybe I'll make a necklace out of it and be a candy raver," he joked.

A heavy feeling crept in. It was time to go. I was tired and still having blurred vision. I didn't think I could drive, so we made a plan that Paul and Clayton would come over to Johanna's Chill

Basement and leave early in the morning to take BART home. Paul would drive.

We floated home to Johanna's and crept in the back door of her house. We threw a bunch of pillows on the carpet and had a slumber party, flirting and cuddling while watching *Who Framed Roger Rabbit*?

Clayton and I kissed a few times. He commented on how sexy my tongue piercing was. I commented on how sexy he was, period. He may have been hard to read the first time, but he was funny and sweet the second time. It could have been the E that made us more friendly. Or our rapping and dancing together. Maybe it was our kisses. Whatever it was, we clicked.

We slept for a couple of hours, and then the boys left. I gave Clayton my home and pager numbers. And my globe. He took a special part of me with him when he ducked out the back door that foggy morning after.

20

REALITY BITES

One weekend I didn't rave because of a trip to Carmel to have family portraits taken. Justin was leaving the next week for college in Oregon. The family portraits were a big, sentimental deal for my mom. She'd insisted on color-coordinated outfits.

It was a typical Northern California summer Saturday with sunny skies and drifting clouds throughout the day. The photo shoot was at the Carmel Mission, a Spanish mission dating back to 1771 with five museums and a romantic courtyard.

My brothers and I vogued, leaning against a column inside the courtyard. Flowers and a trickling fountain were our background. My lips pursed as I stood between my brothers in the sibling photo; I was pissed that the skunk stripes in my hair were an orangey shade rather than platinum blond, and I hadn't had time to fix it before the weekend.

We moved to the beach, and the fog rolled in, its mysterious beauty surrounding us. Sunny frolicked in the surf.

I'm laughing in that family photo, momentarily forgetting my anxieties, portraying a happy sixteen-year-old girl with her nice-looking family and funny-looking dog. We looked like a simple family in that picture, but we weren't—no family is.

I'd been moody all weekend, but I was my quietly depressed self rather than my mouthy depressed self. I was coping inwardly, but my struggles showed outwardly: if you looked at my fingers, you could see my nervous energy in the reddened, bleeding cuticles I'd been ripping and chewing.

I was taking a break from acrylics, which had weakened my nails. Whenever I did that, my cuticles became a sore mess within days. Fake nails helped stop me from picking because it was harder to grasp a hangnail in my skin through the fake nail. It was like every nail was wearing a mask, and when those masks came off, the real me, the raw me, revealed herself as someone who couldn't stop hurting herself. I wasn't satisfied until I ripped a good one, making myself bleed. Then I'd suck the blood, salty and metallic. Maybe I was a vampire after all—nocturnal, soulsucking, damned.

My mom, who had noticed this bad habit, often said, "No picking!" That made me feel more shameful about my uncontrollable urge.

Sober and raveless, I was worried about Justin leaving for college. I would no longer have his company, and I'd be the focal point of our parents. I know some kids crave their parents' attention, but I just wanted to be left alone.

I was dreading going back to the doldrums of high school too. Tommy's complaining had gotten to me, and I felt his frustrations about not being able to rave anymore. We'd had such an amazing summer, and I missed my partner in crime. The only way I knew to channel my feelings was through raving and taking drugs. Real life sucked and rave life rocked, and without my party fix, my fears were tormenting me like Freddy Krueger's knife fingers on a chalkboard.

I was always looking ahead, anticipating the next outfit, the next party, the next drug. I was living in the future, because I was afraid of living in the present. If I kept going, I didn't have to stop to think about everything dangerous I'd done and could avoid facing my thoughts, emotions, fears.

When we were done posing, my family hung out on the beach. The sun vanished, and we were encased in fog. I hugged myself to stay warm. My nose was running. Sea mist made my skin sticky. I stood closest to Justin, avoiding awkward exchanges with my dad. I ran away from the surf. Reed cracked a joke, and we all laughed. Freezing water stung my feet, waking me up, washing away worries.

Later, at our hotel, I took a hot shower and then slipped into my comfy JNCOs and a navy-blue Polo hoodie. I let myself relax and surrender to the love and beauty around me. Real life wasn't all that bad—at least, for a few hours.

The following week, Justin and I had one last stoned night together before he left for college. Mom and Dad were out for the evening, and I was looking forward to a bro/sis night in.

We smoked from Justin's glass bong on his balcony. I choked harder than ever, then saw an alligator in a tree. Sunny was on the balcony with us, snorting around. Justin and I got the munchies and went inside. We were in the middle of a Ben & Jerry's binge when we started wondering where Sunny was. She usually begged around the kitchen, and though we were high and time passed slower than LA traffic, she'd been gone for longer than a typical potty time.

I ran around the house, calling her name, while Justin tackled the backyard with a flashlight. Our parents would be home any minute, and while I'd mastered the art of being high discreetly, I wasn't sure I could keep my cool if we'd lost Sunny.

I found her in my room, her curly tail upright, snorting like a pig and eating something: the colorful tubes and tops of the Lip Smacker lip balms I had displayed in rainbow order on a low table next to my bed. I busted out laughing as I dropped to my knees to stop her from gnawing on the plastic, then called out to Justin.

When he ran into my room and saw what Sunny was doing, he laughed. "Dude, she has the munchies too!"

Sunny ate half of my Lip Smackers collection and survived her first stoned experience.

I missed Justin before he was gone. He had given me the 411 on weed and let me hang with him and his cute friends. He'd never ratted me out to our parents. I was a raver, and he was a Dead Head—we'd both chosen alternative lifestyles. All he had to do was talk to me, and it felt like a warm bear hug. He was a brother and a homie—he was my bromie.

The upside of him leaving, though, was that I was inheriting the Bubble.

The ravemobile was mine. All mine.

Soon after that, I had a date with Clayton in the city to get his tongue pierced. I'd been fantasizing about him going down on me with an adorned tongue. We'd been talking on the phone every day, and I asked his birthday. July 10. I'd missed it. He was a year older than me, and a Cancer, like my mom, Tommy, and Sunny.

I'd read in one of my astrology books that Cancer men like the colors blue and silver. That inspired a baby-blue X-Girl shirt and dark indigo JNCOs. I curled my hair and fastened my fringe to the side with a silver rhinestone barrette. A silver rhinestone choker bedazzled my neck.

I took BART into the city and met Clayton in the Mission. He was wearing long gray corduroy shorts, a beige Stussy hoodie, and a Raiders cap angled to the side.

After a hug and a kiss, I asked him, "Are you ready?"

"Hell yeah." He flicked his cigarette onto the ground and grabbed my hand.

It was the end of August and, though it was nearing Indian summer, the city was sunny but breezy cool. I tucked my other hand into the pocket of my red North Face fleece, and we walked toward the infamous hippie mecca that is Haight Street.

Clayton told me about a graffiti excursion he'd gone on with a friend. He mentioned "tagging" and "getting up" and "throw-ups," and I pretended to know what he was talking about. His graffiti alter ego was Agent 420. It was fitting, since he loved weed. Rebellious street art? I was impressed. Clayton was more than a skater, and he wasn't quite a raver. He was a graffiti writer.

I talked about how much I was loathing the idea of going back to school and asked him when his school started back up.

"I'm not going back," he said.

"Huh? What do you mean?"

"Uh, well, I only have senior year left. I decided to get my GED and start working. Staying in school seemed like a waste, ya know?"

I didn't know. General Education Development. GED. The

concept of getting a GED was something I'd only heard of in the periphery of my upper-middle-class bubble.

"Wait, so you're not going to graduate from high school?" I asked.

"Yeah." He shrugged.

This was a sober mind-opener for me. "And your parents are okay with that?"

He stopped on the littered street to light another cigarette. "I have to help my dad's construction company out while I study for the GED. I can always go to community college, I guess. That's all my folks can afford anyway."

We walked through alluring wafts of weed and Ben & Jerry's ice cream as we got closer to the piercing place.

"Tommy's parents won't let him get his tongue pierced until he gets straight B's this school year. Sucks he has to wait."

"But you didn't wait," Clayton said, smiling.

"Yeah, well, I guess I can hide things from my parents better than he can."

We entered the storefront of the same place where I'd gotten my tongue pierced a couple of months earlier. I knew they weren't strict about the minor thing, since I'd forged my parent's signature on the waiver. While browsing the glass cases filled with jewelry of all piercing sorts, I wondered how long I could hide my tongue from my parents. It was one of the many secrets I'd kept from them that summer. Then a sparkle caught my eye —a silver bar with a crystal-clear gem on top.

"That is so tight. Is that a diamond?" I asked the heavily tattooed dude behind the counter.

"Which one?" he huffed.

I tapped the glass above the beauty in the case.

"It's Cubic Zirconia."

I had to have it. There was no question. It was badass beautiful. A diamond, or CZ, whatever, in my tongue, would be *so* Ferrari Ravioli.

"You ready?" Clayton asked, distracting me from my shopaholic urge.

The piercing only took a couple of minutes. When he was done, the guy handed Clayton a white Dixie cup.

"Here's some mouthwash. Do a quick rinse. It will sting."

Clayton stuck his new tongue out at me, silly.

"Here are your aftercare instructions," the guy continued, handing him a folded pamphlet. "Don't drink alcohol for two weeks, and try not to smoke."

"See?" I said. "Another reason not to smoke."

I didn't like Clayton's chain-smoking. It was a turnoff—except for at raves, where I smoked too. I didn't mind danky marijuana mouth, but ashtray mouth tasted gross.

We paid, and I had the piercing guy insert my new jewelry. I stuck my tongue out in a mirror to admire my new sparkle. Clayton stuck his tongue out in the mirror alongside me.

"Let's bounce," he said, and he grabbed my hand and pulled me out the door.

21 / THE COLOR CLUB

Megga Buzz One, August 1996
Homies: Tommy, Johanna, Luca, Angel, Evan, Julie, Defne
Location: Home Base, Oakland
Drugs: Acid, E, mushrooms, coke, crystal, mescaline, weed

"Ugh, this is so embarrassing," Tommy whined from my passenger car seat. "Who else's parents go to a rave to approve it?"

I took a hit of weed from my glass pipe and exhaled. "I know, dude. Not ideal. But maybe you'll be surprised and they'll let you stay."

Tommy rolled his eyes and took another hit. The idea of running into Tommy's parents at a rave totally freaked me out. It was a Pandora's box that could lead to the end of raving for Tommy and, if his parents talked to mine, the end for me too. But I had to be strong for him and hold optimism tight.

We were sitting in the parking lot for Megga Buzz One, the most talked-about rave that summer. After a three-month raving bender, I was in full stride wearing my best outfit yet: a vintage red Adidas windbreaker, a red-and-white-striped baby tee, dark denim JNCOs, and white Adidas shell toes with red stripes. I was polished off with a classic red manicure with three mini white Adidas stripes airbrushed across my nails and French braid pigtails.

My red Jansport backpack contained my tape recorder and spare AA batteries, glow wand, Lip Smacker lip balms and glosses, Cesar, Blow Pops, Marlboro Ultra Light cigarettes, three lighters (because people always stole them), gum, a pacifier, candy bracelets for friends, tissues, pens, sunglasses, and sidewalk chalk. Just the bare necessities.

Tommy's parents were letting him go tonight under one condition: they were going too. They wanted to check out this rave business Tommy had admitted to and make sure it was safe. Does an illegal warehouse party where people, many underage, consume drugs and dance all night sound like a safe environment for a teenager?

Not ideal.

Megga Buzz One was taking place at an entirely new venue in Oakland—our home turf—called Home Base. The three-fold flyer had listed six Buzz Zones where only Bay Area DJs—Tony, Simon, Frank Nitty, Essence, and Carlos—were all lined up. A play zone, a rave mart, a lost-and-found Chill Room, rides, a tribal dance circle, exotic dancers, and fire eaters were also listed.

Of course, our first massive rave required massive amounts of drugs. Tommy hadn't been to a rave for a month. He was jonesing for it. We wanted to candy flip like we had at Freedom.

We were extra antsy because the school year was about to start and we knew raving wasn't going to be as easy, what with early Monday mornings and homework. And there was a chance Tommy wasn't going to be allowed to party ever again after his parents witnessed rave debauchery that night.

Clayton wasn't coming; he'd told me he couldn't afford to go. I'd offered to buy his ticket, but he'd said he didn't have drug money either. I was bummed but got over it quickly when I realized that meant I could spend more time with Tommy at the party.

Home Base was a 187,000-square-foot retail storage space about five minutes from the Oakland airport. The name Home Base for the rectangular orange building was fitting, because from Megga Buzz One on, the space would house numerous raves where the bass rocked the party all night. Eventually, Home Base was deemed the International Rave Center. In an industrial part of Oakland, and large enough to hold thousands of people, it was the ultimate rave warehouse. Mysteriously, it burned down in a fire in 2005.

"Here, dude," Tommy said, passing the pipe to me. "Can we go over the plan one more time?"

"Yes." I repacked the pipe with the corner of the lighter. "We're going to take our drugs around eleven. Your parents are going to page you with 143 if you can stay and 911 if you have to bounce. At midnight, right?"

"Uh-huh," replied Cinderella.

"What if you run into them?" I asked, thinking he should be prepared in case he had to face his parents high.

"Then I'll just say hi and act normal."

"Right," I nodded, knowing that would be impossible if we were candy flipping. I handed him a piece of gum and straightened the fuzzy dice hanging from my rearview mirror. "You ready for this?"

He put on a happy face. "So ready!"

☺

After waiting in line for forty-five minutes—the longest we'd ever waited to get into a party—we entered Home Base around 10:00 p.m. on a mission to find E, ideally from our latest dealer, Richie Rich, who always wore a bright yellow shirt. Our pants swooshed as we speed-walked down a chilly, dark hallway that led to a pulsating room. Red and green lasers fanned across the crowd, and pinwheel graphics were projected on the walls. White surgical masks glowed, bucket hats bounced, and green glow sticks waved. The uplifting sound of house music comforted me.

"Let's look around," Tommy said, leading me through another hallway. "If you see my parents—run!"

He was joking, but not really.

We moseyed into the Chill Room. It was the prettiest one I'd seen yet. White Christmas lights looped around the room, creating a heavenly aura. Puddles of people sat on sofas and bean bags. In one corner, a few people lay on tables, getting massages. The music was more spa zen than rave massive.

I followed Tommy over to the fruit and water table. There was a banner draped on one wall with "NEXUS" drawn graffiti-style in bubble letters. Nexus was the host of the Chill Room. They were the producers who'd thrown Open in the roller rink.

"What time is it?" Tommy asked, popping a grape into his mouth. "Can we take our acid yet?"

I checked my pager. "Almost eleven. Time to get started!"

"Oh goodie." Tommy smiled. "Wait—are my parents in here?"

We scanned the room and saw kids talking and relaxing, no

middle-aged folks in khakis staring us down. We plopped onto a sofa, and feathers bounced into the air from under us. I discreetly opened my makeup pouch inside my backpack and dug out a clear plastic baggie with two squares of acid in it. We gobbled them up like French fries.

"It's too bright in here," Tommy said. "My parents can see me too easily. Let's walk."

We cruised a hallway that opened to another laser-illuminated room with a door propped open to an outside area where people were walking around what looked like an empty parking lot. A line of porta-potties was to the left. A tall fence separated the party from the city. A stretch of dark nothingness reached to the freeway. The Oakland Coliseum glowed in the distance. I spotted a husky guy in a yellow jersey and grabbed Tommy's arm. "There's Richie Rich!"

We ran over to him.

"It's always easy to spot you in your yellow jersey," I told him after we bought four hits of E.

"That's the idea." He winked.

We left him and posted along the fence. I pressed record on my dictaphone and in my news announcer voice said, "What up? This is Sammy D reporting live from the much-anticipated Megga Buzz One. It's Saturday, August 31, I think, and we're at a new spot in our hometown of Oaktown. It's pretty fresh, and this outside area is quite nice. We have our drugs and we're ready to rave."

Tommy leaned in. "Yo yo!"

I hushed him to say, "There is a special event happening this evening. Tommy's parents are also here. Tonight promises to be action-packed—stay tuned!"

I clicked off recording mode. Golden streetlights gleamed above us, vivid, bright pulses in sync with the thudding music coming from inside the building. Looking around, inhaling my cigarette, anxiety escaped my body with every exhale. A deep breath in and I was far away from the real world, safe inside my raver world.

"Let's dance!"

We went back inside. My body swayed with the booms, shoulders doing their sassy thing. Tommy was doing his cute kick-and-dip move, pumping his fists to the beat, smiling. My superstar self emerged. Energized, I reached into my backpack for my new glow wand. I flipped the switch on and danced with my magic wand, punching the beats with light.

I felt a warm hand on my shoulder.

"Oh my god, Ferrari," Luca said, laughing. "Guess who we just saw. Remember the angel from Open? Tonight she's in a witch costume."

Luca was with Angel, Defne, and a familiar petite brunette girl.

"Hello, darling, you know what? I'm starting to feel my drugs and I'm pretty happy about it, you know?" Defne said, smacking her gum.

Colors brighter. Music louder. Acid activated. "Oh, I know," I replied.

The petite brunette girl was dancing, and I recognized her sharp dance moves from previous raves. We started talking. Her name was Cece, and she had as much personality off the dance floor as she did on. She was eighteen and had been raving for a couple of years. In addition to being a dope dancer, she was a master sound effector. She was a beatbox that turned the snapping sound of opening a Snapple top into song. She was snapping a little ditty when I asked her, "Wow! Does that hurt?"

Tommy stopped dancing and held his left arm out like he was stopping traffic while his right hand held his pager up, close to his face. He held the rectangular device up to the flashing lights to examine it. Then he started jumping up and down, yelling, "143! 143! 143!"

Relief and disbelief washed over me. Tommy showed me his pager, and even though the numbers were blurred, it was 143! We jumped up and down together to the beat of the music, and our friends jumped up and down with us even though they didn't know why. Tommy hugged me and then cried, "Let's take our E!"

I cried back, "Let's take two!" We were celebrating, after all.

"And do the sidewalk chalk!"

Tommy and I downed our E and went back outside. We decided on a soft-lit corner of cement canvas for our art project. I got on my knees and wrote "Ferrari" in pink block letters with arrows pointing to it. Tommy wrote "Adidas" in blue with a smiley face dotting the "i."

"I am going to take this heart and turn it into something so complex the world will not believe," I said as I drew a heart balloon.

Some people stopped to watch us and asked if they could draw too. A skinny, stoop-shouldered kid drew a green cactus. A girl visiting from San Diego drew a two-toned daisy. Cece came over, and we eagerly watched to see what she'd make with the purple chalk. A cluster of purple grapes. Brilliant. We decided we were the Chalk Club, and then everyone dispersed.

Now that Tommy's parents were a non-issue, knowing our E was about to kick in, we set off to find our friends. We walked the perimeter of the gated outside and soon heard a loud, "Hey, guys!" from a familiar, flaming voice.

It was Evan with the Pacifica crew. For a second, I missed Clayton.

They were in a cluster, sitting on the ground. Evan greeted us in goofy, oversize clown sunglasses. We hugged hellos. Johanna was with them, wearing her neon green boa. Her eyes were rolling back in her head, full-on E-ing. Julie was telling a story in her fast-talking fashion. Mike and Mike With The Dreads were there, and so was a girl with star stickers on her face.

"I'm sooo fucked up," Evan said.

"SO AM I," Tommy replied, surprisingly friendly toward Evan.

"We have shrooms," Julie said. "Do you guys want a nibble?"

We nibbled. The cardboard texture made me gag. "Bleh!" I said. "Hook me up with some water." After washing the dirt taste away, I fetched a Blow Pop from my bag.

"Dude, what is that?" Julie pointed yonder. "Is that a giant panda bear? It's, like, bouncing."

"Oh my god, it's having sex with all of us. He's fucking all of us!" I exclaimed. It was a giant panda bouncy house, and that was the E talking.

"Ferrari! You dirty birdy!"

Tommy and I were walking and talking, talking and walking, taking it all in. Our acid was activated, our ecstasy was in effectasy, and energy was spreading through me like wildfire. My arm was linked with Tommy's, and I felt him on the same wavelength as me.

Then, suddenly, throbbing, pulsing, burning—my bladder was one giggle away from exploding.

"I figured out what I want to do," I said. "I have to pee. Hella bad."

We visited the porta-potties, and then it was back to Tommy and me strolling around the outside of the party, talking about how we could always find our dealer because of his signature yellow shirts. We nicknamed him Mr. Yellow. That made me think of the Quentin Tarantino film *Reservoir Dogs*, where the characters adopted color pseudonyms to hide their real identities. If I were in that movie, I would have been Ms. Red—fiery, bold, passionate. Tommy would have been Mr. Blue—friendly, universal, calming.

It dawned on us, what if we had a club where our friends were a color that represented their personality *and* protected their identity? The name of our new club was obvious: the Color Club. Mr. Blue suggested there could be a Mr. and a Ms. for every color. I elected myself president since I was the organized one. Mr. Blue was vice president. The first rule was that we both had to approve any new members and agree on their color.

"Look! It's Dreya!" Mr. Blue yelled. We went over to her and told her about the Color Club.

"What's your favorite color?" I asked her.

"Brown," she said assuredly, hands on hips. "No, wait—Foxy Brown!"

"Hell yeah!" Mr. Blue said.

Moments later, we found everyone, plopped down, and announced our new club. They all jumped in.

"I'm Ms. Blue!" (Cece)

"Can I be Neon Green?" (Evan)

"Orange! I want to be Ms. Orange." (Julie)

"I am Mr. Green, of course." (Luca)

"Darling, I'm Ms. Gold." (Defne)

"I want to be Ms. Hot Pink!" (Johanna)

Mr. Blue came over and sat with me. "Ms. Red, I have a report: we have lost all our sidewalk chalk. Wow, I have never been so high in my life. But I'm so happy, because this may very well be my last party for a while, you understand."

I was sad for a second, but then it was back to having the time of our lives.

For the next four hours, Mr. Blue and I bopped around the party, visiting with friends. We hardly danced. Instead, we did speed bumps with Ms. Gold, lines of coke with Mr. Green, and more shrooms with Ms. Orange. We smoked bowls with anyone who offered, and with anyone we offered to. We were incapable of saying no. When did candy flipping turn into straight-up polydrug abuse? Sometime around 3:00 a.m., when we took our third hit of E . . . around the same time a friend of Ms. Gold's offered us mescaline.

Mescaline. Ms. Gold said it was a hallucinogen like acid. Mr. Blue and I thought about it for about a minute before opting yes —we didn't turn down free drugs.

Shortly after that, I was sitting cross-legged with Mr. Blue and I forget who else when I felt an inescapable itch inside my throat. I was convinced my E was blocking my airway. Mr. Blue assured me it wasn't and told me to drink more water. I did that, and smoked a cigarette, and was fixed. Then excessive burping began. That must have been the mushrooms messing with my digestion. Then a bitter taste in my throat kept making its way up into my mouth, making me cringe. I felt nauseated. I vomited. And then I felt much better, as you do. Another lollipop masked my vomit breath. And then—POP! My jaw loosened right under my left ear. I took out my lollipop to move my jaw around. It sounded like someone was knocking on a door inside my head. It was lockjaw, a physical annoyance I would permanently have courtesy of mastication from methamphetamine.

After searching the black hole that had become the inside of my backpack, I found my emergency pacifier. Struggling to maintain bodily function, I alternated between my lolly and paci. I was so high I couldn't speak. The narcotic mix bubbling inside me was no doubt dangerous. My mind was blowing.

Suspended in a *Twilight Zone* episode both thrilling and frightening, I focused on the characters around me. My fascinating cartoon friends talking and laughing and hugging each other comforted me. Everyone was deep in conversation, with themselves. I couldn't focus on one speeding train of thought, so I had no choice but to give in to Dr. Timothy Leary's way: I turned on, tuned in, and dropped out.

I heard Ms. Orange's voice say, "Oh my god, you guys are purple!"

My upside-down vision refocused in her direction.

"Red and blue make purple, so you guys are purple together. You have Purple Power!"

I smiled through my pacifier.

"We are, totally!" Mr. Blue agreed. "We have Purple Power!"

I clenched the soft mouthpiece between my teeth. At extreme moments of highness, the baby tool indeed relieved my jaw and teeth from constant grinding. To whatever raver who came up with that idea—bless.

"Do you realize what this means?" Mr. Blue asked me. "This means that no one can be purple because we are purple."

In that moment, that rule was the most important rule in the universe.

Overwhelmed by blissful insanity, I sat back, drifting away. . . .

What is this jagged thing on my pacifier? A foreign something is floating around inside my mouth. Gum? Too small. Fuzz? Too solid. Dirt? Maybe. I can't lift my hand to my mouth and take out my delectable toy. Dude, what is stuck to my pacifier? Did I just say that out loud?

No one responded. No one noticed.

Mr. Blue isn't looking at me, so maybe he didn't hear me. Dude, what is stuck to my pacifier?

Again, no response. I inspected the pink object in front of me, the jelly mold a blur. I stuck my tongue out and licked it to see if the particle in question was still there. I searched for an answer while rounding the nipple with my tongue.

"Whoa, Ms. Red! What are you doing?" Mr. Blue and Angel's laughs merged, forming trailing rows of musical notes.

"Dude!" I squealed. "What is stuck to my pacifier?!"

"So that's why you're making out with your pacifier." Mr. Blue giggled.

"I can't see straight, and I've been trying to figure out what the hell it could be."

"What does it feel like?"

"It's small and sharp."

An arm came toward me. "Hand it over."

"Wait!" Ms. Gold snapped. "Was it, like, a little pyramid shape?"

"Yes!"

"It's your mescaline, darling!"

Mr. Green reached over and plugged me back up.

Bowls of weed and bottles of water later, I sobered some. Our posse sat huddled in the outside area of the party for hours. The thudding bass that had been the background music to my highest night eventually stopped. Megga Buzz One ended around 7:00 a.m. But our mega buzz was still in full force.

The sky was cobalt blue, and sunlight was minutes away. The veil of night lifted, and I wasn't afraid of what the aftermath looked like. We were full of drugs and weren't even close to calling it a night. While Mr. Blue and I usually left the party before it got light out, that night we were prepared for extended play. We were equipped with our red-and-blue-lensed sunglasses, which suited our newly appointed Color Club selves.

When someone started calling, "Party's over, dudes!" my friends and I begrudgingly unglued ourselves from each other and left Home Base.

But we didn't go far. Cue a dance party in the parking lot across the street. Mr. Green undulated with my glow wand, a miniature Etch-A-Sketch and water gun dangling from his belt loops. Ms. Blue danced alongside him in silver-rimmed sunglasses. Rainbow glitter made her face sparkle, and a half-eaten candy necklace bounced with her jerks. Ms. Gold, Ms. Hot Pink, and Angel, who so far remained colorless, circled them. Everyone grooved to the breakfast beats.

Mr. Green had popped the trunk of his car, and Mr. Blue and I jumped inside, sitting with our legs dangling, watching our friends dance.

Reality bit when Mr. Blue remembered he had to be home to do a weekend chore. Every Sunday morning, he had to clean the kitchen. I had forgotten this and wasn't going to let my buddy do it alone—so it was time to go.

I took the stuffed bulldog off my head, and Ms. Gold sent us off with two fat lines of crystal to make sure we were sufficiently energized to clean. An eye-watering burn up the nostrils, and zip-a-dee-doo-dah!

On the drive home, Tommy and I prepared ourselves to act normal and scrub as fast as possible so we could take showers, change outfits, and get to Strawberry Sundays, the after-party everyone else was going to, which sounded sweet. After slowly rolling through upscale Piedmont in the quiet of Sunday morning, I pulled over a block from Mr. Blue's house so we could freshen up with eye drops.

I flipped my visor to look in the mirror and immediately wished I hadn't. My complexion was splotchy, my lips rouged from lollipop stains and sore from my biting them all night. My eyes were bugged-out glassy. My cheeks were sore from smiling. My jaw ached and was still popping on the left side when I moved it around. My nose was raw and stuffed up as if I had a cold. My heartbeat, meanwhile, was pumping triple-time through my chest like the tempo of techno.

The Bubble was loud, so I parked a few houses down from Mr. Blue's to avoid waking his parents. We crept in through the back door, the entry door farthest from his parents' bedroom. I expected the worst, that his parents were awake, waiting, wanting to talk. But the house was quiet.

Tiptoeing into the kitchen, Mr. Blue whispered, "Dude, I think my parents are still asleep."

"Then let's get to work and get out of here!"

"I think I can clean everything hella quick if you want to jump in the shower."

"Are you sure?"

"Yeah, I got this. Scram!"

As I was turning on my heels to head toward the bathroom, a woman's voice boomed, "Hi, Tommy."

His bed-headed mom was standing in the doorway of the kitchen in her burgundy velour robe.

Mr. Blue's smile dropped from his face and fell down the kitchen sink drain. "Oh, hi, Mom," he said through a nervous smile.

His mom looked at me with a forced smile. I forced one back.

"So, how was the party?"

"It was fun," Mr. Blue sputtered.

"Yes." She nodded. "I could see how it was fun."

I smiled and nodded. Did that mean she *saw us* having fun? Our special, drugged-up, crazy kind of fun? I really wanted to know what she'd seen but didn't want to ask. I stood wearily next to Mr. Blue, unsure if he needed me. He started spraying something on the countertops, a smooth move since that would be the normal thing to do.

"Is it cool if we go out to breakfast after the kitchen's done?" Mr. Blue dared to ask.

His mom glared at the two of us. She had to notice how tired we looked. And we were all eyeballs. She must have known we were wired too.

"Is it all right if I take a shower?" I asked, attempting an escape.

"Sure," she said coolly.

I crept out of the kitchen, slowing to pass her in the doorway. She watched me as I approached, and I kept smiling, hoping she didn't notice my dilated pupils or hear my heartbeat or smell cigarettes on me.

As I walked down the hallway toward Mr. Blue's room, I heard his mom bellow, "You can go to breakfast. But this is it, Tommy. Once school starts, things are going to change."

We were in and out of the house in an hour. We switched to Mr. Blue's car for this escapade and decided to have a bowl of weed for breakfast. We pulled into one of our smoky spots and dragged from his glass pipe while recounting the action-packed night/morning.

After a few minutes, weed's calming effect blanketed me, and I was ready for more.

We drove to a payphone in Montclair to page Luca. After a few beeps, I typed in the number of the payphone, our pager codes (111 and 629), and then 311 and 911. The 311 meant "party information"; the 911 meant "pronto." Pagers only allowed numbers, so we wrote in numerical codes to communicate messages.

We chugged Gatorade and vegged in Tommy's car near the payphone, listening to TLC, while we waited for Luca to call us back. My head rested against the car seat. It felt good to sit and give my body a break.

"I'm just going to rest my eyes," I said.

"You better not fall asleep on me, Ms. Red."

"No way, man," I said with my eyes closed. "Impossible."

Megga Buzz One's characters flashed before me. Also, rainbow-colored squiggles. A eucalyptus-infused breeze drifted through our open windows. My nose was still raw, and it was a relief to know I hadn't burned away my sense of smell.

The payphone's ring made us both jump, waking us from our daze. I answered, and Luca gave me the 411.

Go time.

The after-party was at Bahia Cabana, a Brazilian restaurant turned after-hours spot on Market Street in the city.

It was about noon by the time we parked. The place smelled of sugary cocktails and last night's sweat. Spastic music played. Shiny black decor glistened. Flyers were stuck to the floor. A few people were sloppily dancing, and familiar faces were nowhere to be found. Mr. Blue and I were standing in the underbelly of the after-party scene, feeling too cute and clean to be there.

We snarled at each other, then walked around.

We entered a smaller room with a row of rectangular booths lined along a wall of windows. A bar was at the far end. Again, there weren't many people, except for, behold—our beautiful, youthful, vivacious friends sitting with dwindling water and beer glasses in a booth.

They perked up as we approached.

"What took you guys so long?!" Mr. Green greeted us. "This party blows bubblesss."

"Whatever, dudes," Mr. Blue said. "You took forever to call us back."

The girls, Ms. Hot Pink, Ms. Gold, and Ms. Blue, had all freshened up, while Mr. Green and Angel were in the same garb from the night before, which they couldn't have been happy about.

"Hey," Mr. Green said, "do you guys have weed? I'll trade you speed for weed."

"Speed for weed! Weed for speed!" everyone cheered.

"Totally, tortellini," I said.

Mr. Green was already scooting out of the booth. "Cool. Let's blow this popsicle stand."

The new plan was to ride out the rest of the day at Sunset, a day party at Point Molate in Richmond. Mr. Blue and I had heard of this after-after-party. To get there, we'd have to turn back onto the Bay Bridge and head north.

But first, we all smoked a bowl and snorted some crystal in an alley.

After an eternal hot box in a parking lot, we flung the car doors open, and oxygen splashed me upside the head. My eyes fixed on the rainbow sherbet–colored sky holding the sun low over a shimmering body of water. Awed by the beauty of my golden state, I stumbled on the pebbly ground like I was tipsy. My Jell-O legs struggled to walk, and my crazy mind struggled to keep things straight.

We descended on a stretch of grass with picnic tables sprinkled around. People were gathering around the turntable island on the beach park. Uplifting house beats stirred the crowd. Dreadlocks, candy bracelets, spent smiles, we joined our funky bunch.

Some people sat on blankets while others stood around talking and dancing. Many faces looked familiar.

My eyes fixated on the sherbet sky and shimmering water again. Mr. Blue and I held hands as we walked through the crowd toward the water's edge. The Richmond Bridge was in the distance, a sleek steel spiderweb floating above the water.

I'd been externalized the entire weekend, obsessing about what was going to happen, who was saying what, what drug to do next. I hadn't once silenced my inner voice (which was multiple voices by then) to enjoy the present moment.

A part of me was afraid to. I hadn't slept in over twenty-four hours, and I'd put my body through the ringer. On previous post-party Sundays, I'd always snuck in a nap or afternoon relaxation, but Mr. Blue and I were chasing this weekend, running from the past, fearing the future. I'd stretched my mind like a rubber band. If I stopped to enjoy the present moment, would I snap?

"Wow. That's all I have to say right now," Mr. Blue said, in awe.

"We've had a pretty bizarre weekend," I said.

"Where did today go? What did we do today?"

"Today we did drugs. Lots of drugs."

"What did we do is what we did," I eloquently replied. "You know, I'm not that into nature, but this is beautiful."

"This is really nice."

"Out there extraordinaire."

Mr. Blue and I had walked to the end of the bluff, where our friends were also watching the sunset. Tunes in the background, splendor in the distance, a dank musk floated by. I inhaled it.

My pocket vibrated. It was a page from my home phone number with a 911 after it. I had been lax about keeping in touch with my parents all weekend and was usually home in time for dinner, which was right about then. Mr. Blue and I left the peaceful scene to find a payphone, but there wasn't one around. It was getting dark. My time was up.

But not without saying goodbye to our friends first. We ran back to the gathering and found them dancing. Nearly everyone was standing up, getting down. We quickly hugged, and then Mr. Blue and I were in the car, racing back to the O.

When I think about Megga Buzz One and that weekend, I can't believe we came out of it with our brains intact. There was the scary part when my body malfunctioned and I couldn't talk. The roller coaster ride was going so fast I thought it was going to fly off the rails. Water, gum, music, my pacifier, another bowl, and my raver tools helped me hang on, but it was my friends that gave me the comfort I needed to keep it together. My "set and setting" was safe.

Megga Buzz One was my eighteenth rave. I'd done the most drugs I'd ever done in one night there, and while I'd survived, I knew I wouldn't do that again.

22 / DANCING QUEEN

The lyrics were muffled, but I recognized the Swedish disco pounding through the walls while I lazed in bed. My dad was subjecting me to something that seemed worse than the Chinese water torture for a detoxing drug addict who wasn't a morning person.

This was the second Saturday in a row my dad had blasted oldies through the house starting at 9:00 a.m. My ideal rise time was noon. It was the Beatles last weekend, this weekend ABBA. Even though I liked the music, the wake-up call was annoying.

School had started, and I was grounded for a couple of weeks because of not calling home the Sunday after Megga Buzz One.

I powered through the first day of school, catching up with Naomi and my high school crew. It was refreshing seeing them, though I felt Naomi and I were on different wavelengths; she'd gone to keggers and BBQs all summer, and I'd gone to raves. I'd tried to get her to go with me to one, but she'd had no interest. She was satisfied with a normal high school lifestyle. She was one of my best friends and I respected her preferences, though I thought she didn't know what she was missing.

I was in my new uniform of JNCO jeans, a baby tee, an oversized sweatshirt, and Adidas. Johanna was sporting the look too. Our overly baggy pants didn't go unnoticed. Guys teased me, saying, "Could your pants *be* any baggier?" and girls complimented me, saying, "Cool pants." I rolled my eyes at the guys—they didn't know fashion.

By the end of the week, we were the token raver girls of the school, of which I was very proud. I felt exotic, like the European supermodels I'd always adored. I'd never felt so cool.

I was also very proud of my new tech accessory: a cellular phone. My parents had given me one "for emergencies," which meant I had no more excuses not to call them when they blew up my pager. It was their latest effort to keep tabs on me. But it also meant no more payphones. I could call and page friends on the go.

For the two weekends I was grounded—no overnights and a midnight curfew—I thought it would be a good time to catch up on the hours of sleep I'd lost over the summer. But now, with my dad blasting ABBA . . . not so much. After tossing and turning, crushing my pillows over my ears, trying not to follow the lively music, I finally rose out of bed, *Exorcist*-style.

ABBA was singing about Fernando as I walked down the stairs with heavy steps and entered the living room, where my dad was lying on a sofa, reading a book, and tapping his feet to the music.

"Morning, babe," he said.

I grunted. "Not cool, Dad."

He peered over his book, looking at me blankly through his glasses.

"Isn't this music a little loud a little early?" I said, turning toward the kitchen, stomach growling.

My mom turned away from the sink to look at me when I entered. "Hi, honey," she said, chipper.

"Is Dad going to be blasting music every Saturday morning?" I asked, opening the fridge.

"Well, your dad likes his music. Want me to make you some breakfast?"

I kept staring at the fridge's contents, holding the door open, wasting energy. "Yeah, maybe."

"Want an egg? I was just going to make myself one."

"Yeah, thanks."

I walked over to the eating nook. Sunny was on her side, sleeping on the wooden floor, quietly snoring. I envied how she could sleep through the booming disco. Sitting at the table in my pj's, waiting for my breakfast, I reached my legs out to pet her with my feet. The crackling sound and buttery smell of eggs reminded me I was home, safe.

Aside from my morning 'tude, our home was peaceful, and I was a normal, sober girl. But normal was boring, right?

Tommy and I had big plans for later that day. We'd found a business card printing place to make official Color Club membership cards. We were both grounded and figured we'd make good use of our partying time off getting our creative enterprise in order. After telling Naomi and a couple girlfriends from school about the club, they wanted in. I wasn't supposed to induct new members without Tommy's okay, but they insisted, and he was MIA, so I did what any president would do and made an executive decision.

A Color Club recap:

1) Ms. Red (President)
2) Mr. Blue (Vice President)
3) Ms. Hot Pink (Secretary)
4) Mr. Neon Green
5) Ms. Orange
6) Ms. Gold
7) Mr. Green
8) Mr. Clear
9) Ms. Blue
10) Mr. Gold
11) Ms. Irie Green
12) Ms. Sapphire
13) Ms. Puke Green

After breakfast, I went upstairs and set my hair in hot rollers. As the curls set, I put on Madonna, tidied my room, and organized my Bad Box, a metal lockbox where I kept all my drug paraphernalia, along with a handwritten master list of every rave I'd attended. And my precious party tapes, each labeled with the name and date of the party. I also hid upcoming rave flyers in there. I kept the key in a bathroom drawer and stashed the Bad Box under my bed. I eventually moved it into my closet, and then my trunk. As long as I kept rotating hiding spots, I thought I was safe from my parents finding it.

I took out the rollers, and dark brown curls and bleached-blond highlights bounced free. I pulled my hair up into a pony-tail and twisted it into a messy bun, secured it with a hair band and bobby pins, and voilà: rave princess. I'd taken to wearing my hair back when raving and drugging because when you're high, your hair can turn into a tangled Medusa mess.

After my beauty session, I went downstairs for a refreshing beverage. ABBA had left the building, CNN was on the TV, and my mom wasn't around. I'd been hoping she would be so she would notice my prom 'do and compliment me.

I opened the refrigerator door. There wasn't anything to drink besides milk. The phone rang, and rang, and rang, and I answered it.

"Hello?"

"Connie?"

"Um, no, this is Samantha."

"Hi, honey. Is your mom around? This is Sharon."

"Hold, please," I said, pressing the Hold button, and then I shouted, "Mom, phone!"

All I could hear was TV commercial chatter. I stepped onto the patio overlooking the backyard and yelled, "Mom, are you out here?"

No answer. Nothing from my dad either.

I went to the entry area at the bottom of the stairs and, from the epicenter of our house, yelled, "Moooooom, phooooone!" Then I ran up the stairs.

My parents' bedroom door was closed. I turned the door handle and barged into their bedroom, which was brightly lit by west-facing windows that showcased a grand view of the glistening bay.

"Mom, pho—!" I choked.

The room was quiet, but what I saw was loud: my dad's hairy butt and the backs of my mom's pale calves flailing in the air, her legs spread open. I tossed the phone onto the carpet as if it were crawling with spiders. Their nude bodies were frozen in a porno position, their faces looking at me, surprised.

"Oh dear!" my mom gasped.

My dad shifted on the bed, and I, knowing a full frontal was a second away, yelled, "Oh my god oh my god!" and ran out of the room, slamming the door behind me.

Cunnilingus. I knew the word from my favorite musical, *HAIR*. I'd heard it in a lyric when I was maybe ten years old and thought it had something to do with being cunning. When I looked it up in the dictionary and learned what it was, I blushed.

And now, at sixteen, seeing my parents engaged in that act on a Sunday afternoon? It was a vision forever embedded in my mind. I kept trying to blink it out, but it was too vivid.

Tommy and I weren't supposed to meet up for a while, but I had to escape. I needed some space to digest what I'd seen. I quickly changed out of my pajamas, left a note for my parents on the island in the kitchen—"Spending the afternoon with Tommy, be back for dinner"—and fled.

23 / SPACE CHILDREN

Space Children Anniversary, September 1996
Homies: Johanna, Clayton, Luca, Angel, Defne
Location: The Deli, San Francisco
Drugs: Liquid acid, nitrous, weed

Back at it again, Johanna and I were taking a break from the main dance room at the Deli, the spot where I'd first made out with Jack. It was called the Deli because it was an operating deli during the day.

"Johanna, darling," I said, leaning against a wall and smoking a cigarette. "Darling," I repeated, unable to form new words because my eyes were bending into spirographs. The hallway was musky and smoky. Movement was fast-flow, then slow-mo.

"Yeah, Red?" she said, ashing on the floor.

"I have something for you!" I remembered. I shuffled through my backpack for my makeup bag and unzipped it. It took me a few minutes to find what I was looking for because I was swimming in liquid acid, and it was hard to stay focused.

I'd been consistently forgetting what I was doing ever since my acid had kicked in. Unless you're the one preparing it, you don't know how strong a hit of acid is, but one thing's for sure: when it's dropped right into the source, it's a guaranteed feast for the eyes. It was like extreme absent-mindedness from smoking weed or sleep deprivation, only the fantastic kaleidoscopic designs I was seeing everywhere were what were distracting me. Every time I blinked, a geometric layer appeared over Johanna's face, the back of my hand, the wall, the dirty carpet. It wasn't a bad distraction, but I couldn't keep a conversation going.

I felt the thin edge of paper. "Found it!" I drew my hand out of my bag and handed Johanna a white business card.

She lifted it up close to her face to study it.

"It's your membership card," I said.

The front of the Color Club membership cards were printed with "The Color Club" in purple block lettering—Purple Power, remember?—under which was parked a stretch limousine. On the bottom half of the cards were my and Mr. Blue's titles and contact information. I'd written "Ms. Hot Pink" in hot pink ink and "Secretary" underneath on the back of Johanna's card.

"Wicked," Johanna said. "Is Clayton in the club yet? I'm so happy you guys are together because he's, like, a tagger, and your hair looks hella tight."

He wasn't in the club yet, and he wasn't happy about there already being a Mr. Red. Julie's boyfriend, Mike, had taken the title before Clayton had the chance to, because he was wearing a red Enyce T-shirt at a party. So Clayton, ever the moody artist, was still deciding on his color.

Johanna and I walked through the square-shaped venue to find our boyfriends. The Deli was intimate, and everyone seemed to be on the same drug—in this case, liquid acid. When you have a communal high scenario, minds run far, far away together. It was a relief when that happened because you could admit to being "so fucked up" and people could relate, and you didn't feel self-conscious.

I was coherent enough to remember Chris, the guy from Concord, whose face I recognized through the kaleidoscope because he resembled the skater dude from *Clueless*.

"Holy shit," he said, stopping me in the hallway, "I met you at Intoxication so long ago."

It had only been two months, but it felt like two years.

"You were walking around with a recorder at that really bad party where I overdosed on GHB. You're what? Seventeen and live in Oakland?"

"I was hella high at Intoxication," I said.

Clayton emerged through the spiraling hallway, his baseball cap facing backward, a cigarette pressed firmly between his thumb and forefinger. He walked up to me and kissed me with ashtray breath.

"Hey!" I said, taken aback.

"Small world." Chris avoided eye contact with Clayton, who was being antisocial, leaning against the wall. "Do you have a pen?"

"It very much is so," I said, reaching into my backpack for a pen. "I'm sixteen, not seventeen."

"Call me before this party next weekend and I'll put you on the guest list," he said, handing me a flyer with his phone number scribbled on it.

Clayton was hovering, so I said, "Later skater," to Chris and grabbed Clayton's hand to walk around.

Around 5:00 a.m., I was exactly where I wanted to be: sitting with my boyfriend on a sofa watching the dance area in front of us. Julie was sitting on the other side of me, hypnotized.

"Here's the scenario," Clayton said, our sweaty palms melting together, our fingers each other's. "You're on acid, and you're just chillin'. You're sitting on a couch that's really really comfortable, and you're, like, sunken in, and it's hard to feel your body."

"And you're in a kaleidoscope," I added.

"And you close your eyes, and you start to pretend that you have no body."

"But you're in a kaleidoscope."

"Okay, you can be in a kaleidoscope. But you're pretending you have no body, and then you start thinking in your mind, *If I can't feel my body, if my body wasn't here, would I still be here? Would my mind still be here?*" He paused, and I looked at him. Flickering lights, like a snowy TV screen, dotted his face. "And then you'd have to say to yourself, 'I don't know, because the only reason I know my body is here is because my mind is here. Because if I didn't have eyes, I wouldn't be able to see my body. And it's all going on in the head. It's all going on in here.'" He pointed to his head.

"You're alone in your head," I said, completely understanding him.

"Isn't this so solitary, what you're feeling?" he said. "A kaleidoscope, yeah, that gives me a picture. What's it like? I can't tell somebody what it's like when everything is going on over there and under there and around everywhere. Is it real or is it just me? Try it, and you tell me."

I closed my eyes and kept them shut, something I'd never

thought to do on acid. I decided to keep them closed and see what happened.

I'm floating in a canoe on a vast body of water. In the dark. Alone. Shadowy blues flood around me as I peacefully row myself through glittering waters. I stop, look up. I'm floating within a giant globe. A snow globe. An iridescent ceiling curves infinitely around me.

To my right, the water is rising, angling itself, forming a flat but slanted wave that looks like a piece of glass. It grows taller and taller, sharper and sharper, closer and closer to my canoe. It's next to me. Crystalline magnificence. It's friendly, and I'm not afraid of it tipping me over. It slowly angles down, swallowing itself, sliding under me as I pass over it. The force rocks me gently. Soothing, surreal. Smaller linear waves follow in its wake.

A small ring in the center of my globe's ceiling opens, and a beam of light shines in, and everything brightens into lighter shades of blue. Azure. Cerulean. Cornflower. Thick lines I didn't see in the dark appear, fanning all around me like tightrope lines. They form a massive spiderweb above me. I slowly stand up in my canoe, balancing, reaching to touch one of the lines. I almost grab one when the ring starts retracting and everything dims back to shadowy blues.

I witness this a few times. Opening, brightening, spiderwebbing, while angled waves gently swish me around. This place is familiar. It's like I'm drifting inside an eyeball opening and closing its lid. *Wait—am I inside my eyeball?*

The white light shines again when it opens. Fading into

weightless darkness when it closes. As it opens again, a giant white figure in the distance appears, coming toward me, walking on water. It's getting closer, a blob of white approaching me.

Closer and closer . . .

Clearer and clearer . . .

"It's the Stay Puft Marshmallow Man!"

"Are you talking to yourself again, Ms. Red?" a girl's voice tugs at me from afar.

Blink. Encased in smoke, I see the voice smiling at me. It's Ms. Orange. Galactic sounds swarm in all directions. A deep bass clenches, smooth and constant. Red laser beams vibrate lines up and down a wall. I'm sitting on a sofa, expanding and contracting with everything and everyone around me, wonderfully overwhelmed by the sensations. I realize that I have vision beyond my ability to see. There's endless creative exploration inside my mind, just waiting to be released into the world.

"Why, yes, I am," I say, clicking off my recorder.

"Let's dance," my friend says, her voice close and clear.

"Hell yeah," I say, slowly standing.

We walk into the rave abyss.

24 / PARANOID ANDROID, SIDE B

"**D**ude, I cannot believe your parents are letting you go tonight," I said to Tommy, stuffing my mouth with French fries.

"I know! It's a trip," Tommy said through Big Mac chews. "But I have a curfew."

"Yeah, sucks, whatever, we'll get there early and just fry tonight. Then we'll leave and go to your house and trip out. Is it cool if I sleep over?"

"Totally."

"Too bad you can't sleep over," I said, sipping my Coke. "This is, like, the one weekend my parents are actually out of town."

He burped. "And they're letting you do whatever?"

"Pretty much. Justin's home for fall break, so it's the two of us. Okay, tell me exactly what you told them."

Tommy and I were sitting in my car in a McDonald's parking lot, chowing down before his first party since Megga Buzz One. Between him going to a different school and not being able to rave, I felt like we were growing apart, even though we spoke on the phone often. When he'd called to tell me his parents had said he was allowed to rave again, I was floored—his parents were even stricter than mine.

He took a long slurp of Coke. "We had this long-ass talk, and I told them that raves were the only place where I feel like I really fit in. I said I was insecure at Piedmont, where people are hella conservative, and that I didn't have any friends, and that there were other gays at raves. I started crying. I think that's what really got them." He paused to giggle. "Little did they know I was crying because I was afraid I would never be able to party again."

"Wow. Then what?" I bit a chicken McNugget in half and inspected it to make sure it wasn't the wet kind.

"Um, they said they were worried about how raves were all night, and we talked about a later curfew. I suggested 3:00 a.m., but they wouldn't budge, so 2:00 a.m. it is."

"Ugh, that means you have to go home high."

"Ugh, I know. Hella annoying."

Neither of us brought up what I really wanted to know: Did his parents know he was doing drugs? Like, hard drugs? First Johanna's lenient parents, then Tommy's parents letting him rave. I still doubted my parents would let me rave. I didn't feel like I had a good reason for drugging and dancing all night. Tommy had played the gay card, which was his truth. What was my truth? Raves were where I fit in too, among the other alternative kids. But I was convinced that, in the words of the Fresh Prince, "parents just don't understand."

We got to the party around 10:00 p.m. and took our acid in the parking lot. It was a typical Saturday night rave at Home Base, aside from the arsenal of drugs I was carrying. I hadn't realized I'd accumulated so much, and I was uncomfortable with having so many drugs on me. I'd wanted to sell most of it that night, and Tommy agreed to help me. We thought it would be fun to play the role of drug dealers. We'd leave for Tommy's at 1:40 a.m. That was the plan.

We walked past the line of people that curved around the side of the warehouse. When we got to the entrance, I asked for Chris. His friend was throwing the party. In no time, he came out to greet us, gave us laminated VIP lanyard necklaces, and led us into the party.

"The VIP room is where the Chill Room usually is," Chris instructed as he led us down a black-lit hallway.

"Cool," I replied, "and hey, if you know anyone who wants to buy weed, or something else, I'm looking to unload tonight."

He slowed his pace and gave me a look that was a cross between surprise and disappointment. Or maybe his weird look was just my acid kicking in.

Thudding beats, musky air, and green lasers engulfed us. Tommy and I went toward it. Chris walked another way, I assumed to the VIP room.

"That was weird," I said to Tommy, stopping. "Was that weird?"

"Huh? What was weird?"

"Oh. Never mind."

We circled the party, ducking into different rooms and the outside area, hugging hellos. We found Luca and Angel. They bought a couple hits of E and some weed.

Tommy and I were smoking cigarettes outside when a lanky guy with a goatee came up to us asking for a cigarette. We were in a kooky state of frying and obliged, asking him his name, where he was from, niceties, etc.

"Nick. Modesto. Do you guys know where I can get some dank?"

In his funny announcer voice, Tommy replied, "Well well well, it's your lucky day, chap. We happen to have some right here."

"Oh yeah?"

In my serious businesswoman voice, I said, "Follow me this way, please." I didn't want to do the exchange under a spotlight.

"How much do you want?" I asked once we'd moved a few feet over.

"A twenty's cool." He twitched.

I put out my cigaroo and reached into my makeup bag within my satchel. I found a tightly packed twenty sack and slipped him the baggie.

He stood staring at Tommy and me after putting the weed in his pocket.

"Uh, the dinero, please?" I said in my serious businesswoman voice, glancing at Tommy, who was putting out his cigaroo, keeping watch.

"How much more weed do you have in there?" the guy asked, pointing at my bag.

"A few more twenties."

"Oh yeah? Why don't you just give me the rest, then?"

Excited by the idea of making a good sale, I reached back into my satchel. My hand grabbed three baggies, and I plopped them into his outstretched hand. He itched his nose with his other hand, said "Peace," and disappeared into the crowd.

Distraught, I couldn't comprehend what had just happened.

A wide-eyed Tommy helped clarify. "Dude! Did he just jack you?!"

Apprehension came over me. I looked at scattered groups of strangers around us. They were staring at us. At me. They were smiling, laughing, at me. "I, I thought he was going to pay me," I said. "He said he wanted the rest."

"Obviously!" Tommy sighed dramatically. "Whatever, that guy was shafty. New rule: money first. Let's go dance."

I nodded, zipped up my bag, and followed him inside to the main room.

The dance floor had filled with people, and the visuals were brighter. The swaying of glowing hats and glow sticks calmed me, but as we made our way through the crowd, I felt like everyone was watching me—like they knew what had just happened and were mocking me for being so stupid. So inexperienced. So high.

"Let's get some water in the VIP room," Tommy said. "Maybe it's free in there."

I jumped to say, "Just don't tell anyone what just happened."

He nodded and took my hand to lead me down a hallway.

The VIP room welcomed us with warm pastel lights and tables spilling with fruit. The familiar faces of Chris and his crew, which consisted of DJs and cute fifteen-year-old girls, filled the room with positive vibes.

"Is that a bar?" Tommy squinted. "Like, alcohol bar?"

I followed him to the bar, like, alcohol bar. But it wasn't serving booze; it was a fancy water station with juice and free water.

Tommy and I sat down on a sofa. Not feeling very talkative, I listened to him go on about something funny and tried to focus on beautiful things that made me feel good. The lotus flower on a flyer on the floor. The rainbow sherbet on the wall. Sparks of glitter on the raver girls' smiling faces. I eyed the crowd, sorting out who was who, and then my jaw locked.

Nick. Modesto.

I grabbed Tommy's thigh and said, "Oh my god, there's Nick."

"Who?"

I whispered, "Nick. Modesto. The dude who just stole my shit."

"Really? Where?" he whispered back.

"Over there, in the corner." I motioned to a tall figure in a dark T-shirt.

He shook his head. "I don't think so, dude. I don't see him. You be trippin'."

I stopped staring at who I thought was Nick. Modesto. and realized I was most certainly tripping. Suddenly, I didn't want to be high anymore. My pulse thumped in my temples. My breathing was shallow. I was afraid someone else was going to rip me off—or, worse, security was going to catch me dealing. Everyone in the room was suspect. They were looking in our direction like something was about to happen. Someone was coming for me. My hands were clammy, my mouth unbearably dry. I couldn't swallow. Anxiety was strangling me.

"Water," I said to Tommy.

"What?"

"Water!"

He handed his water bottle to me, and I chugged the metallic coolness, spilling some down my chin.

I heard him say, "Seriously, dude, are you okay?" but I couldn't speak. I looked at Tommy and then saw Chris, who was walking toward us with a smirk on his face.

"I have to go."

"What you need to do is relax. Want to go outside?"

I started standing up, and Tommy stood up with me. "No!" I yelled at him, not wanting to talk to Tommy or Chris or anyone, just wanting to escape.

I blurted, "I have to go! I need to get rid of it!"

A glimmer flicked across Tommy's confused face.

Go. I turned and ran out of the VIP room. *Get rid of the drugs.* I faintly heard Tommy yell, "Samantha!" over the downtempo music. Trying not to draw more attention to myself—I didn't want the security guards to see me—I slowed my running to a fast walk through the black-lit hallway, looking behind me, around me. No one caught up to me as I raced out the entrance.

And that was when it happened: The terrifying drive through Oakland on acid. Forgetting Tommy at the rave. Flushing all my drugs in a dramatic attempt to find sanity. The brain works in mysterious ways, especially when you're tinkering with it.

I had sobered some after talking to Justin, when I realized I'd had a bad trip. But I was left feeling lost, wound up in an emotional tornado of self-doubt, disbelief, and shame.

After drinking some water, I called Tommy at the number he'd paged me with. He was at the Denny's next to Home Base in a tizzy, saying he'd blown curfew, asking where I'd gone. He'd called his parents to tell them my car battery wouldn't start and we were waiting for AAA to come, but he was sure his parents hadn't believed him.

Hearing this made me want to scream. Had I just ruined Tommy's chances of ever raving again?

"I had a bad trip," I said.

"Dude," he breathed into the phone, "I'm sorry. That's crazy. Are you okay now? Can you come pick me up?"

Fearing what would happen if I got back in my car, I said, "I don't think so."

"Fuck. Okay, maybe someone else can give me a ride home."

Hearing his nervous tone, I rushed to say, "Maybe Justin can pick you up. I just need to see if he's asleep yet. But will your parents let you sleep here? I don't think Justin will take you home."

"Let me call them. Damn, I hope they don't come get me. I'm frying balls."

"I'm so sorry, Tommy."

"It's okay. Go ask Justin, and I'll call them. Call me back in ten."

I hung up and left my room. I put my ear to Justin's door and heard nothing. I knocked twice before hearing a weary response. After explaining what I'd done, he agreed to pick up Tommy. And Tommy's parents said that since it was so late, he could sleep over.

All the organizing drained my last bit of energy. I wanted to curl up in bed and forget the rest. I put on pajamas and undid my prom 'do. I turned off the lights and sank into my bed, watching my lava lamp's purple globs morph on my bedside table. A cow. Salt and pepper shakers. A balloon animal . . .

Just as my eyes started closing, I heard Tommy whisper, "Are you asleep?"

Relieved he was safe with me, I muttered, "I'm so sorry, Tommy."

"Dude, it's okay." He sat on the edge of my bed to take off his shoes. "You totally scared me for a second."

I sat up to look at him in the glow. Shadows under his eyes made him look older—haggard, even. Both of us had almost lost our minds from overindulgence at various points in the last year, but until tonight we'd always managed to fight it off, find the light.

"I am so fucking embarrassed," I said, my words catching in my throat. "Does everyone know?"

"Well, Chris was like, 'What the fuck?' and Luca and Angel came with me to Denny's to page you, but, you know, they were worried about you too. I was so worried about you, dude. I didn't know where you'd gone."

I cracked, and tears started gushing out.

"It's okay, dude! No one will judge you. Everyone is a mess anyway."

"I just never thought that would happen to me," I blubbered. "How did that happen?"

Tommy sighed. "Yeah, crazy shit. That fool who jacked you messed with your head."

Nick. Modesto. was the trigger. But there were other factors. Months of drug abuse had broken me down, wreaking havoc on my dopamine and serotonin levels. I had reached my cerebral cortex limit. Acid had opened so many doors in my mind—but where was I going?

I told Tommy, "I'm never doing acid again."

He didn't respond. He just stood up, took off his clothes, walked around to the other side of my bed, and said in a flirty voice, "Is there room in there for me, Ms. Red?"

Lying back, I patted my bed, and he got under the covers with me. I think I even smiled a little, thanks to him.

It was comforting waking up next to Tommy the next morning. The crazed thoughts and lunatic driving on acid of the previous night were a memory I wanted to forget.

It took months, and many therapy sessions, for me to process what happened that night. I'd learned that my biggest threat wasn't my parents or the cops but myself. And what would have been if my parents were home that weekend? What if I'd come home in an acid-fueled frenzy and my dad had knocked on my door instead of Justin? That could have been my big confession moment.

After that night, I never did acid again, and never went to another rave.

As if. Rave life most certainly went on.

25 / MY SO-CALLED LIFE

Rave life went on, and real life dragged on. I couldn't find any inspiration at school, not even in art class or when I had to write papers. Tired and foggy in the head, I walked the halls like a zombie every morning alongside kids full of vim and vigor. Or so it seemed.

I tried drinking coffee, since my dad brewed enough for a startup every morning, but I found the taste too strong. I usually opted for skipping breakfast entirely. I just didn't have much of an appetite, except for an appetite for destruction.

One morning, Johanna offered me Ritalin to help jumpstart my day.

"It's, like, prescription speed," she said with unblinking eyes. I told her I didn't want to do lines in the school bathroom. That was a hard no for me, just like how smoking weed between classes had always been a no for me. Something had changed since I'd joined the rebels on the fire escape to smoke cigarettes during drama practice. As much as I disliked school, I didn't want to be in an altered state there. That's what raves were for.

This boundary came from the immense importance my parents placed on my brothers' and my education. My dad worked tirelessly, traveling and sacrificing time he could have spent with us to support three kids. I was afraid of getting caught doing drugs at school. And yet I took other risks every weekend, raving and drug driving. What was worse, being suspended from school or getting caught by the police driving on acid? For me, being suspended from school.

Johanna said Ritalin was a pill, so I took one. I was more alert and focused that day, but I was also anxious and restless, and it felt weird to be buzzing like that at school. An unrealized part of me needed the sobriety school forced upon me during the week. If I didn't have school every day, I would be raving more, like Tommy and I had during the summer. Spacing out my exploits allowed me to detox enough to be able to retox a week later, keeping burnout at bay.

I still managed to get in trouble at school.

After I got another C on a test, my math teacher wrote, "See me after class," on my paper.

When I approached his desk, he looked up at me.

"Hello, Samantha," he said, his weathered face serious.

"Hi, Mr. Clara," I said, chipper.

"How tall are you?"

"Uh, five eight. And a half."

"You should consider trying out for the basketball team," he said.

Caught off point guard, I said something like, "Sure, maybe," but I had no intention of playing sports that semester. Raving was my sport.

I'd expected him to talk to me about my dropping test scores, but all he wanted was for me to try out for the women's basketball team.

My mom was enraged when I told her about it.

"I knew he'd be difficult," she said. "I requested you not to have him because he did the same thing to Reed—he pressured him into trying out for the basketball team instead of helping him in the classroom. It's all about basketball for Mr. Clara. He doesn't give a shit about math!"

Mr. Clara being an asshole was something my parents and I agreed on, and they got me a math tutor.

Doodling was my favorite subject. Hearts and flowers had evolved into colorful graffiti scribble. Inspired by Clayton, I practiced my potential tagger aliases in boxy, bubbly letters.

Ferrari. Ms. Red. V-Mob. Even. Dazi. Adidas.

I practiced my penmanship, though I wasn't sure I would have the guts to spray paint a wall in public. Clayton sometimes stuck white sticker labels he'd Sharpied "Agent 420" across on bus stop signs or payphones. I thought maybe I could start with that.

26

24-HOUR PARTY PEOPLE

2nd Chakra, November 1996
Homies: Tommy, Clayton, Johanna, Defne
Location: Home Base
Drugs: Special K, crystal, weed

Razor goosebumps shot up my arms as we waited in line to get into the party. Bone-chilling November nights had made me switch from Adidas windbreakers to North Face fleeces (which I was collecting in every color thanks to the North Face outlet in Berkeley). Me, Tommy, Clayton, and Johanna had been waiting hella long and were bitching about how annoying it was to have to wait in line for parties. The days of people slowly trickling in after finding the Map Point were over. Raves were getting bigger and not necessarily better.

I had a loopy buzz from doing a line of Special K in the car; my body was liquid loose. Ketamine, a dissociative anesthetic, wasn't a speedy high. It was more of a drunk feeling. Medically used as an animal tranquilizer, recreationally it was more popular on the East Coast than it was in the Bay Area. But Johanna had found a local hookup.

A fluffy white powder, it tasted cleaner than coke, or at least the coke I'd done. It burned sniffing it. Not as intensely as ecstasy, though, and I was getting used to the burn of powders up my nose. I kinda liked it, actually. It was like that triumphant pain of ripping off a nagging hangnail or biting through a blister inside your lip.

I felt Special K after a few minutes of doing a line, and the high tapered off after about forty-five minutes. We'd started dabbling in K more because of Tommy's curfew—we were seeking shorter highs.

It was crowded by the time we got inside the familiar rooms of Home Base. We found a dark corner and did a few more bumps of K, and then Johanna announced she was going to find Josh and left us.

"Who's Josh?" I asked Tommy.

"Whew!" Tommy sniffed. "I don't know."

I grabbed Clayton's hand. "Let's roam."

We rotated around the rooms, swirling lights and pounding beats guiding us. We posted near a speaker producing a steady stream of energetic sounds. My body felt lightweight, my mind flooded with stimulus, but I was also having uncontrollable jaw-popping problems.

"Whoaaaaa," Tommy said, reading my mind.

"I don't think I can dance," I said, my voice slowed in my head.

Clayton lit a cigarette. "I'm fucking high as hell."

"Let's go outside to get some air," I suggested.

I locked arms with the boys, Tommy on one side and Clayton on the other—a Ms. Red sandwich—and we zigzagged our way toward the back door.

After slowly making our way outside, I recognized Dreya strutting past us and called out, "Hey, Foxy Brown!"

She stopped, smiling at us. Every weekend I'd tried to have a conversation with Dreya as she breezed by me. Through my best attempts, I'd learned she was eighteen, a party promoter born in Hawaii, didn't do a lot of drugs—i.e., she was always able to carry a coherent conversation (not so much me, on the other hand)— and was friends with tons of DJs. I always tried to find out which party she was going to the next weekend, since that was obviously the best choice.

We were still talking with Dreya when a tall dude with a sideways-slanted baseball cap came up to her and said, "Hey, whaaat's going ooon?" kinda slurred.

I looked him up and down, admiring his cute hip-hop style: cargo pants and a Nautica jacket.

"What's your name?" I asked him.

Clayton was busy working on a chalk graffiti piece on the ground a few feet away. Some people had gathered around to watch him.

"Vince. Vincent Antonio," he replied.

"I'm Samantha." I smiled at him.

"What's up, dude? I'm Tommy."

"Bomby?"

"No, Tommy, but Bomby, hmmm, that's tight."

"Sam and Tom, stocking down with your favor, what's the flavor when your neighbors be doing favors?" Vincent Antonio freestyled.

"Not Sam, Samantha," I corrected Vince while Tommy pondered another nickname. It irked me when people assumed calling me Sam was okay. I'd been Sam when I was a little girl, but now I'd grown to appreciate the sophistication of my full name. At the beginning of junior year, I'd informed my friends that my name was "Samantha now, not Sam." (More like "Samantha the Diva.")

Dreya mentioned to Vincent that she was Ms. Foxy Brown in the Color Club.

"That's tight," he said, putting his arm around Dreya. "Can I get in the mix and be Mr. Foxy Brown? I've always wanted to marry this girl."

"But of course," I said, and we shook on it.

Then I was talking to Kenji, or Benji with a K, whose eyes were heavy until he saw my tape recorder's little red light. "You're recording this shit?" he asked. "Oh, I'm awake now. What's up?" He started freestyling: "Take it from this one but it's just begun. . . . Do you understand the spoken one? The rhyme the time, trying to find the words, the time passes but it never does, always going. A little spoken word. I'm radical, radial, spun out metallic, spacious. . . ."

After idling around outside, Tommy ran up to me, saying, "Dude!" and holding something in front of my face so small I couldn't tell what it was. "This fool went to Japan and brought back Adidas thumbtacks, paperclips, and toilet paper. Adidas thumbtacks! And he gave me one, look!"

I studied the teeny thing with my night vision, squinting to see what could very well have been an Adidas flower on the flat end. Tommy asked me to put the tack in a safe place. Eventually, he glanced at his pager and said he had to go. I walked him to the exit gate.

"Page me if you and Clayton want to come over," he said, leaning in for a goodbye hug.

I watched him leave the party, his JNCOs floating across the ground, his right hand gripping a half-full water bottle. Wind blew across the back of my neck, sending shivers down my spine, and I quickly walked back to the party to find Clayton. We danced for a bit, then found Johanna, who had run out of K but had a baggie full of crystal, and soon after ran into Defne, who was also on crystal.

Off acid and ecstasy-tolerant, I was all about powders, whether it was a downer like Special K or an upper like crystal. Around 2:00 a.m., when I could have easily fallen asleep after a faded night of Special K, I opted to keep going via crystal.

It stung. In a good way. My nose was stuffed up and running from doing Special K, and crystal cleared up my sinuses, burning everything in its path up to my brain. It jolted my body, perked up my mood, and motivated me to keep going.

I usually mixed crystal with other drugs. The morning after Megga Buzz One had been a legit meth buzz, but this felt like the first time I'd really experienced the singular rush of meth-amphetamine. For the first time in months, all I wanted to do was dance. Keep dancing. Dancing in heaven. Don't let the party end because when it does, you have to face life. Boring, normal, confusing life. Coke has the drip, crystal has the burn. You talk fast you dance cool you don't get tired and you, are, the, shit.

I ran up to one of the giant speakers and danced my heart out. Footloose and fancy-free, free as a bird, free form, free to be you and me, I was freestyling. House, trance, breakbeat, jungle, whatever the DJ spun, I spun with it. My body took over, and my mind surrendered to moves, sharp and focused.

Like when I'd gotten lost in the dancing zone at my first rave, I eventually noticed the dance floor clearing away around me. Clayton was still dancing, sweat dripping down his face soaking a ring around the neck of his shirt. A cigarette dangled between his fingers. Hours must have gone by. I reached for his arm. "I'm hella thirsty! Let's find water."

We went outside. The sky was sapphire blue, the air dewy. The lightening sky made the empty water bottles and flyers scattered on the ground more obvious. Kids drifted aimlessly across the spread. The remaining ravers were sitting by the fence along the perimeter, huddled together, keeping warm like penguins. I spotted Johanna and Defne in one of the huddles.

"Hey!" I said, surprising myself with my alertness.

"Hello, darling!" Defne waved us over. Fake eyelashes punctuated only one of her cartoon eyes. The other eyelash must have fallen off.

Itching for a change of scenery, I said, "I think we're ready to go."

"Yeah, we were just talking about that," Defne said. "We're probably going to Strawberry Sundays."

Johanna was whispering and giggling with the guy sitting next to her. He had a sharp jaw and wide-set eyes. He looked slightly reptilian, in a sexy way.

I didn't want to dance I didn't want a cigarette I didn't have to pee I wanted to leave and go somewhere else but I didn't know where and I was totally wired and I needed a piece of gum and I pulled my backpack around and got a piece of wintergreen out.

"Anyone want gum?"

Everyone answered, "Yes!"

And like that, I was out of gum.

Johanna stood up, brushed off the back of her pants, looped her satchel around her torso. In her breathy voice, she asked, "Do you guys want to come to my place to shower and stuff, then we can go to Strawberry Sundays?"

The reptilian guy was the elusive Josh, and he came with us to Johanna's Chill Basement. We took turns showering as daylight emerged outside. And we took turns doing lines of crystal. The guys lay around drawing in either Josh's journal or whatever paper they could find. Josh drew graffiti too, sketching in what he called his Book. Johanna and I bopped around the basement talking, getting ready, organizing our stuff, talking, doing our hair, reorganizing our stuff, talking, getting ready, organizing our stuff, talking, doing our hair, reorganizing our stuff.

Once 9:00 a.m. rolled around, I paged Tommy. My fingers shook as I dialed his pager number, waited for the beep, and then entered Jo's private number, "111" (my code), "311" (party info), and "143" (I love you).

He called right back.

"What's up, dude?" he asked.

"Hey, babe, we're at Jo's freshening up and we're going to Strawberry Sundays soon and do you want to come?"

"Oooh, interesting," he said. "I can probably swing that. Should I just come over there?"

"Whatever's clever."

"What time are you guys leaving?"

"If you can leave soon just come over here we can all go together," I said.

"Copy that. I just finished cleaning the kitchen. Assume I'll be there in, like, thirty."

We hung up.

After more talking, getting ready, organizing our stuff, talking, doing our hair, reorganizing our stuff, we heard a tapping on one of the side windows. Johanna peeked through the curtain, and Tommy made a funny face at us.

He entered the room looking fresh and clean. "Okay, what are you guys on, and can I get some?"

Johanna had tucked her kit away, fearing her parents would come downstairs, but she got it back out. "Okay, two for Tommy one for us."

Even after hours of dancing and staying up all night, my body wasn't tired. But my eyes were heavy and dry, and my heartbeat pounded through my toes. I dropped some Visine into my eyes and kept drinking water. Tasteless and refreshing, it was the only thing I could stomach.

I volunteered to drive everyone in the Bubble, and we set out for the city. Sun shining, cool breezing, it was a blue-skyed Sunday as we bounced along the Bay Bridge listening to De La Soul while everyone talked talked talked, especially Tommy. After a good night's sleep and crystal for breakfast, he was on fire, performing a one-person show sitting shotgun. He reminded me of Max Headroom, a pixelated AI character from the '80s who spoke fast and distorted, like a robot on speed.

Following Johanna's directions, I drove toward the water's edge in San Francisco's Dogpatch neighborhood. After parking, we entered a nautical-themed restaurant at the marina, wove through disarranged dining tables, and ran upstairs to the second level, where we found a DJ spinning next to a bar in front of a makeshift dance area full of people dancing elbow-to-elbow to house beats. White pillars and golden wood created a modern space naturally lit by windows, some of them portholes, like on a boat. It was indoor/outdoor, and outside, people were dancing and sitting around on benches mixed with tables.

Alcohol was served, but crystal was on our menu. We circled the party, too busy too distracted too spun too cool. We prattled on about nothingness. I was restless I was free and everything was crystal clear.

The views were glamorous, but the scene wasn't. It was daylight, and ravers in the light weren't as fabulous as they were in the dark. Whether you were coming down or trying to stay up, every blemish, acne scar, hangnail, and snaggletooth was under a magnifying glass. That person you recognized from the night before didn't have the same *je ne sais quoi*. The shine from the night was gone, the veil lifted.

Not everyone had the luxury of going home and taking showers like we had. Most had gone directly from party to afterparty and were unkempt. Complexions were blotchy. People stunk of BO. Girls' hairdos were in tangled disarray. Everyone reeked of cigarettes.

But hey, I was having an okay time.

Reality reared its ugly head after I got a page from my parents sometime in the afternoon. We were over the party by then—we being me, Tommy, and Clayton—and out of crystal. My jaw was tired from talking, my ears sore from pounding sounds, and my body finally wanted to rest. We agreed to go somewhere quiet and smoke bowls to help us come down.

After saying our goodbyes to the others, we walked toward the Bubble and I realized I couldn't find my keys in my backpack. After checking rechecking checking rechecking all the pockets, it was official: my car keys were missing.

"Shit shit shit!" I stomped. "What should I do?"

But I knew what I should do first: call my parents. I dialed home on my cell phone, and my mom answered.

"Hi, honey," she said. "Where are you?"

"In the city with Tommy at the Esprit outlet I'll be home soon," I said, looking at Tommy, who gave me a thumbs-up. I could be somewhat truthful about what I was doing since Strawberry Sundays took place at regularly functioning hours.

"The Esprit outlet? You haven't been there in years."

"I know, Tommy and I were out and about and I thought it would be fun to pop in."

"Can you be home for dinner?"

"Yes bye!"

Back to the problemo. I thought maybe somehow Johanna had my car keys, so we went back to the party to find her. She checked rechecked checked rechecked her bag and didn't see them. "Maybe they fell out of your bag," she suggested.

The remaining partiers helped me search the entire restaurant for my keys. Even the DJ made an announcement reporting my missing keys. But they didn't turn up—they were gone missing spinning gone missing! I was dangling from my last nerve, trying not to freak out, when Defne asked, "Darling, are you sure you didn't lock them in your car?"

Insight from a seasoned raver, I hadn't thought of that. We went back to the Bubble to check. Circling my car, peeking through the windows at the black leather seats and half-empty water bottles inside, I saw the glimmer of my disco ball keychain on the passenger-side floor.

Relieved, we went back to the party, and I praised Defne for solving the mystery. We asked around if anyone knew how to break into a vintage car, and one willowy kid offered to jimmy my window if I had a hanger, but I resolved to call AAA—I didn't want to have to explain a broken window to my parents.

We waited in the parking lot, smoking, talking, yawning. We decided Clayton would be Mr. Ruby Red in the Color Club. He couldn't be Mr. Red, but he could be a precious red gem.

Tommy blurted, "Dude! Do you have the tack?!"

I dug around my makeup bag to find it. Holding it up in daylight, we admired its glory: a white plastic thumbtack with a black Adidas flower emblazoned on the flat head. Beautiful. I gave the tack back to Tommy.

The sun was shining. I'd found my keys. The Adidas tack was intact. The rave gods were watching over us.

In the empty time slot post-rave, pre-Sunset party, the idea behind Strawberry Sundays was good: a legal venue where ravers could gather when the party was over and they had nowhere else to go, where the DJs kept spinning, trying to keep the vibe alive. Only, the kids I knew who went were tweakers. Speed freaks. Meth heads. How else would they still be up?

27 / SWEET 17

"I love your nose," Clayton said, tracing his finger from my forehead down the ridge of my nose.

The sensation relaxed me.

I rolled over in his waterbed, turning from my back onto my side to face him. When the bed settled, I found a cozy nook in the pillow.

It was a Saturday, and we were hanging out in his room, a private back-house detached from his parents' house, not unlike Brandon's guest room. His room was typical teenage boy messy, with clothes draped on chairs and in lumps on the floor. He had a TV and VCR, but his CD player was his primary entertainment center. He spent the most time at his drafting-style desk, where pencils and markers mingled with books and paper, practicing graffiti. Navy and white plaid curtains covered a couple of windows.

I was hanging out at Clayton's on weekends more now that Johanna often wanted privacy with Paul in her Chill Basement. My parents thought I was sleeping at either Tommy's or Johanna's. They didn't check up on me as much anymore since I was managing to keep up a B average. I powered through classes and homework knowing that once Friday came, I was free to be the real me.

"I have a present for you," Clayton said, his eyes red from smoking weed.

He sat up to get off the bed, sending a tidal wave under me. Relieved that he'd remembered my birthday was the next day, I watched as he stood over his desk in boxers and a T-shirt with his back to me, shuffling through papers. Smatterings of dark hair on the back of his thighs and calves outlined pale, muscular legs. He was the same height as me, build average, chest hairless. He didn't have a tall, athletic body I wanted to admire all the time. What I admired most about him was his creativity, his passion for graffiti and hip-hop. I also admired that most days he worked for his dad's construction company while studying for his GED. The rest of the time he skated, got high, and drew. He was taking an alternative route to adulthood, and I thought that was cool.

Peter Tosh's reggae beats were playing, and smoking earlier had made me groggy. I shivered in my underwear and T-shirt, pulling the blanket up over me, as I sat up as gracefully as I could in a waterbed. I was reaching for the oversize sweatshirt I'd tossed overboard when Clayton turned around to face me, holding something behind him.

His hair messy, his smile unsure, he said, "You know I can't afford much, but this is the first of two presents." He stepped toward me and handed me a piece of paper.

Sitting cross-legged, I leaned forward to take it from him and flipped it over. It was my name in sharp graffiti-style lettering alive in red-, orange-, and silver-colored pencil. The tips of the letters expanded into arrows. Mini Adidas pyramids were sprinkled within the letters, along with smiley faces. Shaded purple bubbles surrounded my name whimsically. He'd signed his alias, Agent 420.

The gesture warmed me. Suddenly, I was awake and happy, leaving groggy and indifferent behind. No guy had ever given me such a thoughtful gift.

"Wow! This is amazing!" I sloshed onto my knees and pulled him into me, our bodies slapping together against his bed. "You are so good." I kissed him and looked at my name, admiring it again.

"You really like it? It took me hella drafts, but this one is you."

"It's so dope, seriously. I love it. Thank you." I kissed him again and again, and he kissed me back, our tongues diving for each other. He grabbed at my breasts, and I felt for his boxers. He was hard. It was on.

FANTASY #1

Clayton's waterbed. Satin sheets. A mirrored ceiling. Lit candles everywhere. Dark and sexy Portishead drifts through the Tahitian vanilla–scented air. We're in violent throes of passion, like the sex scenes in *Basic Instinct*, minus the ice pick. Riding him, my hair wild and sticking to my face, my hips circle around and around in belly-dancing formations. My breasts bounce, and my nipples are hard as bullets. He's under me, his chest soaked with sweat, his smooth, strong hands caressing my hips, pulling me down while he thrusts his rocket cock up into me. Moans and groans and aches and yeses. We break to catch our breath. Our eyes lock, and beams of blue fire connect us—blue fire because that is the hottest.

REALITY #1

Clayton's waterbed. We didn't spend long on foreplay, though it was something I'd come to appreciate—there is an art to it. Clayton had given me tips on how to give a good blow job: relax your throat, use your hands, the wetter, the better. When it was my turn to receive, I tried to lie back and not squirm while I felt the sensations, guiding him while he tongued my most sensitive spots. Through his patient tutelage, I overcame my cunnilingus trauma.

Foreplay was less confusing than having sex, than the idea of losing my virginity. And it was fun. When the moment came to have sex, though spontaneous and exciting, I was nervous. And when I get nervous, I get impatient, and with impatience comes impulsivity, and after making out for five minutes, I slid my hand around his dick under his boxers, squeezed, and whispered, "I'm ready."

Clayton was prepared for this moment. There was a condom, one candle, and The Fugees. Then one minute of penetration—not enough time to break a sweat. Not enough time to enjoy it. I was just getting to the point of being relaxed enough to surrender to the slippery, sweet penetration when he grunted and stopped. It hadn't been hard for him to get hard, but after he entered me, it was over before the song was.

I didn't realize anything premature had happened until he rolled off of me. I thought maybe he wanted to change position—that's it, grab me, throw me around!—but instead he looked down at his shrink-wrapped manhood and muttered, "I'm sorry."

I was speechless, my fantasy obliterated. I was pretty sure one minute of penetration wasn't the norm. But I was sure that one minute of penetration meant I wasn't a virgin anymore. Splat. Just like that. One could argue that Brandon had technically taken my virginity since he'd popped my cherry with his fingers, but after that messy, embarrassing experience, I had decided a P inside my V was the real deal.

I wanted to say, "It's okay," but it wasn't. I had waited to find the right guy to experience my first time with, and now it had ended before I could even quiver. Or feel something more than what I'd felt so far with fingers. All I'd gotten was a little discomfort.

Goose bumps popped up across my legs. I glanced at his crotch. At some point, he'd grabbed his boxers and placed them over himself. I pulled the blanket over me and swished onto my side to face him. He was on his back, staring at the ceiling.

"Hey" was all I could say.

He looked at me. The whites of his eyes were pink, but he didn't look stoned anymore. He looked like he might cry. Concern creased his forehead. His feet twitched under the covers. I forced a smile, trying to show him it was okay without having to tell him.

"I can probably go again," he said. "I just need a minute."

It was a fluke, I thought. *He got too excited and just had to get a quickie out of his system.* I'd heard about that before. He pulled me into a cuddle, and I buried my face into his chest, inhaling his comforting scent of laundry detergent and weed, soft and sour.

"I'll be right back," he said abruptly. He kissed my forehead and sprung off the bed, the quick motion smacking me around.

"Okay," I said, holding the blanket, waiting.

FANTASY #2

Sandy beach. Crashing waves. Sherbet sky. Misty air quenches my sun-warmed skin at the end of a dreamy day at the beach. In a red string bikini, I stand facing the ocean, watching a glistening Pacific. Two smooth, strong hands come from behind, wrapping around me like a beach towel. I grab his hands as they reach for my breasts, and I flip around and kiss Clayton, who is tanned and ripped in his black board shorts. He's taller and buffer and more distinguished than I've ever known him to be. It's definitely Clayton, but he's older than seventeen. He's a man. Kissing and feeling one another, we sink into the sand. As we splash and roll around in the frothy water, my top and bottom untie, and Clayton's suit floats away. The water is warm like the air. Clayton slips inside me. I throw my head back, moaning in ecstasy.

REALITY #2

A scraping sound startled me. It was Clayton's annoying door that sometimes got stuck in the doorway. Clayton walked over to the bed and took off his shirt and jeans with the swift intention of a lover. I sat up, pulled him down by his boxers onto the bed, and smothered him with kisses. He smothered me back. It was on, again.

The positioning was nearly identical to the first time—he was on top, and I held my breath underneath. The sounds of crashing waves were miles away, but the bed swooshed underneath us.

He grunted and stopped moving. It may have lasted a little longer this time, maybe one and a half minutes, because I'd felt a frisson of pleasure when he was inside me. A preview of what could be.

"Man, I don't know what the problem is," he huffed, pulling out of me and flopping onto the bed.

"It's okay. I'm nervous too. I mean, I don't even know what to do. I've never done this before, remember?" I reassured him while noticing how tingly I was inside.

"Well, I have, and this has never happened before. What the fuck?!" He punched the bed, creating a Mavericks-size wave underneath us.

"Let's just keep trying! I mean, we don't have to again tonight, but I liked it. It was fun."

"Yeahhh. . . ."

I couldn't tell if I'd convinced him it was okay, but I'd convinced myself. It was okay because I cared about him and knew he wasn't broken. I was disappointed, but the experience had been short and sweet and on my terms. And I was hopeful. I knew in my heart it was right and would get better. It had to. After all, my friends who had told me about their first times, or at least the honest ones, had all said it hadn't been what they'd expected either.

What had I expected?

I'd expected it to be perfect. Multiple orgasms, or at least one. One huge eruption that made my boobs bigger, my hair thicker, and my life meaningful. I would be as sexy and powerful as Madonna. Or Julia Roberts, who was unconventionally pretty and likable and funny, with a smile that melted hearts. Or Paula Abdul, who was exotic and could dance her way out of anything. The sacred O would make me feel like a woman. And look like a woman.

I'd expected Clayton to tell me he loved me afterward. I'd expected time to stop. I'd expected flowers and lace lingerie and chocolate. I'd expected to feel different.

It could have been worse—it could have been with Brandon. And I did feel different. That was one expectation that was met.

After a few hours of watching TV with Clayton, my pager struck midnight. I was seventeen. Sobered and discontented, I got dressed and gathered my stuff.

I had to be home by 1:00 a.m.—my parents had pushed my curfew as an early birthday present.

Clayton gave me a goodbye birthday kiss, and I took off. Thoughts kept me alert as I drove home in the Bubble: *What is his other birthday present for me? What are my parents getting me? How does Justin like college? What am I going to wear to Be Here Now next weekend? How can seventeen possibly be better than sixteen, the best year of my life, the year I found raves, house music, JNCO, acid, ecstasy, nitrous, mushrooms, tongue piercings, my glow wand, Cesar, candy jewelry, the Color Club, Luca, Angel, Julie,*

Evan, Defne—everyone? And Clayton and sex? Confusing sex, but sex nonetheless. And Ferrari Ravioli and Ms. Red. And my therapist. And a community.

When I got home to a quiet house, I tiptoed upstairs to my Chill Bedroom. My Jansport backpack fell onto the carpet, my JNCOs landed on a chair. My emptied head plopped onto a pillow and fell fast asleep.

Sunday morning, I woke with a revelation: I wanted to go blond. Not bleached blond, like Tommy recently had, but I'd been rocking the skunk stripes in my brown hair since sophomore year, and I needed a change. A physical change. Something people would notice. Something seventeen.

It was my first sober Sunday in a while, since a promising rave hadn't presented itself the weekend of my birthday. A hair appointment, shopping with Tommy, and a family dinner was on my special day's agenda.

After a birthday breakfast of French toast and sauteed bananas, my mom offered to take me to my hair appointment in Montclair.

"Why? I can drive myself," I said.

"Oh, I thought maybe I could go with you. I can run errands around the Village while you get your hair done."

"Aren't we having a family dinner later? For my birthday?"

She wiped the kitchen counters clean with a sponge. "Yes, that's what I need to get groceries for. Do you want to come with me to pick up Justin from the airport later?" Justin was coming home since it was Thanksgiving the following week.

"Not really," I said, flippant. "I want to go look for new sneakers with Tommy after my hair."

She sighed. "Okay, well, dinner's at seven. You still want ravioli, right?"

"Yes. And Tommy's coming to dinner."

Reed also joined us for dinner. His update was that he was working at a restaurant and dating a woman named Pam, whom he called "Pamcakes."

Justin was mellow and didn't seem very enthused about college. I got the sense that he was stoned all the time in Portland.

After dinner, I opened presents. My dad gave me one of those pop-up cards with an *Alice in Wonderland* theme. His note on the back of the card read:

> For the greatest daughter ever —
> even if she hasn't yet figured out how to
> accept help and love.
> James

28 / GIRL TALK

A couple weeks went by, and I didn't tell anyone about having sex with Clayton, not even Tommy. I locked the memory away in my Bad Box with all my drug paraphernalia, pretending it hadn't happened, because it was such a disappointment. Denial. I'd seen Clayton since the attempt, but we hadn't tried again. Quiet and distant, he was still embarrassed. We didn't talk about it. We didn't know how. But there was one person I could talk to about it: my therapist.

Karen sat across from me in her high-back chair, nodding and listening. I'd just finished telling her about the math teacher/basketball debacle when she asked, "Is there anything else bothering you?"

I twirled my hair between my fingers. "Actually, yes. I haven't told anyone about this yet, and it can't be normal. I just started having sex and my boyfriend is totally sprung and I know he cares about me but . . . he didn't stay hard for very long. Like, at all. We tried a couple times, and now things are weird, and I don't know what to do, and . . . do you think this is a big problem?"

"So you had sex for the first time?"

"Yes. Finally." I sighed. "I really wanted to with Brandon, but thank god it didn't happen with him because he turned out to be a total jerk. . . . Yeah, I wanted it to be with someone special. I know that sounds cheesy, but I guess it was kind of a big deal for me."

"Is this the boyfriend you've mentioned before? Clayton?"

"Oh, yeah," I said, forgetting what I'd already told her.

"How old is he?"

"Seventeen."

"Does he do any drugs?"

"Well, yeah, sometimes we rave together. He smokes weed. Like, a lot of weed. Almost every day."

"It could be affecting his sex drive," she said. "Is he doing anything else?"

"He's done all the stuff I have, but not as often. He can't afford to rave all the time. We've been doing crystal lately."

Her bangs inched up again. "Crystal meth?"

"Yeah. I started dabbling in it. It's not like it's the best high or anything. It just . . . keeps me awake. And it's cheap. I don't know." I looked out the window. Power lines crossed with drooping eucalyptus trees against a cloudy backdrop.

I was trying to come off as aloof about doing meth. I knew it was a harder drug than all the others I'd told Karen about, and I'd told her about nearly everything. But crystal meth was insidious, and before I realized it, I was doing it every weekend. It wasn't a daily habit, like my brother Reed smoking cigarettes or Clayton smoking weed, so I didn't think it was something I needed to discuss in therapy.

"How long can he penetrate for?" she asked.

I curled my hand around the side of my neck, which was

getting warm. "Um, like, a minute? And he was so embarrassed. And now I have to get birth control. My parents haven't even met him yet."

"He may have premature ejaculation," she said.

"So this is curable?"

"Sure. I have a book that may help." She uncrossed her legs, stood up, and walked over to the bookshelf. She continued talking as she scanned the books. "There are exercises you can do together to slow him down so he doesn't get excited too fast."

Sexercises.

"Cool. Wow. Thanks!" I said, suddenly motivated to learn all about this penis problem and fix it.

With an upswing in her voice, she said, "Here it is," and handed me a book with "P.E." in large letters on the cover. She sat back down and glanced at the short table below the window, where the antique clock was. "Well, we're almost up for time."

I sighed. "I should get birth control. I'll tell my mom soon, but, in the meantime, where can I go?"

"That would be a good thing to talk to your mom about," she said.

A few weeks after that session, my mom came upstairs to talk to me. I was sitting at the desk in the guest room, doing homework to the beat of En Vogue's sassy tunes.

She sat down on the white wicker daybed behind me. "Honey, your father showed me a recent charge on the emergency credit card."

My pulse quickened. I put my pen down and turned to face

her, churning through what the charge could be: *Was it the AAA charge from the spun Strawberry Sunday when I locked my keys in the Bubble? (Emergency.) Was it that shopping spree at Foot Locker? (Fashion emergency.) Or was it my secret visit to Planned Parenthood to get birth control? (Emergency.)*

Firm but friendly, she said, "It was a charge to Planned Parenthood."

Not my slickest move. Of course that charge would have jumped out among Safeway and the dry cleaners on the statement. I hadn't mustered up the nerve to tell my mom about it. Clayton and I had been practicing slow, safe sex with condoms according to the book my therapist gave me, but I'd wanted to get on birth control ASAP, and Johanna had suggested Planned Parenthood.

She said it was free, but it wasn't. I had to visit with a doctor to get the pill, and it turned into a physical and lecture about safe sex. The doctor urged me to still use condoms to prevent STDs and gave me a paper bag full of free ones in a rainbow of Color Club colors.

"I'm glad you've taken the initiative to get birth control. And whether you're having sex or planning on having it, you can tell me that when you're ready," she said. "But we have health insurance through Kaiser. We could have gotten your birth control for free through there."

Surprised by my mom's acceptance, I felt bad for not being more open with her. I'd hidden so much from my parents I'd gotten used to hiding everything from them.

"Your dad and I really wish you felt comfortable telling us about these things. They're important. We knew this would happen. I wish I could have been there for you and taken you to Kaiser to see a proper OB-GYN."

"Uh, mom, Planned Parenthood is legit. It was clean and everything."

"I know, Planned Parenthood is great. Wonderful, actually. But once you start having sex, you need to have an exam every year, so you'll need a regular OB-GYN. Okay?"

I stared at the blue carpet of the guest room, realizing I couldn't help myself from going behind my parents' back anymore. Being sneaky had become my default, a bad habit I could lump together with smoking, drugging, and lying. My parents had evolved to trust me more; why couldn't I trust them more? Discouraged, I looked into my mom's moss-green eyes and said, "Sorry, Mom, I wasn't thinking."

She looked around the guest room I'd taken over. Pillows were thrown on the floor. Stacks of VHS movies sat on the dresser where the TV was. Textbooks and notebooks were shoved inside the bookcase. Colored gel pens and pencils were scattered across the desk.

"Did you get the pill?" she asked.

I nodded.

"Do you know how to use it and everything?"

"Yeah, I already started."

"And you feel all right?"

"Yeah, I feel the same." I shrugged. "I didn't know birth control could help with cramps and pimples. That's a bonus."

She smiled. "Yes, it can. I wish I'd had a place like Planned Parenthood when I was your age. Birth control wasn't easily available for women in the '60s. Especially in Ohio. And my mother would have gone ballistic if I'd told her when I started having sex." She inched closer to me. "I accidentally got pregnant when I was with that jerk boyfriend I've told you about. The one

I followed to California. It was after my parents split up and I was living with my dad. But I didn't—couldn't—have a baby. I was desperate and had an illegal abortion. I bled out. Ended up in the emergency room. I was terrified I was going to die."

I couldn't believe what I was hearing. My mom had a back-alley abortion? The idea made my stomach turn.

"Did you ever tell Grandma?" I asked.

"God, no. I called my dad from the hospital, and he picked me up. He was good about it. He never told my mother. That's what a lot of women did back then. We didn't have many choices if we weren't ready to have children."

She put her hand on my knee. "That's why I'm not mad at you for doing this. I'm so relieved you have safe options."

I felt myself nodding with her, relieved I had safe options too.

"And that's why I'm passionate about women's rights. Those were very different times. Worse times for women."

As she told me this, my heart broke a little. Sadness, surprise, gratitude, fear, sympathy—they all swirled around inside me. An impromptu talk with my mom had gone from birth control to profound emotions about my mom's near-death experience. It was a lot to take in. I wanted to comfort my mom, and to thank her for surviving. If she hadn't gotten help, my family would have never existed. But my words stuck in my throat.

"Well." My mom stood up. "I'll let you get back to your homework."

She leaned over to hug me while I sat in an emotional stupor. Her gentle embrace lifted me to standing, and I hugged her back, eagerly and fully. It had been too long since we'd hugged. She was soft and safe and smelled like chamomile. Her hugs were naturally soothing, like the simplest, best things in life. A sunset. A bath. A good song. I felt a tightening in my chest like I was going to cry, but just as I was about to, she pulled away and said, "I love you, sweetheart."

I knew if I opened my mouth to say it back, I'd start crying and wouldn't be able to stop, so I just stared into her eyes, holding back, toughened from the strength she'd just given me. I decided then that every woman should be able to choose what to do with their body. Period.

29

SUPERGIRL

Clayton was wearing a big goofy smile when he plopped into the passenger seat of the Bubble.

"Hey, doll face," he said, leaning in for a kiss. He tasted more like cigarettes than weed that afternoon.

"Hi! So are you going to tell me where we're going? And what my second birthday present is?"

"We're going to my friend Dan's place. He wants to be a tattoo artist. We've talked about getting tattoos, and I really want you to be there when I get my first one. And if you want one, it's my treat."

I'd woken up nervous for Clayton that morning. Instead of going to a rave that night, he'd reserved me for my second birthday present. I'd been admiring his handmade present, which I had propped up in my bedroom above my stereo. It would be hard for him to outdo himself with another gift. He didn't have the money for the North Face fleece I wanted, and his idea of dining out was a trip to Taco Bell.

"Oh, really?" I gripped my furry zebra-print steering wheel. I stared at the street ahead of us, unsure I wanted to move forward.

Getting tattoos together would be bold, naughty. It was like we were Clarence and Alabama in *True Romance,* about to stamp ourselves with our eternal love for each other. It had seemed more romantic when we'd talked about it some stoned night. Clayton wanted to draw his first one. I didn't know what to get, but I knew it wasn't a heart with his initials in it. Back then, I didn't have reservations about what to put *in* my body, but I always knew what looked good *on* my body. I didn't want to dedicate my first tattoo to someone else.

"Who is this Dan guy?" I asked, starting the car up. "Is he for real?"

"He's a friend's older brother, and yeah, he's cool. He's just not established yet. I've been talking to him about this, and he's stoked to meet you and practice on us. Everything is sanitary and professional, you'll see."

I shifted into first, and we chugged toward the freeway. The words "practice on us" sounded dodgy, but I couldn't stop thinking about what tattoo to get. *What statement should I make? And where? It can't be anywhere my parents could see it.* I'd just turned seventeen. I was still a year away from the legal age to get a tattoo. Even after the heart-to-heart with my mom, I didn't consider asking my parents for permission. They wouldn't authorize my tongue piercing, and I'd done it anyway and successfully hidden it from them for six months. Hiding a little tattoo seemed like a cinch compared to a metal bar in my tongue.

Clayton was talking about the design he'd drawn, a thin-lined tribal pattern with ghostly faces throughout. "Just get back on the 1 going south," he said.

Curving onto the highway, I flashed to the tribal tattoos of some raver chicks, their tramp stamps centered on their lower backs, peeking out from baggy pants. The swirly black lines seemed masculine and ambiguous. That spot, though somewhat hidden, was too obvious. I wanted something that represented who I felt I was: empowered, independent Ms. Red.

Bouncing in his seat like a kid raring to go to Disneyland, Clayton said, "Take the Collins Street exit."

As we exited off the highway, he pointed to the right. We drove past simple one-story houses, many weathered and stripped of any brightness.

Driving along, I thought about how Clayton and I had different ideas of sanitary. I often reminded him to scrub underneath his gunky skater boy fingernails. I remembered learning about HIV in junior high, and how you could get it from contaminated tattoo needles. *Can you really sanitize properly in a DIY tattoo shop?*

"Park here," Clayton told me, and he clicked his seat belt free before I turned off the car. Through his passenger window I saw a white house with navy-blue trim. When I walked around the front of my car, I noticed a splotchy grass lawn with a nearly naked tree on one side. Pebbles crunched under our sneakers like Pop Rocks as we walked the path up the front.

We stepped onto a wooden front porch, and just as Clayton lifted his fist to knock on the door, it flew open to reveal a stocky guy with a ready smile. "Hey, man!" he said in a raspy voice.

They gave each other a bro half hug.

"Come in, guys," Dan said, waving us inside.

Clayton pulled me into the entryway. "This is Samantha." The pungent stink of canned tuna fish hovered in the hallway with us.

"Hi, I'm Dan." He extended his hand. "Great to meet you."

I shook it—awkwardly, since most ravers greeted each other with a hug, and I wasn't used to handshakes.

Dan's smile exuded natural ease while I gripped his hand loosely. "I'm really excited about you guys coming over. I've got the studio all set up." He motioned for us to follow him.

I had expected a greaser guy wearing a white T-shirt with a cigarette pack rolled up one shoulder, arms covered with tats, his hair slicked back. Dan, with his Levi's blue jeans, navy-blue T-shirt, and vanilla-plain haircut, looked more like the guy behind the counter at Blockbuster video.

We walked past a living room, where two brown leather reclining chairs sat front row to an enormous television framed by shelves of VHS movies (kind of like Chandler and Joey's apartment on *Friends*). Under a window, a mahogany bookshelf housed magazines, more videos, San Francisco Giants bobbleheads, and—wait—*is that a Slinky?* On top of the bookshelf stood a half-full bottle of Jack Daniels with the cap off. Next to that was a framed photo of two dudes and two older folks, presumably Dan and his brother and parents. Sweatshirts and T-shirts littered the dirty beige-carpeted floor. There was one wall decoration: a dartboard.

"As you can see, me and my brother are clean freaks," he joked as we moved through the kitchen toward the back of the house.

He took us to a den-like room with a couple of windows with drawn curtains. A black leather chair was the centerpiece. Filmy pieces of paper with drawings on them were tacked to the wall. They flapped like an audience wave as a desk fan rotated its blow at them, a subtle crackle with each flutter.

Dan handed me a thin black binder. "These are the pieces I've done, in case you want to look," he said. "You think you want one?"

I looked at Clayton, who was urging "yes" through a closed-mouth smile.

"No pressure." Dan walked to a cluttered counter by the window. "Let me know if you need any ideas. Do you guys want water or anything?"

"Yeah, man," Clayton said as he took off his baseball cap and shirt and sat in the black leather chair. He explained his design to Dan as I wandered around the room.

A tiger, a sun and moon, an old-fashioned sailor girl curling through an anchor. Nothing spoke to me.

Dan left the room, and I went over to the counter to examine his spread. There was a gun that looked like a hot glue gun made from metal rather than plastic, cloudy plastic bottles of every possible color of ink, pens and tracing papers, little plastic caps. I inspected the power box with cords coming out of it and relaxed when I saw a six-pack of needles sealed in plastic. I reached a hand out, and Clayton breathed, "Don't touch!"

Dan came back carrying two glasses of water. "Is Creedence cool?"

I hadn't heard Creedence Clearwater Revival since one of my dad's weekend-morning home concerts. Dan pushed play on a CD stereo, and twangy classic rock lit up the room, transporting me to the *True Romance* scene I'd envisioned earlier.

He assembled things on a small metal tray propped on the arm of the chair. He copied Clayton's drawing to a piece of tracing paper, then water-transferred it onto the inside of Clayton's upper left arm, like you do with a fake tattoo.

The buzz of the tattoo gun blew like a swarm of bees into the room. I watched as Dan bent over Clayton, eyebrows squished together in concentration.

Ten minutes in, Clayton was sweating. "Aw, man, I'm dying for a cigarette."

"Sorry, you're going to have to wait until I'm done."

Clayton was tapping his toes together and gripping the sides of the chair tight.

"Does it hurt?" I asked.

"It's more of a sting," he said through gritted teeth. "Not too bad."

"Uh-huh, right," I said, turning to the black binder. A red image flashed at me. "I've got it! I know what I want."

Two hours later, Clayton's upper arm was bandaged in Saran Wrap, and we were smoking cigarettes on Dan's front porch. Anticipating my turn, I ducked back into the house to empty my excited bladder.

Upon entering the tattoo den where the guys were waiting, I announced myself by taking off my baby tee, revealing a burgundy lace bra. Confident as two pairs of eyes admired my body, I jumped onto the leather chair and undid my belt and zip fly before slithering my pants and underwear down a few inches.

"Right here," I said, pointing to a smooth patch of skin just above my tuft. Instead of back and center, I opted for front and center, right above my liberated womanhood.

"That's hot," Clayton said.

"Yeah, it is."

Intoxicating rebellion washed over me as I looked down at my exposed target. Excited by the adoration of two guys, I asked Dan if my needle was fresh out of the plastic. He stopped, serious, as if I'd offended him, reassured me that every person's needle was always a new one, and quieted to draw my simple design onto tracing paper.

I looked at Clayton, who was holding a hand mirror up to the underside of his arm, although all you could see was a plasticized blur. I hoped Dan was going to take pictures of our tattoos to put in his binder, but I was too nervous to ask.

He did the water transfer, and because it was a weird angle for me to see straight, Clayton confirmed it was in the right spot.

"Are you ready, Supergirl?" Dan asked me, gun in hand, prepared to fire.

"Hell yeah."

The loud buzzing interrupted the song "Midnight Special."

"Oh my god, I know this song," I said. "Do you guys remember that driving scene in the *Twilight Zone* movie?"

Dan laughed. "Yeah, I do actually. I forgot about that."

I laid my head back to relax. The ceiling was a dull wash of white, so I turned my head to watch the animated papers on the wall. There was a tug on my skin, and then the swarm of bees banded together to sting me, a hundred at the same time. The pain of a tattoo needle was more of a sting—the sharpest, hottest sting I'd ever felt. Within seconds, beads of sweat bubbled on my forehead and wetness spilled out of my armpits. I focused on staying still, surrendering to the pain.

I kept reminding Dan to make my tattoo as pretty as possible. He quietly said, "Okay," every time.

The buzzing stopped after about forty-five minutes. I peeled my sweaty body off the black leather to sit up and looked down my chest at a swollen patch of pink skin that appeared redder because of the red ink of the design.

The size of a big strawberry, the Superman symbol was forever stamped on me. A black outline intended to define the diamond shape looked blurred. When I pointed this out to Dan, he said, "Don't worry. When it's healed, it will be clearer."

The rush of adrenaline left my body depleted and my targeted spot warm and numb at the same time. But my mind was alert—I couldn't wait to see the final result.

After two weeks of cleaning our wounds and applying Lubriderm lotion to crazy-itchy scabs, the tattoos revealed themselves. Clayton was satisfied with his raw, ambiguous styling. It was the beginning of his deep connection to tattoo art, igniting what many tattooed people know as an addictive means of self-expression.

Mine wasn't perfect. The black outline was still blurry after it healed, and it wasn't as pretty as I'd wished. It was also off-center, floating slightly to the left. My Supergirl had blurred lines and misdirected angles, a symbol of a girl not trying to be perfect but to be superhuman.

30 / TOO COOL FOR SCHOOL

Candyland. The Gathering. All in the Family. I raved every weekend leading up to the holidays, culminating with a New Year's Eve rave called Origin that was broken up. At least it was broken up after the midnight countdown, so we got to have our whistling, hooting fun.

Spun out on crystal, a bunch of us ended up having an after-party in Johanna's Chill Basement, spiraling into 1997 while rain consumed the Bay Area. What was my New Year's resolution? I had a feeling my parents wouldn't be on the same page, but I went for it anyway.

During the first week of school in January, I entered the kitchen one evening and told my mom, "I'm not going back there."

"What?" she answered.

I tried again, this time with eye contact. "I'm not going back there."

She stopped cutting some potatoes. "Not going back where?"

I raised my voice. "I mean what I'm saying, Mom—I'm done with O'Dowd. I can't go back there."

"Did something happen at school?" she asked.

I lost control of a hand, and it flew up in the air. "No, nothing happened! It just sucks, and I don't want to be there any-more. How is that so hard to believe?"

"Have you talked to Karen about this?"

"No," I said quietly.

"I think you need to talk to Karen about this. And your fa-ther." My mom walked over to the eating nook, sat down, rested one arm on the cushioned back of the chair, and pulled at some hair. "But Karen first."

I wanted results quicker than that. Frustrated, I looked away from my mom to avoid misfiring at her. I organized some things on the kitchen counter while a TV commercial agitated me fur-ther.

I took a deep breath and exhaled. "Fine. Can we move up my appointment with Karen to ASAP then?"

She nodded. "I'll see if she has an opening. And I won't say anything to your father until you've talked to her and really thought this through. This is very serious, Samantha. I hope you realize that."

January had been cold and gray. I was trapped in high school purgatory. I barely spoke to anyone. I stopped doing my home-work. Classroom chatter irked me like the buzz of a fly stuck against a window. Cue the girl with her elbow on her desk, face resting on her fist, sighing deeply, doodling defiantly. All I could think about was how much I wanted out. I didn't need a gradua-tion to feel accomplished. I was beyond high school.

Karen saw me for an emergency session. Talking it out didn't change my mind, but she helped me realize that I still wanted to go to college and should make that clear to my parents. She pointed out that my parents' biggest fear would be that I was going to mess up my chances of going to college.

I was open to options other than getting a GED. But what were they?

When I got home, I told my mom I was ready to speak with my dad about it. It was cuticle-biting times like this that I wished Justin were still home. He was a buffer. I wrote him letters but hardly ever heard from him and had no idea how college was going. I envied how he was out of the house, free to do whatever he wanted. It was that freedom that I craved. Having my own space, not needing to sneak around, quitting lying once and for all. I was tired of high school, but I was also getting tired of having a secret life.

That evening at dinner, my dad asked, "So what's bothering you, hun?" He wiped his face with a napkin, pushed his emptied dinner plate into the center of the table, and stretched out his daddy long legs under the glass-top table.

My nervous stomach had left a gooey pile of beef stroganoff on my plate.

My mom turned off the TV—this news was more important than Princess Diana wanting to ban land mines.

I pushed my plate to the center of the table like my dad and sat up in my seat, forming a confidence wall, bracing for resistance. "I have decided that I don't want to go back to O'Dowd."

My dad stared at me and then looked at my mom, whose unblinking eyes encouraged me to go on.

"I've been thinking real hard about this, and I am not inspired at school anymore." Sigh. "I'm not interested in my classes, and the teachers don't care. School is . . . unsatisfying." My dad was opening his mouth to speak when I remembered Karen's advice and quickly said, "But I definitely want to go to college, eventually."

"Hmmm, I don't know," my dad said, calm. "You may have to tough this out, at least until the end of this year. That would give your mother and I time to figure something out."

I started shaking my head. "I don't think I can. I'm sick of it."

"Honey," my mom said, "I don't think it's very easy to find a solution in the middle of the school year. In order for you to get into a decent college, you need a high school degree."

"That's not true. The GED test is given every month. I can take it and then I'm done. Then I can apply for colleges." My delivery was shaky.

"The GED?" My mom balked. "Honey, no."

"What's wrong with getting a GED? It's better than flunking out of school, isn't it?"

"Well, yes, but the GED is for kids who . . . kids who don't have a lot of options. You have options. This is because of Mr. Clara last semester, that sexist jerk. He didn't support you."

"Yes! Exactly. There are lots of jerk teachers that don't support me."

"Here's the thing, Sam." My dad sat up in his chair. "The chances of getting into the kind of schools you'll want to go to are much lower with a GED."

"But I don't know what kind of college I want to go to," I said.

"Not now, but you have to start thinking about it. Senior year you'll need to apply to schools and start studying for the

SAT. Soon you're going to need to seriously think about this stuff. It's a process, but it's important. This is your future."

Thinking about the mother of all high school tests—the SAT—made my entire body tense. But there wasn't any aggression behind my dad's words. I became aware of a shift. My dad was speaking to me like an adult. He wasn't angry or awkward or about to chase me around the kitchen. Since I'd been in therapy, my communication with him had moved past combative into constructive. I was prepared for a fight, but I wasn't getting one.

"You know that neither your mom or I completed college. We've created a fund for you. This is one of the most important decisions you'll make."

His words repeated in my head while I stared at the wooden floor. The idea of staying at school suffocated me. My breathing quickened every time I thought about it, blocking my flow of positive thinking, opening the anxiety floodgates—making my chest warm and flush. I had a physical reaction to the idea; I'd become allergic to school.

I had always been able to pull an idea out of a hat, but this conversation left me speechless. I didn't move except for my hands under the table, my fingers searching for hangnails to rip open. I wanted the solution right then. If I thought hard enough, I knew it would come to me.

"Samantha?"

"I just can't go back there," I said, shaking my head. A tickling sensation on the skin under my nose made me sniff.

"We just need to figure this one out." My dad leaned forward, reaching his hands toward me across the table. "Together."

I looked up at my dad, wishing I was as confident about figuring it out as he was. Something trickled down my lip. I itched my nose and felt a warm wetness. My stomach leaped into my throat.

"Oh shit," I mumbled, holding my nose with my hand.

"Is your nose bleeding?" my mom asked, standing up quickly. "Let me get you a tissue."

I jumped up. "No! I have to go to the bathroom. I'm fine!" I yelled before running out of the room.

My allergy to high school caused a bloody nose. Lie. Snorting crystal on the weekends had, but I swept that truth under the faux fur rug to focus on my pressing school problem. I decided to protest, like my dad had against the Vietnam War, and I refused to get out of bed the next morning. Since we had evolved past kicking and screaming, my parents didn't force me to go to school. But they didn't approve.

My parents and I talked about me getting a job while they scrambled to sort things out. They recited learnings from *Reviving Ophelia*, a book about how culture affects adolescent girls. None of it felt like it applied to me. They upped my therapy to two times a week and told me I had an appointment with an educational psychologist.

The first two weeks out of school were chill. I caught up on sleep, watched TV, and planned outfits. It rained nearly every day. Not one to be a couch potato, I was antsy for action, but my parents were watching me closely, so I didn't think I should chance going to a rave and getting caught since they'd been relatively cool about the whole high school dropout thing.

I spent hours in my Chill Bedroom doing a massive reorg, cleaning out my closet, organizing makeup and mixtapes. I bought a blank canvas book to bring to parties for people to write in. I wrote the current count of the Color Club on the front pages of my Book—we were at twenty-five members—and listed all the rave hotlines in the back pages. I decorated it with my favorite stickers and Band-Aids.

I moved my Bad Box from underneath my bed to the back of my closet. It now held razor blades, mirrors, and tooters, along with my recorder, notes from raver friends, and any drugs I was holding—all my top-secret stuff. I hid the key to my box in a bathroom drawer.

I'd hidden my pipes all over. My glass pipe, named Tabatha Toes, was in a zebra-print pouch inside my bra drawer. A 12-inch-long pipe made from bamboo was tucked behind folded sweaters in my closet. There was a pipe in the Bubble disguised as the cigarette lighter: a small, silver metal pipe with a screw-on plastic lid with a white cigarette drawing on the front.

There was proof of Ms. Red everywhere, and yet my parents didn't know I was a raver girl. They were too busy making sure I wasn't a high school dropout.

The two weeks after that were busy. Couch time turned into crunch time. My mom and dad kept me updated about their progress, from researching homeschooling to taking a trip to

meet with a man named Loren Pope, a college placement counselor on the East Coast.

My days were filled visiting other high schools and doing psychological and LD (learning disorder) testing. I visited a public
school where some raver friends went. I was turned off by the mo-
bile classrooms and intimidating looks from hard-looking girls
eyeing my phat pants. Maybe I wasn't as badass as I thought.

I didn't mind the testing and enjoyed the Rorschach inkblot
test. Lions, a dance party, sombreros, I saw all kinds of animals
and fun acid flashbacks in the black splatters. The personality
tests didn't reveal a severe mental problem but did show "some
depression within an anxious young lady who tends to internal-
ize feelings but may release them in an impulsive manner."

Touché.

My parents insisted that we make a cultural trip out of the
visit to Loren Pope. We flew into Washington DC and stayed a
few nights, touring the capital and visiting the Air and Space Mu-
seum, where I stocked up on astronaut ice cream and nifty pens.

We drove to meet Loren Pope at his home in Virginia. A
slim white-haired man with bushy white eyebrows who looked
like a tall gnome welcomed us. After a pleasant chat, he recom-
mended I apply for colleges early. He thought I was ready, even
mature for my age, and knew of some schools that would be
open to an early applicant. He could write a recommendation
for me to be considered.

But as reassuring as Mr. Pope's confidence in me was, I
wasn't ready for college. The more I thought about it, the more
the idea freaked me out. I didn't want a fresh start. Justin and
Reed had both left home for college, and I figured I would too.
And leaving home meant leaving my rave scene. Yes, I wanted

the freedom of going away to college, but I wasn't going to give up raving for it. Of course, I didn't tell my parents that.

The psychological and LD testing answered more questions. I qualified for attention deficit disorder (ADD), something as familiar as Facebook now that was only beginning to be diagnosed as a real disability in the '90s. We also learned that I had an auditory processing disorder. It would have been clear to the perceptive teacher that I was a visual-motor learner who responded best to lessons that used creative examples, pictures, and diagrams and who experienced a slippage in comprehension when I was only lectured to.

This had nothing to do with hearing. I could hear what a teacher was saying and follow it; I just had a hard time translating it into notes I could understand later on. It affected my reading and spelling. As much as I enjoyed reading, I was a slow reader, which made me less confident. It also explained why I'd preferred comic books and magazines at an early age—words accompanied by photos were easier for my brain to digest.

ADD. An auditory processing disorder. Performance anxiety. It all made sense that I was frustrated trying to learn in a traditional teaching environment. Of course, there were a couple other "A" words interfering with my learning as well: an attitude problem and addiction.

> *"While this examiner cannot specifically cite drug usage on Samantha's part, it is highly likely that, if she attends raves, some pattern of drug usage is likely and does enter into her overall behavior, concentration, and heightened distractibility. This needs to be 'ruled out' in a more careful and considered approach to Samantha's behavior in her current peer group."*

31

BUZZ
KILL

Splish, February 1997
Homies: Tommy, Johanna, Evan, Julie, Defne
Location: On a boat in the San Francisco Bay
Drugs: Crystal

"**D**ude, did you see clubville back there?" Tommy asked, referring to a couple of people in skintight clothes we walked past.

"Seriously," I said. "Kiddy clubville. They're, like, thirteen years old."

"Oh my god, trying to look hella sexy and just looking like skanks from fuckin' Mars," Tommy scoffed.

Tommy, Johanna, and I were in Oakland's Jack London Square boarding a boat for a Valentine's Day rave. It was one of those triple-decker boats tourists take to cruise the San Francisco Bay. We did lines of crystal in the car. Clayton opted not to come because it was a boat party, which he thought sounded lame. But the rest of us were excited for a change of scenery.

"Aliens! They're coming!" some candy raver yelled, pointing up at a plane, as we walked along the deck looking for a good spot to watch the boat leave from. Water shimmered over the depths of the Pacific. White boats of all sizes bobbed around us. Even though I'd dressed in extra layers, the icy wind was inescapable. It was ruining my up-do, and Johanna's neon green boa was strangling her.

"It's hella cold, yo!" Johanna yelled over the wind.

My teeth chattered. I told Tommy and Johanna I was going inside. When warmth and bad lighting welcomed me, I was standing alone. Stompy house revved me up as I walked toward the DJ tables at the front of the boat, looking for a familiar face.

Partygoers swayed on a dance floor in front of the DJ, a twenty-something dude with a goatee wearing a T-shirt that read "Emerica." People sat in booths and at square tables. No lasers, no light show, I definitely needed to be more high.

I saw a dark-haired girl sitting with a smiley guy with a blond Cesar haircut like Tommy's—Ms. Orange and Mr. Neon Green—and walked over to them.

"What it is?" I asked.

"Hey, girlfriend!" Julie smiled.

"What it is?" Evan smiled.

"Mind if I join?"

They scooted over to make room for me. Water bottles, flyers, and Pez dispensers decorated the table.

"You'll have to excuse us." Julie chuckled. "We're really fucked up!"

"We took our E thinking this boat would have sailed away by now but oooh weeelll," Evan said.

"I'm just spun," I said. "But E sounds fun fun fun."

"I can find you some," Evan whispered to me, offering me a Dracula Pez dispenser.

"Are these Pez dispensers loaded with E?!" I joked.

"That would be such a good idea!" he blurted. "Oh my god, Ferrari, do you remember taking that picture last weekend?"

"Um, no."

"Duuuude, we thought the camera didn't have any more film so you made the cheesiest face and then it flashed. You had the funniest look on your face!"

"Can I come with you to develop those so I can, like, steal that shit and burn it?" I asked.

He laughed. I was serious.

I looked at the dance floor, and even though I was feeling the music, I didn't want to dance. The freezing wind had sucked the joy out of me.

I whispered to Evan, "Can we do lines here or do we have to go to the bathroom?"

"Oooh, can I have some?"

"What up, y'all?" Johanna said, walking up to us.

"Oh! Just in time," I said. "Let's just do them here."

Evan and I huddled over Johanna so you couldn't see her make lines. We watched as she used a razor blade to crush shards into a fine powder on a small mirror. They sparkled like Swarovski crystals.

I pressed record on my dictaphone. "Hello, hello, okay, we're at Splish and today is Valentine's Day 1997. I'm sitting here with Johanna and we're about to do *(sniff)*, you know. I lost Tommy. I don't know where he is—"

"Hello!"

"That was Evan," I continued. "I lost Tommy. I don't know where he is, so hopefully he'll see all of us. I'm sitting with Jo Jo. Say hi."

"Dude," Johanna said, "I've lost, like, ten pounds in the last month."

Evan gave her a sidelong glance. "Yeah, on the crystal meth diet."

"Crystal Light, baby." Johanna smirked.

(*Sniff, sniff, sniff.*)

I felt a vibration under my bum and heard the hum of an engine. The boat shifted. A few people cheered while the vibration got stronger, the hum louder. We were leaving, finally.

The music got faster, the dance floor filled up, and the vibe was alive. Tommy and Defne found us, and we all sat around the table, high on either E or crystal or both, mostly talking about how high we were.

Then the conversation turned to socks. Someone mentioned they were wearing white socks with black Adidas flowers on the sides. Someone else said they were wearing the same socks. You know I was wearing my Adidas socks. Same, same, same, same, same. Five of us lifted our baggy pants to reveal the same socks.

"Fuck Nike!" Tommy said.

"What about Puma?" Evan asked.

"Puma's okay because the guy who started it was the brother of the guy who started Adidas," I said. "So they're, like, brothers."

"Yeah, so you can mix Adidas and Puma, but you can never mix Adidas and Nike," Johanna added.

We mixed other street and outdoor brands with Adidas since they weren't our beloved brand's biggest competitor, but we were adamant about not wearing Nike. I think Tommy and I were the most committed to this. And would you believe we still are? Brand. Loyal.

The music stopped about an hour after cruising. The vibration halted. Ho-hum. This kind of lull was what usually happened when a party was being broken up. Everyone looked around, wondering what was going on.

"Hey, everyone," the DJ announced. "We stopped the party because two men have gone overboard. We're going to circle the area for a while to try and find them."

Say what? I couldn't believe it. And then I could. Earlier, while eating mac 'n' cheese at Boston Market, we'd joked about how a boat party was a death trap for ravers. I knew acid had to be involved. Or some crazy drug like PCP. I mean, if I'd had my bad acid trip at a boat party, would I have jumped overboard? Scary thought.

The situation was disturbing. After the announcement, we tried to put on happy faces, but sadness lingered like smoke, thick and toxic. Laughs hushed into whispers; it felt wrong to laugh. It felt wrong to have fun.

The easiest way to escape the melancholy was by doing more drugs.

"Let's do big lines again," Tommy said to Johanna. "I mean, not little ones like before."

"Totally tortellini," she said.

"You guys!" Evan walked up to our table we'd been sitting at for hours. "There's, like, helicopters and police boats circling us!"

We went to the windows to look, and a couple boats drove by, flashing lights. Firebird lights. Whenever I saw flashing strobe lights, my stomach dropped and my pulse accelerated, forcing me to remember when I was pulled over on acid. I stepped away from the window and sat down, unsettled. I heard someone say, "I wonder if we're going to be on the news," and I had to get up and walk around. Being on TV was something that couldn't happen, because then my parents would see it. Everyone would see it. Raves didn't have a good reputation, and this news would ruin them. They were changing, becoming bigger and more commercial, and I knew they wouldn't be around much longer if people were dying at them.

Of the 104 raves I attended, Splish was the only one I knew of where someone died. Two people, actually. Overdoses, bad trips, arrests—I'd witnessed shady stuff at raves but never a death.

Splish became infamous. About one hundred people were there, and we all carried the weight of it after getting off that boat. I tried to lose the weight by going to another rave the next night. My friends and I rarely talked about Splish, and if we did, minimal words were said, and the subject was quickly changed. Like everything else that was scary and disturbing, it was easiest to pretend it never happened.

SFWEEKLY

WEDNESDAY, FEBRUARY 26, 1997

Lost at sea early Saturday morning, Feb. 15, DJ party promoters Nomad Interactive hosted "Splish," a Valentine's Day cruise held aboard the vessel Jack London Commodore. At 2 a.m., not even an hour into the cruise, 20-year-old Tavaris Willis, a visitor from Murietta, GA., jumped from the rear of the third deck and fell 26 feet into the 55-degree water at the mouth of the Oakland Estuary.

Security guard Richard Ortega, 28, a San Francisco resident, immediately leapt into the bay without a life jacket. He was last seen swimming away from the boat toward Willis. No bodies have been recovered.

32 / SLEEP-WALKER

1 1:11 p.m. Toss. Turn. *What time was that last line? Should I wear khakis or jeans tomorrow? Khakis, they're more studious. With my sky-blue sweater vest and white Polo underneath. And my red-and-white running shoes. Hair down. I wonder if there are any ravers at this school. I wish I'd gotten my nails done. My hands are a mess. I'm hot. What the fuck? I thought a two o'clock cutoff was fine to be able to get to sleep. But we did do a bump once we got to Sunset. What time was that? I'm cold. I can feel my heartbeat through my whole body. Maybe on my side I can't feel it.*

Toss. Turn. 12:52 a.m. *I am so fucking tired and my first day is tomorrow and I can't fall asleep and this fucking sucks. Okay, new cutoff time for crystal is noon. No bumps, only bowls after that. Maybe I should go get Sunny. At least I can listen to her snoring and not hear my heartbeat.*

1:36 a.m. Toss. *What's next weekend? Clayton's family BBQ reunion thing. Clayton's dad is kind of creepy. I'm getting a manicure this week. Did I write down the new Color Club members from this weekend? Mr. Ultra-Violet. Mr. Navy Blue. Ms. Citrus. Maybe I should wear my watch facing the inside of my wrist. I wonder if Tommy and Jo are having this much trouble sleeping tonight. I just wish I didn't have my first day tomorrow. I hope no one notices the pimple on my cheek. Does baby blue offset pink? Yes, white and baby blue will brighten my face. And khakis are crisp and smart.*

Turn. 2:23 a.m. *Ugh, I'm not looking at the clock anymore. I wish that glowing green light wasn't hovering over me. Maybe I can dim the light down like how you can make it not so bright. No, I'm comfortable and don't want to move. I think Josh likes Jo. His style is cute. Maybe Jo cheated on Paul with him. I know she's getting crystal through him. Wait, did I set my alarm? I must have. Mom said we have to leave at seven-thirty, so I set it for six-thirty. Right? I should check. No. I can't look at it. I can't know what time it is. I can't believe I'm still up! Fuck me. Okay, so definitely manicure this week.*

3:32 a.m. Toss. Turn. *Is Johanna promoting parties now? She keeps showing up at every rave with a stack of flyers, talking about how she got in for free. And she's selling drugs? How come she didn't mention any of this to me? Whatever, Tommy and I hung out with DJ Dan this weekend. Where did Luca and Angel go? I haven't seen them in weeks.*

Toss. Turn. 4:13 a.m. *I think I slept for a few minutes. This is bad. I've never had this much trouble sleeping before. I'm not doing crystal anymore. Should I read something? When was the last time I actually read a book? Is a half hour of sleep enough? No, absolutely not. Ugh. Tomorrow is my first day and I already fucked it up. Me, ready for college? Who was that DJ I really liked at Sunset? Simon. And now I'm hungry. Should I have a snack? Warm milk helps you sleep. Ew. No, I can't let my parents know I'm awake at . . .*

5:41 a.m! *Really? What the fuck? This sucks. Khakis, sky-blue sweater vest, white Polo.*

33

GIRL YOU KNOW IT'S TRUE

I survived my first day at my new school unslept, unkempt, etc. After six weeks of being a high school dropout, my parents enrolled me at a continuation school in Orinda, a charming town twenty minutes away from Oakland. The campus was compact and the classes smaller, and the kids were alternative like me. We'd finally found a school for misfits.

At some point that week, I told my mom the Bubble had almost blown off the Bay Bridge from the wind while I was driving in the rain. The truth was, I'd hydroplaned while driving a carload of chatty ravers on crystal to Johanna's house after a party.

"I think I'd feel safer driving a newer car," I said, knowing any mention of the word "safe" would help get me what I wanted. I loved the Bubble, but it was work to drive it, and I'd become wary of driving in the rain while high. The drive the morning after the Santa Cruz rave still haunted me. My mom said she would talk it over with my dad.

Soon after, we sold the Bubble to a family friend. RIP.

Our new car—which I quickly dubbed the Lude—was a black '92 Honda Prelude, a newer version of my dad's '84 Prelude.

New school. New car. New me.

☺

The next weekend, I accompanied Clayton to a family reunion in Pacifica. We endured two hours of a snore fest talking to grandparents, cousins, and uncles I would never remember the names of while Clayton and I shot each other flirtatious glances.

The first thing we wanted to do after leaving was smoke a bowl. I zipped the Lude around a corner and parked us not so privately on a nearby street, and we rolled our seats back and took hits from Clayton's glass pipe.

I exhaled, blowing smoke up through the open moonroof. Clayton was obsessed with the Wu-Tang Clan, and we were listening to the *36 Chambers* album he'd been playing on repeat lately. As the weed relaxed me, I meditated on the word flow, following the trails of the harsh yet poetic lyrics.

"They have a new album coming out in June," Clayton said, breaking my concentration. "It's supposed to be a double disk. It's gonna be hella tight, yo."

I rolled my head to the right to look at him. "Dope."

"So how's your new school?" he asked, lighting the bowl.

"It's cool," I said as he exhaled out the moonroof. "There's only, like, eight kids in my classes. And we can go off-site for lunch."

"Word." He handed me the pipe.

I lifted my palm up to pass. "The best part is I'm done at, like, one o'clock three days a week."

"Whaaaat?" He lit the bowl again.

"I know," I said, looking up through the moonroof. Clouds crept above eucalyptus tree with glistening leaves. "You pretty much just have to do the minimum requirements to graduate."

Clayton coughed smoke. "Right on."

I took one more hit and entered the sweet escape of lost time, any day, nowhere. Clayton smiled at me, gap-toothed goofy.

He might have been a broke-ass, chain-smoking graffiti artist, but he was also sweet, cute, and creative. And he had excellent taste in weed. Most importantly, I knew he was committed and would never cheat on me.

I plunged toward him to kiss him. My focus turned from lyrics to circles with his tongue. The metal balls on our tongues clinked together, jolting the wild kiss. I grabbed the back of his neck, drawing him closer. He reached for my breasts. We lunged at each other, pawing for warm flesh. I lowered my hand onto his crotch, feeling a hot mound. We stopped kissing, and I started undoing his belt buckle. He tried to help me, and I swatted his hands away.

Once I'd wiggled his boxers down, his dick popped up, ready to rocket. I stared at it. I'd never realized how pink the head was and how much pubic hair he had. His dick looked strong, like flexed muscle. Something primal urged at me, making me want to wrap my mouth around it.

I bent over him, and he moaned before I made contact. He sank down farther in his seat, prodding himself at me as I consumed his stiffness. I teased the head, then ran my piercing up and down the sides of the shaft, gently. I ran my hand over his fuzzy balls, lightly squeezing them. I opened wide and lowered my mouth down as far as I could, seeing how low I could go before gagging.

Clayton was getting harder and larger, and I didn't want him to come yet, so I stopped and went back to kissing him.

"Wow," he mumbled between kisses. "That was amazing."

"Get in the back with me."

He shimmied out of his pants, flung his door open, and hopped in the back seat like a bunny. I poked my head out of the moonroof for a 360. Trees, a couple houses, no cars. I flung my door open, pulled off my JNCOs, and got in the back seat.

We were cramped in the two-door back seat, giggling and panting with anticipation while we wiggled off our underwear. I tried to take off my pink Polo shirt but didn't have enough elbow room, so it stayed scrunched above my chest, revealing my white lace bra. I straddled Clayton, feeling around for his hardness. He was holding it upright. My eyes fixed on his as I lowered myself just barely onto the tip of his cock. I closed my eyes, tuning in to the sensation of penetration, knowing that I would get wet once I felt the warmth.

My body welcomed him with slippery surrender. When he was entirely inside me, I rode him up and down as fast as I could without giving myself a concussion hitting my head against the roof of the car. He noticed my discomfort and kicked his legs out to lie down more. I propped a foot onto the seat, bending my leg to get a different angle. It clicked, and we throbbed together, sex musk replacing dank drift.

"I'm going to come," he warned. "I'm going to come!"

I was on the pill, but I was still afraid of getting pregnant, so I quickly pulled myself up, allowing him to pull out, just before he erupted.

I fell face first into the back seat—my hair sticky, my body tingly. A leg was sprawled across Clayton's lap. He didn't move, didn't bother with the mess in his lap.

"You know I love you," he whispered.

He finally said what I'd been feeling. I brushed my hair out of my eyes to look at him. "Say that again."

"I love you," he said with the conviction I craved.

I felt myself blush under warmed cheeks. "I love you too."

34

FROZEN

"It's awfully chilly. It's awfully chilly. It's awfully chilly." I thought I'd only said it once. And I couldn't tell if I'd said it out loud or in my head.

It was nighttime, and I was sitting in the back seat of Johanna's parked car. A damp breeze blew through the open car window. I wasn't bound or tied down in any way, but I was stuck. Stuck in a K-hole, an overdose on Special K.

Fifteen minutes earlier, Johanna and I had been at a house party in the Berkeley hills, a typical high school beer-drinking house party. The kind of party I hadn't been to since before I started raving.

At the party, a heavyset guy I was 50 percent sure was named Gerald offered me a drink, and I scoffed, "Alcohol? What's that?"

He looked at me blankly through geeky square-shaped glasses.

I rolled my eyes, annoyed at yet another person who didn't get my humor at the party. Minutes before that, I'd joked about the bathroom being so swanky I wished I had some coke to some girls I'd once been friends with. They'd smiled at me nervously, red plastic cups clutched in their hands.

Planning for a more chill night, Johanna and I had chosen Special K as our party favor. After catching up with Naomi and some other friends I didn't realize I'd kind of missed from O'-Dowd, the room started spinning, and Johanna suggested that we go outside to get some air.

She held my hand, leading me down winding stairs. My vision tunneled on a curved street lined with driveways, mailboxes, and trees. I stumbled into the street and saw a blur of city lights in the distance.

"Out of the street!" Johanna yelled, grabbing my arm, pulling me back onto the sidewalk.

"Where are bushes?" I asked, hoping to barf out the evil.

"Everywhere."

I would have barfed in the middle of the street if it helped get the horrible feeling out. She stood there quietly as I groaned, clutching my stomach, holding my forehead. The evil spread to my legs, and I lost the strength to stand. Both of my legs had fallen asleep. I fell to follow them, wherever they went.

Johanna broke my fall and held me up, repeating, "Let's just get you to my car, let's just get you to my car, let's just get you to my car," as I dragged myself along with her.

Her baby-blue Volvo wagon appeared. She propped me against cold metal as I heard the jingle of keys.

"Here," she said, opening the car door. "Just sit in the back seat, and I'll roll down the window in case you need to puke. Do you think you can get in the car by yourself?"

I couldn't form words, so she helped me inside. The leather was cold as I slid my hands across the seat, twisting my bottom to propel my legs into the car with me. She grabbed my feet and put them on the floor, shut my door, and walked around to sit with me on the other side. I tried to think of what shoes I was wearing and couldn't remember.

"Do you still feel sick?" she asked. "Do you want some water?"

I heard the swish and crackle of plastic and knew she was handing me something, but I couldn't open my hand. And I couldn't answer her questions. She was sitting within arm's distance. A weight fell into my right hand. I clenched it but couldn't lift it. My usual dissociative Special K state had gone from invincible to immobile, and I lost my grip on the water bottle. I didn't know if Johanna took it or if it fell to the floor or if it disappeared into thin air.

I'd witnessed Paul in a K-hole at a rave before and knew it wouldn't last long. You had to let it run its course. You could go to the emergency room, but that was the last resort. Special K is a short-lived high, and the K-hole usually lasts fifteen or twenty minutes. When it happened to Paul, he sat cross-legged with his back against a wall, appearing drunk, slurring his speech, and rolling his head around. Johanna sat next to him, talking him through it, just like she was with me. I watched this for a minute and then left because it made me feel uncomfortable. When I saw Paul dancing at the party an hour later, he seemed fine, so I figured it couldn't have been too bad.

But I was frozen within my body, unable to move.

Looking out the window, I strained to see a blur of gold lights but mostly saw darkness. My eyes were heavy and burning like hot glue. I thought maybe I could sleep off the bad trip, so I closed them.

"No!" Johanna yelled from down the street and around the corner. "Don't fall asleep." Cue the survival rule of *Nightmare on Elm Street*: Don't, fall, asleep.

My body swayed, but only because Johanna was shaking me. I mumbled, "Don't touch, I'm going to puke!"

"That's why your window is open," she said. "In case you need to puke."

I sensed her watching me, probably glad she wasn't suffering too. We'd snorted the same amount, why had I fallen into a K-hole and she hadn't? Of course, if she did, we'd both be screwed. We could have passed out at the party, and maybe Gerald and his friends would have found us sleeping in a bed together and had their way with us. It was terrifying, imagining what it would be like to watch what was happening around me, or to me, and not being able to stop it. Or I could have gone out like Jimi Hendrix, choking on my vomit while Johanna snoozed inches away. Or what if we'd both passed out in the street, been run over, and woken up in a hospital to find ourselves really, truly paralyzed.

"Let me put some music on. That might help." She leaned forward through the seats and reached for the car stereo. "Just try to keep your eyes open, okay?"

"Eyes open. Eyes open. Eyes open."

I couldn't move my body or my head, but I could move my eyeballs. So I focused and looked to the right, then down, then left, then up. Right, down, left, up. That made me feel woozy again and I yelled, "Fuck! This sucks!"

The breeze coming in through the window helped me stay awake. I focused on breathing the cold air in. I turned my eyes downward, and my heavy head followed. Looking at my chest underneath a gray sweatshirt, I took a deep breath and squinted to see if the upside-down "Timberland" embroidered across my chest moved. It took a few tries to see it. I was still breathing. Things were looking up.

A Tribe Called Quest's playful rhymes drifted around, soothing me with their familiarity. The K-hole already felt like it had lasted for hours. It had to be over soon. I retraced the evening and sort of remembered the house party, but I couldn't remember anything from earlier that day. Or yesterday. Or from the week. It was all thick and heavy and lost.

"Tell me a story, Jo. Keep me awake."

She was quiet for an eternal minute, then began. "I was just reading about DMT, a hallucinogen that comes from rare, exotic plants in the Amazon. You can smoke it, and you get super high for only, like, thirty seconds after one hit. You're in an entirely different world. Everything around you disappears. You can hallucinate so strongly that you're out-of-body, like, for real. You have out-of-body visuals for, like, five minutes, then you have a hella strong acid trip for only forty-five minutes. Doesn't that sound cool?"

Who talks about getting higher when your best friend is struggling to find her way back to sobriety? Crazy shady bitch. I wanted a funny story with a happy ending. Paul had seemed fine after his K-hole, but I was so far from fine I couldn't remember what fine was like, and I knew this was in the opposite direction. I mean, I couldn't remember what shoes I was wearing.

I blurted, "I'm fine!"

"You are?"

Remember my snow globe? Glittering, calming, full of magic? It was empty now, drained and lifeless. Somehow it had ended up in the gutter, tossed aside. That's what the K-hole felt like; I was a ragdoll, limbs flailing, face stuck in a fake smile. I was lost, chasing something I'd already found. Lost and found.

Black Adidas shell toes.

My limbs awoke from a deep sleep. My thighs, stomach, arms, neck, I smoothed my hands along my body to make sure everything was there, resting them across my chest like a corpse. The nausea was gone. I took a deep breath, but it didn't create any space or relief in my body. Nothing.

Within twenty minutes, I went from frozen to thawed. Sober, but not fine. Another drug had betrayed me. I couldn't believe that the quick thrill of Special K could have such an intense bad trip. It didn't make sense.

I turned to look at Johanna and, through a fake smile, said, "I'm fine."

35 / KEEP PUSHIN'

One evening in May, my mom approached me in the TV room. Her eyes were red and swollen, and I knew something was very wrong. She sat down next to me and said she'd just gotten off the phone with the father of a family we were friends with. His wife had suffered a stroke and was in the hospital in a coma.

I instantly thought about her kids, a boy and a girl we'd grown up spending Thanksgivings with who were close in age to Reed and Justin. I'd always looked up to the daughter because she was friendly and a superstar swimmer. And the brother was super cute; I'd always had a secret crush on him. My heart sank for them knowing their mother could die. I didn't know what to say or how to react, and I couldn't help but cry too. It was a shock of unbelievable sadness.

My dad was in Seattle for business, and he was coming home early so they could visit Adeline in the hospital. "To say goodbye," my mom said as I held her, crying with her, silently thanking somebody, something, that it wasn't my mom in a coma.

"It's okay if you don't want to come to the hospital." She sniffed. "It will be hard."

"I want to come," I said, wanting to be there for my parents and our friends, to say goodbye to this other mom who was a special person my parents loved.

Justin had finals at college in Oregon, so he couldn't make it. My parents and I met Reed at the hospital soon after we heard the news. There were hugs and tears, and not many words exchanged that could make the situation more bearable. It was real life at its worst. I hoped my being there helped in some way.

When I walked toward the hospital bed where Adeline was lying, everything was dim and still. I hardly recognized her. Her face, which I remembered as beautiful—glowing olive skin and red lipstick—was pale and stuck in a distorted look. She had wires going into her nose and wrapping around her arms. Slow beeps on a machine provided a gloomy soundtrack. Reed and I held hands. I couldn't speak, but I said goodbye.

My parents suggested I go back to Oakland with Reed in his car. Irish diaspora folk-thrash infused with alcoholism was playing on the stereo as he drove. My brother said it was The Pogues. I'd never heard of them. I told him about my new school and then ran out of things to say. He started crying, and the car swerved. I asked him if he was okay to drive.

He shook his head and I said, "Take the next exit."

He exited and pulled over at a gas station. He got out of the car, and I did too, and I walked around the car to hug him. We stood holding each other, sobbing, while the rest of the world zoomed around us.

"Everything's going to be okay," he told me.

"Everything's going to be okay," I repeated.

With the help of tutors, I finished my junior year without having to attend summer school to make up for the time I'd lost being out of school. I managed to rave, do crystal every weekend, and keep my grades up. I was a functioning meth head. Tommy and I regularly smoked bowls after school, with the occasional nitrous binge.

When the last week of school rolled around, I was looking forward to something that was my parents' best idea ever: a ten-day educational trip to Greece with Johanna, Naomi, and some other girls from my old school.

My parents had registered and paid for the trip in the fall, and even though I'd left the school, I was still eligible to go. It was the first time I'd travel internationally without my parents. I packed my khaki JNCOs, white jeans, sundresses, and bikinis, with my sights set on the island-hopping part of the trip after the first days spent touring Athens.

Johanna offered me some crystal after we'd arrived at our foreign apartment in Athens, choosing roommates and claiming beds. I hadn't brought any drugs since I didn't want to risk flying internationally with it, but Johanna dared.

We watched cheesy Euro TV, spun out, trying to get comfortable on a small couch in the dark, while the other girls slept the first night. It was warm and balmy in the entry room of the apartment. White linen curtains blew around like ghosts, the French doors open on the terrace overlooking the exotic city below. I wondered why I'd chosen to be awake when I knew I should be sleeping and recovering from the jet lag. It felt wrong to be awake still, and I envied the girls who hadn't taken drugs and would adjust to the time change easier than me.

The rest of the trip, I soaked up naturally induced freedom in a blue-and-white country with delicious food and welcoming locals. Our troop of nineteen American girls and one boy (lucky guy) explored the Greek Isles by way of an intimate cruise ship, tour buses, and cool teacher chaperones. I drank alcohol, skinny dipped in the Aegean, and had healthy teenage girl fun. It was the longest I'd been drug-free in months, and it gave me a glimpse of life with a clear, positive mind.

36

DA BOMB
SQUAD

Infectious Grooves, July 1997
Homies: Tommy, Johanna, Clayton, Josh, Krista, Jill
Location: Second and Jackson, Oakland
Drugs: Crystal

Greece kicked off my summer, and I returned home re-freshed and tanned. I continued therapy every week and started a job working at a smoothie shop in Montclair. Crystal was my go-to drug, and Clayton kept an erection. He finally met my parents, and we were totally in love. All was well.

I found out that Luca and Angel had burned out and quit the rave scene. Evan, Julie, and Defne were still around, however, and they were getting deeper into crystal too. We made some new friends who also enjoyed insomnia and burning brain cells. Mr. Frosty White. Ms. Aquamarine. Ms. Metallic. Tommy and I had become part of a clique. We called ourselves Da Bomb Squad.

The Second and Jackson warehouse in Oakland was the venue du jour. It was in the Jack London area, close to the marina where we'd boarded for Splish. The rest of the neighborhood was industrial warehouses, which made it a prime spot for raves.

Da Bomb Squad got to Infectious Grooves early, before it started, because of VIP access we got through Clayton. He was doing graphics for a local clothing company called Estilo that had a booth at parties—a job that was boosting his ego and his bank account. I was proud of him.

While he helped set up the stand, the rest of us started doing lines. The DJ and water tables were still setting up. No one seemed to mind the group of kids standing together snorting loudly, fast talking, talking shit. We didn't care. We were VIPs who owned the party.

"Damn it!" Tommy stomped his foot. "Pardon me." He rushed off toward the porta-potties.

"What's up with him?" Krista asked. She was a petite blonde with ocean-blue eyes who looked innocent but was the first person I ever saw smoke crystal (rather than snort it).

"Oh." I sighed. "Tommy has this problem. Whenever he starts doing lines, he pukes. He's usually okay after the first line though."

Looking back, it's obvious his body was rejecting the drug. Clearly, we didn't know how to listen to our bodies when they were crying for help.

The music started, the lights dimmed, and the two rooms started filling out. Bored, I did some bumps. I had a ring with a small mirror on it about the size of a dollar coin. All I had to do was tap-tap my baggy of crystal onto my ring, and a bump appeared. Then disappeared.

Jill walked up to us. "What's up, you stylin' bitch?"

She was a year older and leaving for college in SoCal at the end of the summer. She always had a full face of makeup on (even in the wee hours, post-shower, cracked out, and hanging in Johanna's Chill Basement) and wanted to be an actress.

One look at Jill and I was annoyed at her for wearing an outfit too similar to mine: khaki JNCOs and a red tee. The raver style of our clique was preppy-pretty, and we layered tees and vests over Polo shirts, and rhinestone necklaces. There was something ironic about dressing prim while doing hard drugs.

"Ugh, asshole Cosmic forgot to put me on the list." Jill rolled her eyes. "He's lucky I had extra money, or else that motherfucker would be serious toast. I have been taking a month-long vacation from crystal, and this is my first party since, thank you. I just had a line and thought I was going to come. Oops, was that vulgar?"

I was going to answer "yes" when she continued, "This party's kinda shafty, but I'm having fun, just looking super fly in my new gear my ex-boy bought me."

I grabbed Clayton's hand. "Let's go find the circle."

Swiftly walking away, I vented, "Ugh, her new gear that is completely unoriginal. Did you not notice that she's, like, wearing the same 'fit as me? Leggo my Ego."

Clayton shrugged and lit a cigarette.

"Didn't you just smoke one, like, a minute ago?" I asked him. "You fucking smoker."

He looked at me with sad puppy dog eyes, which further agitated me. I took off and joined Johanna, who was watching the breakdancing circle.

Tommy ran up to us. "Oh my god, you'll never believe what's going on over there." He pointed to a corner. "There's a dog on Ecstasy."

"What?!" I exclaimed. "Let's go see."

We followed Tommy through the crowd.

"It's so fucked up, it's so fucked up, it's so fucked up," he repeated.

There was a crowd standing around a large brown dog. A Lab, maybe. A girl and a guy were sitting on the floor, petting the dog obsessively. Empty water bottles surrounded them. Between the flashing lights, you could see the dog was panting. The girl was holding the dog by the collar and shaking her head, crying. There was a large bowl of water. The dog was restless and kept circling while the girl held on to him, trying to calm him down.

We stood watching, shocked. My stomach twisted. I wondered if I should do something, but I didn't know what the right thing to do was. I couldn't think right.

"What the fuck?" Johanna said. "Who would give a dog ecstasy?"

"It's so fucked up. I can't watch this," Tommy said, already walking away.

I silently agreed. It was the definition of bad vibes. I pushed my emotions aside and followed Tommy to do another line.

Me, Johanna, Krista, and Jill tried to pose for a picture together, but we couldn't stop talking.

"I've been up for twenty-seven hours now, and no matter which way you look at it, it sure as hell ain't normal," Johanna told me.

"Honey, I'm all kinds of tired."

Clayton popped by, handed me a half-full baggie, said, "I'm hella spinnin' off this shit, word!" and ran back into the crowd.

"Dude, can you get Clayton a nose plug? He's out of control," Johanna said.

"Jill was being mean," Krista pouted. "She just tried to apologize, and do you know what she said? 'I didn't mean to hurt your feelings, I just wanted to see you cry.' What a biotch."

We stopped talking because Paul walked by. Johanna had just broken up with him.

"Can you guys stand still for one picture, please?!" Tommy yelled.

"Um, maybe it's not us and it's you!" I yelled back.

"Whatever! My hand's all jittery, but I'm dealing with it! You all need to chill and smile for the camera."

"Do you know the deets about what happened with Jo and Paul?" Krista asked me.

"All I know is he's been fucking up and totally slacking. He can't hold a job and he's always broke. She was just over it."

"I was sitting next to the fan, and my hair got stuck in it," Jill said, smacking her gum.

"I'm so happy you're a Scorpio too," Krista said. "There could not be a more bomb-ass, kick-ass, wonderful, outright tops sign."

"My mind is thinking faster than my mouth," I said.

"My nose has issues with tissues," Krista said, wiping her nose.

"Well, now that I'm swingin' single, I'm less stressed," Johanna said. "I hope Clayton treats you with as much respect and love as you deserve. Never settle for less than you deserve. It hurts too much."

I nodded fast to the thudding trance.

I was going to ask her for another line when she smiled and said, "I spy with my little eye a cutie and his name is Josh."

I'd always thought something was going on between Johanna

and Josh, and not just him supplying her with crystal. I wondered once again if they'd hooked up while she and Paul were together.

He walked up to Johanna. "Yo, I've got a grip of money and no meth—can I buy some off you?"

Clayton came back around. "What it is, man?" he said to Josh, grinding his jaw. "I'm going so fast. Word!"

"I want what he's got, damn it!" Josh said. His sideburns were expertly groomed.

Johanna smiled at him. "I'm sure something can be arranged."

She totally cheated, I thought. *Scandalicious.*

"My eyes are wiggin' out," Tommy announced.

After a long sniff, Josh turned to me. "Hey, thanks for the bracelet. I've never actually worn one but maybe, if you're lucky, I'll wear it."

I gave him a fake smile and said, "Let's go dance."

"I'm not in the mood," Josh whined.

"Okay, well then, you can stay with your girlfriend Jo Jo," I said, and headed for the dance area.

I danced for about five minutes before I got bored and wanted another bump.

Tommy and I ran into a friend of a friend.

"Hey, babe, hey, doll face," he greeted us. "Mr. Peach in the house, sucka!"

"Um, dude, you're not Mr. Peach," I corrected him. "You're Mr. Platinum."

"Fact," Tommy said.

"I'm surprised you actually remember, tweakers," Mr. Platinum snapped, walking away.

"Oh no he didn't!" Tommy yelled after him. "What a tool."

I waved him off. "Whatever, we look better than him. You know, I don't even think he should be in the Color Club anymore, because you need to be nice to us. We are the presidents, after all. "

"For real, though."

The Color Club empowered me and Tommy. We weren't DJs or promoters or producers of raves, but it gave us a sense of ownership in the scene—made us feel important, like we were leaders, not followers. It was a creative idea that people liked and wanted to be a part of, a piece of art we'd created together. The growing membership of the Color Club was validation that we had arrived in the rave scene.

I dug into the fifth pocket of my pants to get my crystal. Looking at the mini baggy in my palm through blurs of blue and green, I saw that it was empty.

"We have a bigger crisis on our hands." I turned to Tommy. "I'm all out of crystal."

"Damn."

37

BREAKDOWN

"Did you hear that?" Clayton asked, sitting up in bed. The waterbed swished me awake.

"Huh?" I muttered.

"I think there's someone outside," he whispered.

The red numbers on the clock by the bed read 3:32 a.m. It was early on a Monday in August, and we'd been sleeping for a few hours. We'd gone to a rave Saturday, then Strawberry Sundays, before leaving our friends and heading to Clayton's to clean up and come down together. By then, I'd already been fired from my job at the smoothie shop for calling in sick every week. Oops.

Clayton paced next to the bed in the dark, mumbling to himself. Or was he mumbling to me?

"I don't know. I'm pretty sure I heard someone out there." He went over to the window, peeked out the curtain. "Should I go check?"

I listened and didn't hear anything. Shivering, I bent over to get a sweatshirt from the pile of clothes next to the bed. I couldn't see in the shadows and reached for the floor lamp switch, the bed clapping against my bare thigh.

He whisper-yelled, "No! They'll see the light."

Whoa—he had my attention now. *Who is "they?"* I wondered.

Moonlight gleamed through a crack in the curtains. Clayton's hair was spiked and his boxers swam on him. The slim, toned skater physique he'd had when we first met had dwindled to skin and bones. He was pacing again, still mumbling.

"Clayton, are you okay?"

He came over and knelt next to me. "I'm going to go check. You stay here. Keep an eye on me through the window. Do not turn on any lights, okay?" The red numbers of the clock illuminated his eyes, giving them a devilish tint.

I cautiously stood up to put the sweatshirt on. He opened the door to the outside, and noticing he was only wearing boxers, I said, "Wait! It's freezing out there. Here," and threw him the sweatshirt. The sweatshirt hit him and fell to the floor. He slowly held his finger up to his mouth and said, "Shhhh."

The door closed behind him.

I picked up the sweatshirt, put it on, and walked to the window. I peeked through the curtains. The backyard was small, square-shaped, with a splotchy grass lawn and random tools lying around.

Clayton was clearer in the moonlight, a rare occurrence in foggy Pacifica. Stoop-shouldered, he darted back and forth across the lawn. At certain angles, you could see his ribs rippling through his skin. His lips were moving, and he kept stopping and holding his head, pulling at his hair, and then walking again. He glanced at me, his face hardened. Intense, wild, lost, I recognized that look. My stomach clenched.

Paranoid Android.

I rushed out the door to help him.

He hurried over to me. "What are you doing? Go back inside!"

"I was thinking maybe it was Ginger out here making noises," I said calmly, pretending to look around for his dog.

He grabbed my arms, turned me around, and pushed me back toward his room. "They're out here. It's not safe!"

"Clayton." I took his icy hands into mine. "It's just Ginger. I think I saw her," I lied.

He stared at me, then his hands broke from mine and he violently scratched his head, shook it, held it tightly with his eyes squeezed closed. I reached to grab him to make him stop, but he broke his fit by throwing his hands down and calling out, "No! Stop!" like a kid throwing a tantrum.

Then he took off running toward the side of the house.

"Clayton!" I yelled, chasing after him, wet grass prickling my bare feet. I followed him along the path that hugged the side of the house, slowing past a lawn mower and garden junk stowed along the sides. On the other side of the front gate, the grass became hard gravel.

I ran onto the sidewalk. Moonlight switched to golden street light. Houses with dimmed windows stretched around me.

Clayton ran into the middle of the street, dropped to the ground, and hugged himself into a ball. I followed him, kneeling, pieces of gravel piercing my knees. He was holding his head, shaking it, saying, "They're going to get us," again and again.

I threw my arms around his shoulders. "Clayton, it's okay, it's just us." I tried to pull him up to stand. "It's okay, it's just us," I repeated. "It's okay, it's just us." I kept grabbing at him to get him to stand up, hoping he'd wake up from the dark place he was stuck in. *Paranoia.* The dark place I'd been before. *Paranoia.* "It's okay, it's just us." *Paranoia.*

After a few minutes, he stopped talking. I stopped grabbing. He stood up. I mirrored him, steady, ready in case he took off again. His eyes were bloodshot, pleading. I hugged him. We stood holding each other in the middle of the street in the middle of the night in our underwear (plus one sweatshirt). I didn't know what had just happened, but it was unpleasantly familiar.

38

SPUN OUT

The next week, we were on a bender. Blame it on DJ Paulina Taylor's happy hardcore mixtape, *Bounce*. It kept us going going going (along with an endless crystal supply). We'd been up for three days, going on four—the longest I'd gone without sleep. We hadn't planned it that way, but Therapy Thursday had turned into a sleepless Friday night in Johanna's Chill Basement and then a rave called Kundalini on Saturday night. We'd looped around Berkeley and Pacifica and the city, snorting, showering, smoking, and forgetting to eat. Who needs food when you're feeding off crystal?

It was a sunny Sunday, and I was driving Johanna, Clayton, and Josh back to Pacifica, cruising along the 80 freeway through San Francisco. We were in the Lude, Johanna passenger-side, the boys in the back. With heavy eyes and a delirious head, I was on autopilot. Josh was protesting about listening to *Bounce* yet again.

"Tough shit," I said, turning up the volume. Johanna and I bobbed our heads and shoulders.

A lot of people hated on happy hardcore. It was nonstop, hyper, super cheesy. Rainbows. Glitter. Flowers. Methamphetamine. If happy hardcore came in a capsule, it would be the best antidepressant. It's about four times faster than house music. Faster than trance. So fast it's exhausting to dance to. Mood waker. Brain shaker. Crazy maker.

Going a cool seventy in a middle lane, a ninja car crossed in front of us into the fast lane. I perked up when I heard a familiar purr over our fantastic boombastic beats. It was a Ferrari. Fast. Sexy. Black.

Get closer. Catch it. I edged my way over to the fast lane and sped up to get behind it. Thudding claps mimicked my speeding pulse.

My vision on the Batmobile narrowed. Its sharp lines and sequin lights pulled me in, seducing me. My speedometer crept to eighty. Our turnoff onto another freeway was soon, but I needed to get closer and faster. Closer, faster. Closer faster.

A jolt pushed me out of the lane. I tightened my hands on the wheel, eased off the gas, trying to get back in the lane. It was too late. I was going too fast. Fast-forward. Rewind. I lost control.

The Ferrari disappeared. I eased off the gas more, jerking the wheel left, then right, trying to stay away from the cement divider. *This isn't happening.* Gray, black, and white streaked across the windows. *Fuck, this is happening. We're spinning out.* My hands froze on the wheel. My foot pushed the brake. The car threw me to the left. The Lude took over. Everything disappeared.

We stopped, and my back slammed against the seat. I heard Johanna gasp over the music. We were in the middle of the freeway. Sideways across four lanes. The cement divider was in front of us. No Ferrari, no cars. *Where did everyone go?* Around us was a halo of open road.

I looked over my shoulder. A row of cars was coming at us.

Is this a dream? Game over. *Wake up!* I shoved the car in reverse, shot us backward.

The Lude smashed into the bushes along the shoulder of the freeway. Cars blurred past us. I was holding my breath. My hands were stuck to the wheel. My body shook from adrenaline. The music was too much, too loud, too fast, and I unlocked my hand from the wheel to turn it off. My jaw popped, releasing itself. Johanna's hands were gripping the front seat by her thighs. She was ghostly pale.

Exhale.

"That was fucking awesome!" Josh blurted from the back seat.

"Unreal!" Clayton yelled.

"Oh my god," Johanna whispered. "Samantha, are you okay?"

I wanted to scream, "What the fuck just happened?!" but I couldn't speak. It had all happened too fast for me to feel anything but survival instinct. So I just sat, realizing. Shock consumed me. It was surreal. I knew I'd just pulled off an impossible maneuver, but what had compelled me to drive like Mario Andretti in the first place? Ferrari Ravioli. Ms. Red. Who did I think I was?

What's crazier? Pumping yourself full of drugs or chasing a Ferrari in a Honda Prelude? The spinout may have impressed the boys, but it had terrified me. I knew I'd gone too far and was deeply disturbed. I could have killed myself and my friends. Somehow we were unscathed, but clearly, I'd finally snapped.

"Uh, guys," Josh said. "We should go before a cop sees us."

"I, I can't drive," I stammered.

"I got you, girl," Josh said, already unbuckling his seatbelt.

I reached to open the door to trade seats with Josh, but then I paused—I didn't want to leave the safe cocoon of my car.

"We're okay," Johanna whispered. "But we need to go."

The door clicked and I pushed it open. I stepped into the bush, fluffy ivy cushioning my feet. Hair blew in my face. The loud, whipping sounds of cars passing scared me. I hurried to flip my seat forward. Josh stepped out, and I got in the back seat with Clayton. He tried to wrap his arm around me, but I felt claustrophobic and stiffly sat back in the seat. I buckled my seatbelt and looked out the window at the freeway. It was sunny, clear, flowing, as if something miraculous hadn't just happened.

In a daze, I kept applying and reapplying strawberry Lip Smackers as Josh drove. All I could think about was my family and how heartbroken they would have been if we'd crashed. With how fast the cars were coming toward us, we would have died on impact. My parents would have found the Bad Box, listened to the tapes, and known the truth about me—that I was a materialistic, lying, raving addict. An ungrateful daughter. A spoiled brat. A selfish asshole. I thought I'd successfully dulled all my bad feelings with drugs, but the guilt was torturous. My demons were attacking me like a jackhammer, loud and violent.

I hoped once we got to Clayton's and smoked a bowl, I'd feel better. That was my usual fix for the cracked-out blues. But I wasn't sure I could smoke away what had happened. The countless times I'd driven on drugs had caught up with me. Karma. Carma.

Yet I'd lucked out, again. In the seconds the spinout happened, someone, something, had been watching over us, protecting us from catastrophe. It was a miracle.

But it was also a warning. This was the closest I'd ever been to death. I knew then, I didn't want to take another chance with my life.

39

HAPPY HARDCORE

In the weeks following the crazy Clayton episode and the spinout, with around fifty raves on my list, I came to the sobering realization that I needed to change direction. I'd spooked myself enough to want to live past seventeen. What had started as trippy escalated into self-destruction. An epiphany had become insanity.

I concluded that Clayton had had a nervous breakdown that night he ran out of his room. It wasn't a bad trip like when I was a Paranoid Android on acid; we'd been sober-ish when it happened. But we had also been seriously sleep deprived, and raver life had caught up with him too.

It was catching up with all of us. The wheels were falling off our Further bus, and it was Clayton's turn to crash.

Only after that, instead of feeling empathy for Clayton, I was resentful. And I wasn't just resenting him. Since I'd started raving, I went from being in the drama club to being in a drama clique. Bad trips. Dying ravers. K-holes. Tweakers. Drugged dogs. Nervous breakdowns. Spin-outs. The excess I loved about raves had gotten to be too intense. I'd had enough.

I remember taking an epic shower where I cried the hardest

I ever had—a soul-shaking cry where I purged emotions, questioning and cursing and yelling at myself, rage spilling out of me and down the drain. I'd been holding all my traumas in, and crying was a cathartic way I could process them. I don't know why I was holding back. Trying to be tough, I suppose.

I felt a little better after that shower. My raving life had consisted of lots of mindless trips, but they accumulatively helped me reach a mindful decision: cut out the toxic drugs and people in my life. In the last weeks of summer before my senior year, I changed course.

Clayton was different after his breakdown. He was needy, smothering me when I wanted space to figure things out. The way he held his cigarette, the way he said "word" all the time, his lack of ambition, everything about him annoyed me. I broke up with him. It may sound cruel, but I couldn't look past who he'd become. I saw in him a side of myself I'd come to hate. We were broken, and we needed to move on.

I broke up with crystal too. I realized what a dumb and dangerous drug it was. And the insomnia was killing me. I'd lost weight, and not in a good way—I'd dropped a bra size, and my hip bones jutted out. My senses had dulled, and I was operating on a lesser level every day. I was tired of being tired. I was only seventeen! I should have been in my physical prime.

Above all, crystal was hindering my creativity. I'd stopped tape recording when I started using it every weekend. I wasn't as social as I had been in the acid and ecstasy days, and I didn't care about capturing rave moments anymore. The weekends had started blurring together. My passion for raving had fizzled.

I broke up with the clique. I was friendly with everyone at parties, but I didn't do lines with them anymore. I kept my distance and hung out with Chris's crew, kids who smoked weed and did the occasional hit of E. Johanna and Tommy continued to do crystal. When I saw them sneak off at parties together, my heart would ache from jealousy. Not because I wanted crystal but because I missed them. I was confident in our friendships, though, and was sure they'd come around and quit crystal too, eventually, hopefully.

I'm sure I went through withdrawals, but I don't remember feeling any worse than being burnt out. Maybe being seventeen helped me there.

It wasn't all bad. My parents and I were getting along. I was kind of excited to start my senior year. And I didn't break up with raves. They were still my happy place. I thought maybe I could be someone who could have fun without being fucked up. Someone like Dreya, the coolest girl of all.

I had always believed in signs, believed that things happened for a reason. And, starting from this point in my life, I also became a believer in gratitude. When you find yourself in stressful or dangerous situations, there are doors that will lead you into a darker world. Which door you choose to go through isn't necessarily wrong or right—it's your choice which way you go—but if you read the signs, you can avoid going deeper down the rabbit hole. I followed the signs in the wrong direction for a while, until I was so lost that I stopped reading the signs altogether. I just sped past them. Lucky for me, I was given more than one second chance.

During my senior year of high school, I still raved almost every weekend. I swapped lines of crystal for vanilla lattes from Starbucks at 10:00 p.m., smoking weed, and then heading home to sleep in my bed.

It's no coincidence that when I found my new sober, my parents gave up on holding me to a curfew. Each time I went out, I told my parents I was going to "a party" and would be home late. And every time, they reiterated that I should call if I ever drank and needed to be picked up—anywhere, anytime, no questions asked. To think, after everything, my parents were concerned about me drinking and driving. But there was nowhere else I wanted to go but home once the music got redundant, the warehouse got stuffy, and my eyes got heavy.

I reintroduced myself to the rest of the world, religiously watching *Friends* every Thursday night, devouring the pages of *Vogue* every month, and taking up Billy Blanks' Tae Bo. After months of sparring and hitting punching bags, I regained my appetite and physical strength. My sleep habits regulated and my head quieted; I felt strong and focused.

The Bay Area rave scene was heavily influenced by hip-hop and turntablism toward the end of the '90s. Talent like De La Soul and Cut Chemist headlined rave flyers. I saw Run-DMC perform at a small club in Alameda, Adidas out, attitude on. I became a fixture alongside the breakdancing circles, sitting in my tripod chair with my prom 'do watching the cute breakers, admiring their athletic moves and dope styles.

In my last semester, I wrote my senior report on "Aerosol Art," a history of graffiti. I approached it with the same enthusiasm as the papers I'd written before I started raving. It ended up being of coffee-table book proportions, complete with colorful examples animating the pages and interviews with local artists. I got an A+ and a note saying it was the best project in class.

Taking E at a party still felt good once in a while, but that A+ felt better. And I know I wouldn't have been inspired by graffiti or tattoos (which I continued to get throughout my life) if it hadn't been for Clayton.

A turning point for me in this whole journey was when I started therapy, which was my dad's idea. My therapist not only helped me identify feelings and problem solve but also paved the way for me to be more open and trust adults. I still see the same therapist in Oakland.

Here's some math. By the time I was twenty, I'd attended 104 raves in California. I'd taken about fifty pills of E, thirty hits of acid, ten doses of magic mushrooms, a handful of Ketamine lines, five caps of GHB, one hit of mescaline, and countless nitrous balloons. I couldn't tell you how many bowls, joints, edibles, and bong loads I had. And I'd like to forget how many lines of cocaine and crystal—two highly addictive drugs I don't see any spiritual benefit in doing—I put up my nose.

I dropped acid one more time, in 1998, at Nocturnal Wonderland in LA. I didn't get paranoid and had a fabu time riding my trip out in the hallway of a motel with a friend (carpets really are so fascinating on acid).

I kept in touch with many of my friends after we were past our raving prime. The bonds we forged while raving together were strong; we'd survived together. That was something we could always look back on, knowing we were a part of historical magic. Some of us went to college, some entered the workforce, some sobered up, and some battled addictions as adults—and some didn't make it. RIP Mr. Neon Green.

Sex and the City debuted in June 1998, igniting my fantasy of living the fabulous single girl life in New York City, which then became a reality. I soon moved across the country to attend the Fashion Institute of Technology. Raving had fizzled by then, the early 2000s, and became what is now EDM and festival culture, but I had my sights set on something bigger: landing a job at *Vogue*.

If I were to choose a color to represent myself now, it wouldn't be red. Ms. Red seems too fiery and aggressive for who I've become: writer, editor, sister, daughter, wife, mother, traveler, Californian, yogi, retired raver. My color today would be purple.

One of the rules of the Color Club was that no one could be purple because red and blue made purple, and Tommy and I had Purple Power. I'm breaking our rule now because, well, I'm a rule-breaker, and when it comes to creativity, there are no rules. It's an expansive process without rules and bounds. It's magic that comes from within. It took me a while to understand that, but eventually—with some falls along the way—I found that magic for myself.

But I couldn't have done it on my own. I was able to come into my power because of the boundless love of my family, the people I always knew would be there, no matter how many wrong turns I made.

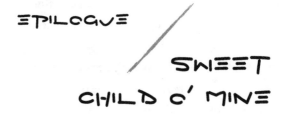

EPILOGUE / SWEET CHILD O' MINE

When I found out about the Day on the Green concert happening in Oakland in September 1992, I begged my parents to let me go. They'd taken Reed to see Judas Priest when he was twelve. Same same, right? This was my chance to see my favorite band, Guns N' Roses.

My dad said yes, but only if he and my mom went too. I was annoyed by the idea of parent chaperones, but I didn't have any other choice. And really, my dad also liked their music and was looking forward to it.

Guns N' Roses' *Use Your Illusion* albums had come out the year before. On the verge of adolescence, I was lifted and soothed by the tumultuous rock. It provided an outlet for all the conflicting emotions I was feeling for the first time. I had also developed an immense crush on Axl Rose. His swagger, squeal, arrogance, he was a bad boy with extreme talent.

I hated his girlfriend, Stephanie Seymour. I knew her from the *Victoria's Secret* catalogs I studied, hoping I would grow up to look like the models in them. Perfect bodies, seductive looks—they were impossibly gorgeous. Stephanie and I both had a cleft nose, and I'd liked her as a supermodel before I found out she was dating Axl in real life. The "November Rain" music video broke me, and she became the enemy. An enemy whose high-heels I wished I could step into.

Of course, I couldn't have Axl, because he was famous—and only because of that reason—but I wanted to be his object of affection more than anything.

Justin said he wanted to go to the concert too. Relieved, I made a secret plan: my best friend, Jamie, and I would ditch my parents when we got there and hang with my brother, especially since I had a crush on his friend. (At that age I crushed on all his friends. But Axl was my #1.)

Jamie and I dressed nearly identical for the concert: black bodysuits, baggy jeans, flannel shirts tied around our waists, and Doc Martens. Entering the Oakland coliseum, I was in awe and intimidated by the tough crowd in their black leather and tattered denim. At twelve, Jamie and I may have been the youngest people there, but at least we'd dressed the part.

Two years earlier, I'd gone to my first concert at the Oakland Coliseum: New Kids on the Block. I'd also worn denim that night, but of the acid-wash variety. Now, instead of romance and the right stuff, I was more interested in hearing about sex, drugs, and Molotov cocktails.

I listened to GNR alone, turned way up in my bedroom, playing dress-up and experimenting with makeup. None of my friends were into them. Jamie was just along for the ride. From pop to rock, my fire had been ignited through music.

Back to 1992. I followed my parents up the bleacher stairs, where they sat down. I looked at the older people around us with their beards and heavy eyeliner and said, "Uh, is it okay if we go closer to the stage?"

As my mom pulled earplugs out of her purse, my dad looked down at the lawn in front of the stage that was filling up fast with people.

"Okay," he said. "But your brother's going with you. And you have to check in with us every hour."

It was fair, and it wouldn't be hard to find my mom and dad in the crowd with her floral cardigan and his clean-cut hair.

During Body Count and Metallica's performances, I saw mosh pits and people smoking joints for the first time in real life. Jamie and I turned down an offer to smoke from a stranger, a word of advice from Justin that I stuck to. Beer spilled on me, secondhand smoke wafted, and my ass was grabbed countless times. I didn't necessarily like my ass being grabbed, but the naughtiness was exciting.

Waiting for GNR to start, people threw plastic cups and yelled, "Fuck you!" They tore up the grass lawn, throwing lumps of it at each other. I covered my face with my hands, trying to avoid eating a dirty amuse-bouche. A large chunk hit me in the back, leaving a tender spot. Dirt crumbled down my pants. I laughed it off, pretending to be cool when I was edging on scared. We'd lost Justin and his friend. It was a good time to escape the fray and check in with my parents.

After showing my mom and dad we were still alive and promising we'd stay out of the mosh pits, we walked back down the steps toward the stage, my mom yelling, "Be careful!" behind us.

The sun had set, making it harder to navigate through the dense crowd. Saying, "Excuse me," wasn't working very well, so I followed behind a pushy guy who was elbowing his way through. I held Jamie's hand, pulling her along.

A reverberating strum of a guitar commanded the coliseum. We stopped. Everything went dark. I held my breath. The crowd went crazy, yelling and whistling. "Welcome to the Jungle" began. I started jumping. An arm pushed into my shoulder blades, forcing me to step forward. Jamie screeched. I grabbed her so I wouldn't lose her. Standing on my toes, I saw Axl illuminated, standing over a bright white light. He was a vision, belting out his signature squeal.

Clapping echoed around me as I swooned, raged, jumped, quivered, thrashed, and sang along to every song. Strobe lights created full moon spirals when I blinked. My arms pumped, my hips shimmied. Dancing came to me as naturally as breathing.

Then, mayhem. The crowd shoved us closer to the stage. Jamie and I held on to each other while hands pawed my hips. We were squished, trying not to fall, while the crowd pulled at us. In a mosh pit near us, shirtless maniacs ran around playing human bumper cars. I couldn't see Axl anymore. Too many people were in the way. Smoke and BO suffocated me. We were stuck.

"Hey, honey," a deep voice beside me said. "Wanna get on my shoulders?"

Barrel-chested and boasting a walrus mustache and leather jacket with patches all over it, the guy looked like a member of the Hell's Angels. I looked at Jamie. She shook her head. I couldn't leave her to fend for herself.

"All gravy," he said. "My friend can help your friend."

Standing next to him was another badass dude who side-smiled while a cigarette dangled from his mouth. I hadn't sat on a person's shoulders since I was a little girl in our pool. On the count of three, my dad would catapult me, and I'd dive into the water. It was exhilarating.

So, I dove in.

There was a refreshing breeze above everyone. I felt safe, supported by strong shoulders. My feet dangled free. The sky was endless. Gigantic images of the yellow and blue *Use Your Illusion* album covers flanked the stage.

A flannel tied around Axl's waist flapped in the wind. His red-topped microphone looked like a cherry lollipop. Powerful, magnetic, dangerous, he was a tornado. Slash's chiseled torso, meanwhile, shone above tight black leather pants. His top hat bobbed as he played guitar. I couldn't help but notice the sensual thrusts of his hips, one leg bent outward. Matt, with frizzy hair and a manic look, banged the largest drum set I'd ever seen. Duff, also shirtless, was rail thin and pale, with bleached hair and black roots. He shifted around on the bass in sunglasses, so cool.

Brilliant lights flashed up and down, circling the sexy rock gods on the stage. Sweat trickled down Axl's bare chest. One more push and I could smell the Jack Daniels on Slash's breath.

I looked over at Jamie. Her dirty-blond hair was blowing in her face à la music video. She gave me a nervous smile, but her eyes twinkled. She was having fun, the wildest fun she'd ever had.

My seat raised his hands, holding something up to me. It looked like he was holding up a snake. He nudged for me to take it. Stomach fluttering, I reached for the creature. Goosebumps ran up my arms as its smooth, cold skin twined around my fingers, its tail coiled around my wrist, its head pointed in Axl's direction.

My boyfriend sat at a piano under a purple haze on the stage. Everything went quiet, and he drifted into the beautiful piano solo of "November Rain." The crowd howled. I raised the snake in front of me, offering it to Axl, the music, the moment. I swear Axl saw me and smiled. My heart bulged, squeezing out a teardrop of blood.

I was high on life. Okay, I probably got a contact high from the smoky air, but I didn't touch booze or drugs that night. I didn't want any of that. I had everything I needed to have the best experience.

THE COLOR CLUB.
EST. 1996

"Respect & Represent"

1) Ms. Red – Samantha
2) Mr. Blue – Casey
3) Ms. Burgundy – Teagan
4) Ms. Hot Pink – Johanna
5) Mr. Frosty White – Jason R.
6) Mr. Ruby Red – Mason
7) Ms. Irie Green – Micaela
8) Ms. Sapphire – Alexis
9) Mr. Neon Green – Isaac (RIP)
10) Ms. Orange – Jeanette
11) Ms. Gold – Deena
12) Mr. Green – Neilo
13) Mr. Clear – Angel
14) Ms. Blue – Danielle T.
15) Mr. Gold – Dale
16) Ms. Glow in the Dark – Emily
17) Ms. Puke Green – Stephanie
18) Mr. Orange – Eric
19) Mr. Pink – Perfecto
20) Ms. Pink – Shannon
21) Mr. White – Mike B.
22) Ms. White – Margaret

23) Ms. Rainbow – Jenn O.

24) Ms. Beige – Barbie

25) Mr. Platinum – Brian

26) Ms. Foxy Brown – Moana

27) Mr. Foxy Brown – Joel C.

28) Mr. Black – Mark O.

29) Ms. Black – Sarah B.

30) Ms. Yellow – Megan T.

31) Mr. Yellow – Bob C.

32) Mr. Navy Blue – Jim

33) Ms. Light Blue – Tori

34) Mr. Ultra-Violet – Leo

35) Ms. Translucent – Octavia

36) Mr. Fluorescent – Dale R.

37) Ms. Metallic – Anne S.

38) Mr. Red – Nic T.

39) Ms. Citrus – Danielle

40) Mr. Leopard – Steve

41) Ms. Lemony Lime – Natalie

42) Ms. Midnight Blue – Eleanor

43) Mr. Light Blue – Nick L.

44) Ms. Teal – Mary

45) Ms. Bronze – Veka

46) Mr. Silver – Ryan

47) Ms. Frosty White – Annette

48) Ms. Magenta – Tessa

49) Ms. Puce – Nicole

50) Ms. Chartreuse – Abi

51) Ms. Periwinkle – Rebecca

52) Ms. Mandarin – Lindsay L.

53) Ms. Strawberry – Kimberlee

54) Mr. Two-Tone – Jordan

55) Mr. Chrome – Matty

56) Mr. Khaki – Adam

57) Ms. Green – Audra

58) Ms. Apricot – Sunny

59) Mr. Blueberry – Nathan

60) Ms. Peach – Nicole C.

61) Mr. Fuchsia – Ian B.

62) Mr. Pineapple – Joe T.

63) Ms. Iridescent – Katie B.

64) Mr. Jungle Green – Jake

65) Mr. Baby Blue – Jeremiah

66) Ms. Aquamarine – Elle

67) Ms. America – Azure

68) Ms. Root Beer Brown – Babs

69) Mr. Mauve – Jerry

70) Mr. Cerulean – Mike R.

71) Mr. Turquoise – Mike O.

72) Ms. Poppy – Melveena

73) Ms. Scarlet – Nicola

74) Mr. Charcoal – Tiger

75) Mr. Brindle – Diablo

76) Mr. Calico – Rumpy

77) Mr. Hot Orange – Travis

78) Ms. Mochachino – Abby

79) Ms. Indigo – JR

80) Ms. Lemon Meringue – Lindsay

81) Ms. Emerald – Melisa

82) Ms. Jungle Red – Sara S.

83) Mr. Cobalt Blue – Eric N.

84) Ms. Blonde – Robin

85) Mr. Sunkist – Ian

86) Mr. Crystal Clear – Max

87) Mr. School Bus Yellow – Tyler

88) Ms. Pomegranate – Raffaela

89) Mr. Bomb-Ass Blue – Moshe

90) Mr. Infrared – Nils

91) Mr. Mustard – Brenton

92) Mr. Lavender – Peter

93) Mr. Lemon Lime – David M.

94) Ms. Camouflage – Anna S.

95) Mr. Aquamarine – Peter

96) Ms. School Bus Yellow – Morgan

97) Ms. Turquoise – Laura V.

98) Mr. Periwinkle – Kevin

99) Ms. Opal – Erin

100) Mr. Gray – Rob T.

101) Mr. Night Rider Blue – Dre B.

102) Ms. Silver – Kelly

103) Ms. Crimson – Katie M.

104) Mr. Peach – Jonathan

105) Mr. Purple Haze – Mike N.

106) Mr. Royal Blue – Rick C. (RIP)

107) Ms. Alexandrite – Lachelle

108) Mr. Emerald – Andrew F.

109) Mr. Champagne – Jeremy

110) Mr. Green Bud – Goodyear

111) Dr. Plum – Tadish

112) Mr. Butterscotch – Diego

113) Ms. Icon – Maya G.

114) Ms. Baby Pink – Rachel

115) Ms. Diamond – Maya A.

116) Ms. Yellow Polka Dot Bikini – Izabel

117) Ms. Smurfette Blue – Katie H.

118) Ms. Khaki – Nyki

119) Ms. Safety Yellow – Katie B.

120) Mr. Ion – Brian Y.

121) Mr. Onyx – Jono

122) Ms. Indigo – Cyndi

123) Ms. Snow White – Janele

124) Mr. Olive Green – Corey R.

125) Ms. Blaze – Nicole M.

126) Mr. Black Light Responsive – Danny

127) Mr. Mellow Yellow – Rich G.

128) Ms. Butta-scotch-on-the-rox – Mariah

129) Ms. Tan – Lucia

130) Ms. Razzle Dazzle – Emmanuelle

131) Mr. Mango – Jared M.

132) Ms. Ballerina Pink – Judy

133) Mr. Kronic – Dre

134) Dr. Green Thumb – Cris

135) Ms. Cyantastic Sparkle – Reyna

136) Mr. Nitrous Oxide – Mike R.

137) Mr. Pewter – J5

138) Mr. Lani Moo Blue – Jevon

139) Ms. Corona – Theresa

140) Mr. Cinnaman – Antoine

141) Ms. Fuchsia – Anna G.

142) Mr. Creme-de-la-creme – J-Dubb

143) Mr. Wintergreen – Dan B.

144) Mr. Cornflower – Greg J.

145) Mr. Storm Gray – Chuck

146) Ms. Bubblegum – Sarah C.

147) Mr. Bloody Mary – Jim

148) Ms. Purple Mountain Majesty – Nadia

149) Mr. Mocha – Carson

150) Ms. Lady Jade – Catherine

151) Mr. Sapphire – Yates

152) Ms. Blue Jeans – Andrea Z.

153) Ms. Marigold – Mom

154) Mr. Salt & Pepper – Dad

155) Ms. Salt & Pepper – AB

156) Ms. Plum – Linda D.

157) Ms. Glitter – Melissa G.

158) Ms. Sunburst – Dreya

159) Mr. Peanut Butter – Sherman

160) Ms. Dusty Rose – Cara

161) Mr. Marled Gray – Rich

162) Mr. Cuddle Yellow – Donovan

If you're going to party, party safe. Educate yourself with these harm reduction and drug education resources I wish were around when I was coming of age in the '90s:

☺ DanceSafe (dancesafe.org)
Promoting health and safety within the electronic music community

☺ DPA (drugpolicy.org)
Drug Policy Alliance

☺ Drugsco (drugsexco.weebly.com)
Drugs, harm reduction, and counterculture

☺ Erowid (erowid.org)
Documenting the complex relationship between humans & psychoactives

☺ MAPS (maps.org)
Multidisciplinary Assocation for Psychedelic Studies

☺ SSDP (ssdp.org)
Students for Sensible Drug Policy

☺ Zendo Project® (zendoproject.org)
Psychedelic peer support

Acknowledgments

How do I send enough thank-yous to everyone who helped make *Raver Girl* possible? And helped make me me? The love begins at my core: my family.

To Mom and Dad, who weathered every storm, never giving up, instilling the confidence that gives me the strength to make changes for the better. Your teachings have enlightened me more than you realize. You installed my moral compass; thank you for bearing with me while I found it. And thank you for all the hugs.

To my brothers, Nathan and Tadish. I've always looked up to you, and you've always treated me like an equal. You also give the coziest hugs. Thanks for being the best bromies a bis could have.

To my husband, Rich, who was there for my writing highs and lows, reminding me that my story is worth being told, and I am worthy of telling it. You are a beautiful soul. Thank you, New Zealand and the Bryants, for my Prince. Thank you to the Universe for sending him to me so we could create our family.

To my son, Donovan. You're the reason I survived this story. You are the greatest gift. I promise to teach you everything I know, practice patience, and read you any book you ever want (except mine). You are my rave now.

To my SILs, Linda and Cara. Thank you for being cool chicks who honor my brothers and my family. You bring warmth and divine energy to the Durbin clan.

To my ancestors who passed on their creative DNA to me and guide me. Thank you for visiting in my dreams, meditations, and rainbows. I'm listening.

To my best friends who were there during every phase of hairstyle: Alexis, Micaela, Elisa, Fiona, Casey, Sarah B., Natalie, Jeni, Sarah C., Nadia, Tracy, Jevon, Andrea, Johannah, Hristo, Sonya, Jill, Danny, Dreya, Chris, Anjali, Lauren, and Brando (you get extra credit for suggesting Sweet Child O' Mine be the last chapter). You are angels and amazing people who've enriched my life. An extra-long hug to my besties who were my first readers and encouraged me to keep going despite having read my memory vomit.

To Brooke Warner at She Writes Press, for giving *Raver Girl* a chance. You're a pioneer, and I'm honored to be a part of your stable. Thank you.

To my editors: Paul Shirley, Ali Lawrence, Lisa Locascio. Every draft got miles better because of your insights and tough love. You're terrific teachers; I've learned from you in many ways.

To the staff, teachers, and fellow students at the Mendocino Coast Writers' Conference. You inspired me every foggy August, teaching me the ways of the craft. Elizabeth Rosner, Sheila Bender, Linda Joy Myers, Reyna Grande, Judith Barrington, Susan Bono—you are wise women and admirable writers. I always left the conference knowing I had a lot more work to do but feeling like I had the tools to do it.

To Mysti, Gary, and Beth: The Oakland Scribes, a small, mighty writers group who gave me different perspectives and offered new directions when I totally thought I was on point and wasn't.

To writers before and after me. Writing a book turned me into a bona fide reader. There are some books I read while writing RG that were especially interesting and now have lots of dog-eared pages: *Altered State: The Story of Ecstasy Culture and Acid House* by Matthew Collin, *Just Kids* by Patti Smith, *Bird by Bird* by Anne Lamont, *The Doors of Perception* by Aldous Huxley, *On Writing* by Stephen King, and the cult classic *The Electric Kool-Aid Acid Test* by Tom Wolfe.

To my therapist since I was Raver Girl. LK, you've always helped me recognize my demons and strengths. Thank you for being much more than a listener.

To my tutor, Hilda, whose patience and passion for teaching made learning enjoyable.

To my healers Lindya, Tobe Hanson, and Liya Garber. You've helped me evolve energetically and spiritually. The work you do is exceptional; thank you for sharing it with me and the world.

To the Color Club, Intercrew, SWB, Village Mafia, and every raver and retired raver out there—we're connected in spirit. Thank you to the DJs who showed me a whole new world of music. Kudos to the promoters, producers (Vlad!), crews, and rebels that made this part of Bay Area history happen. It was epic.

To anyone who reads my story: Thank you. Keep dancing. PLUR.

ABOUT THE AUTHOR

Photo credit: Natalia Yasmine Hayden

Samantha Durbin is a multifaceted writer from Oakland. Her writing has appeared in *POPSUGAR*, *PureWow*, *Zagat*, and *The San Francisco Chronicle*, among others. She lives in the Bay Area with her family and her Adidas collection.

She Writes Press is an independent publishing company
founded to serve women writers everywhere.
Visit us at www.shewritespress.com.

Queerspawn in Love by Kellen Kaiser. $16.95, 978-1-63152-020-4.
When the daughter of a quartet of lesbians falls in love with a man
serving in the Israeli Defense Forces, she is forced to examine her own
values and beliefs.

Being Ana: A Memoir of Anorexia Nervosa by Shani Raviv. $16.95,
978-1-63152-139-3. In this fast-paced coming-of-age story, Raviv,
spirals into anorexia as a misfit fourteen-year-old and spends the next
ten years being "Ana" (as many anorexics call it)—until she finally
faces the rude awakening that if she doesn't slow down, break her
denial, and seek help, she will starve to death.

Hippie Chick: Coming of Age in the '60s by Ilene English. $16.95,
978-1-63152-586-5. After sixteen-year-old Ilene English, the youngest
of six, finds her mother dead in the bathroom, she flies alone from
New Jersey to San Francisco, embarking upon a journey that takes her
through the earliest days of the counterculture, psychedelics, and free
love, on into single parenthood, and eventually to a place of fully
owning her own strengths and abilities.

The Art of Losing it: A Memoir of Grief and Addiction by Rosemary
Keevil. $16.95, 978-1-63152-777-7. When her husband dies of cancer
and her brother dies of AIDS in the same year, Rosemary is left to raise
her two young daughters on her own and plunged into a hurricane of
grief—a hurricane from which she seeks refuge in drugs and alcohol.

Fourteen: A Daughter's Memoir of Adventure, Sailing, and Survival by
Leslie Johansen Nack. $16.95, 978-1-63152-941-2. A coming-of-age
adventure story about a young girl who comes into her own power,
fights back against abuse, becomes an accomplished sailor, and falls in
love with the ocean and the natural world.

CPSIA information can be obtained
at www.ICGtesting.com
Printed in the USA
LVHW020726261121
704404LV00002B/2